Corporate Security Management

Corporate Security Management
Challenges, Risks, and Strategies

MARKO CABRIC

AMSTERDAM • BOSTON • HEIDELBERG • LONDON
NEW YORK • OXFORD • PARIS • SAN DIEGO
SAN FRANCISCO • SINGAPORE • SYDNEY • TOKYO

Butterworth-Heinemann is an imprint of Elsevier

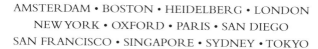

Acquiring Editor: *Tom Stover*
Editorial Project Manager: *Hilary Carr*
Project Manager: *Punithavathy Govindaradjane*
Designer: *Mark Rogers*

Butterworth-Heinemann is an imprint of Elsevier
The Boulevard, Langford Lane, Kidlington, Oxford OX5 1 GB, UK
225 Wyman Street, Waltham, MA 02451, USA

ISBN: 978-0-12-802934-3

British Library Cataloguing-in-Publication Data
A catalogue record for this book is available from the British Library

Library of Congress Cataloging-in-Publication Data
A catalog record for this book is available from the Library of Congress

For information on all Butterworth-Heinemann publications
visit our website at http://store.elsevier.com/

To Jelena with love

CONTENTS

ABOUT THE AUTHOR

Marko Cabric is a security professional, with more than 20 years of top-ranking security experience from Europe, the Middle East, and Africa. The long list of engagements includes the Israeli military service (IDF) and high-ranking security positions in governmental and international organizations and multinational corporations. Marko helped establish the corporate security setup for numerous corporate clients. He performs internal investigations, teaches, consults, manages, and trains corporate security teams of all levels.

Marko has realized that very few books professionally analyze corporate security management and that there is a big gap between corporate security practices and information presented in literature. *Corporate Security Management: Challenges, Risks, and Strategies* is the product of 20 years of Marko's all-round experience in homeland security and as security manager and consultant in various corporate industries, combined with his formal and informal education, numerous articles that he has written, courses that he has delivered, thorough research, and his passion for writing, presenting, and teaching.

INTRODUCTION

Corporate Security is probably still one of the biggest mysteries of the corporate world. The role of Corporate Security is often misunderstood, filled with controversy and overshadowed by internal conflicts. The perception of security as being an unnecessary cost is slowly changing, and businesses increasingly realize that security does not only protect assets, but actually adds value to key business processes. Unfortunately, the actual trust and understanding are still missing in many organizations.

Security is also to blame for this lack of understanding, particularly due to its traditionally introvert nature. Many security professionals fail to understand that corporate security is far more than just a set of security processes that are physically performed in a corporation. Most corporate security practitioners originate from military or law enforcement and they switch to corporate security quite late in their careers. The transition from "shooting targets to meeting targets" can be a true challenge, and not only because of the need to add soft skills to hard-line security doctrine. The true challenge lies in managing to successfully match security principles and philosophies with the, usually completely opposed, business mindset and entirely different perspective that require new competencies and contemporary skills. Basically, as security professionals mostly originate from environments where security is the core business, when transferring to a profit-oriented enterprise they are overwhelmed, not only with different priorities, "poles apart" philosophies, and opposed perceptions, but also by incomparably lower budgets.

An example that can illustrate the lack of understanding in this arranged marriage type of relationship between business and security is the different perception of terms such as risk, protection, value, and efficiency. Unlike security, business perceives risk as financial and investment risk while protection is perceived more in the legal and insurance sense than in the actual one. As for value, business counts the value of its product in terms of cost and profit while security understands the value of a product in terms of motive to commit crime, and calculates risks based on that value. Finally, in security jargon, efficiency implies achieving an objective regardless of the financial cost, while for business, in order for a process to be efficient it must be cost-effective.

My main motive for writing this book was certainly to close the gap between theory and practice, and explain not only how it should be but also how it actually is. In order to succeed in my mission, I am not only explaining and analyzing, but often criticizing.

This book is intended for security professionals who are making the transition to corporate security, for acting corporate security managers who are looking to expand their knowledge and skills and move upward in the corporate world hierarchy, and for business leaders looking to gain an in-depth understanding of one of the crucial corporate functions.

The concept of the book relies on the 5W1H argumentation model based on which we research and introduce the corporate security management role and philosophy and practically explore its challenges, risks, and strategies. We start by clarifying the essence, principles, and philosophies of security and various types of commercial enterprises and how they interact and influence each other. We continue by introducing competencies that are essential for any senior corporate engagement and how they translate to the role of a corporate security manager and the performance of the corporate security team. Consequently we turn to thoroughly analyzing external and internal risks that threaten commercial enterprises. Finally, we base tactics on the identified risks and go to details to give actual corporate security tools by practically explaining strategies aimed at addressing risks that threaten tangible and intangible assets of different commercial organizations in their various parts and during key processes.

As much as I have tried to think of all the possible questions and answer them as descriptively as I could, no single book has the capacity to be used as the only source of knowledge. I believe that mastering any subject requires extensive practice and thorough research using numerous sources and exploring various opinions. Probably the biggest strengths of this book lie in its ability to guide its readers in developing a logical and methodical approach to corporate security and trigger further study of specific subjects.

Marko Cabric

What: Define

CHAPTER 1

About Security

SECURITY AND ITS ESSENCE
About Security

Instead of trying to explain security by analyzing the linguistic source of the word and its meaning, to really understand the essence of security we will concentrate more on exploring its real origins, essence, and principles. Basically, even though some other professions are believed to be the oldest ones, which might be true, security is definitely one of the oldest processes, dating to the beginning of life and the instinct to protect it.

The principles of security at the time of our distant ancestors did not change. The caveman guarded his cave with a spear while another was on the lookout on the edge of the settlement with the mission of spotting the danger at the earliest possible stage and alerting the others. Everyone in the community knew exactly what to do in case of danger and who was in charge of making the decisions.

We have the cave as the physical element of security, the spear as technology, information about the proximate danger, communication among community members, all members of the community as the human element and procedures, both as division of tasks in routine as well as emergency procedures, and the community chief as the management. If any of the elements were missing, the system would not work properly.

Then, as well as now, we had the seven pillars of security:
- Physical
- Technical
- Human
- Information
- Communication
- Procedures
- Management (control)

What changed over time is not the essence of security but its technology.

Now that we have cleared the pillars of a security system, we will continue by exploring the periods and the focus of protection. The protection periods, the focus of protection and its value, together with the probable type of threat that we are facing and its impact on our tangible and intangible assets are the elements that will shape our protection strategy and determine how we allocate the seven essential security pillars and transform them into a successful security system.

Protection Periods

We usually divide protection into three phases:

- Prevention
- Reaction
- Recovery
  Protection phases correspond with incident phases:
- Prevention corresponds with preparation, which consists of target selection, collection of information, and planning. The preparation phase can last long—days, months, and sometimes even years before the action.
- Reaction corresponds with action, which consists of arrival, action, and escape. Depending on the type of action, it can last a few minutes or even seconds.
- Recovery corresponds with consequences, which can have a devastating impact on people, property, morale, and so forth. Consequences can be felt for a long time after an incident.

Focus

To be able to design applicable security strategies and recognize the threat, the probability of action, and its modus operandi, understanding the protection focus is a crucial starting point. For example, our focus can be on:

- People
- Property
- Process
- Product
- Information

Our focus can also be on the combination of all of the elements with the same or different levels of priority, for example. Different strategies are applied and different resources are used depending on not only what we are protecting but what the situation is and the probable risks, protection obstacles, and worst-scenario consequences. For example, although people are our primary concern, it is different if we are protecting clerks in an office, VIPs, or patients in a hospital. If we are protecting the product, we must first understand its value in terms of the motive for committing a crime against it.

Type of Threat

If we understand the nature of what we are protecting and its value, we also understand the type of threat we are facing (terrorism, theft, hooliganism, political violence, etc.) as well as the type of perpetrators we can expect: a planned organized group, an unprofessional perpetrator, and so forth. When we talk about the type of threat, we are also talking about different probable risks associated with the probable modus operandi of perpetrators. Different types of risk are associated with different types of threat. For instance, a lone drug addict bank robber who needs money immediately is targeting a smaller amount of cash but is more likely to cause greater damage than an organized criminal group that is targeting a much larger amount of cash. A group of criminals will plan the robbery so as to accomplish their goal as efficiently as possible and is completely aware of the different consequences concerning different types of damage.

Concept of Value

One of the key elements of security is the concept of value. Security does not calculate value based on cost, but on a motive for committing crime and in terms of the justified cost of security measures. Basically, the value of what we are protecting gives us the probability of the item (process, product, person, etc.) being a motive for an action against it. It also tells us the type of threat that we are facing and the modus operandi of perpetrators.

If we take a product as an example, tin cans manufactured for a soft drink factory have a value in terms of cost but no value in the security sense.

Furthermore, value can be divided into primary and secondary value:

Primary value is basically the immediate value of a product. For example, cash, jewelry, alcohol, cigarettes, and branded clothing are primary value products. These items can be used immediately by a criminal or easily be sold. As such, they can be attractive as a motive for opportunity crime by a lone perpetrator, but also for organized crime.

Secondary value applies to items that have no usability in their current form: for example, branded shirts are primary value items whereas the textile used to produce them is a secondary value item. It cannot be used directly by the perpetrator but can be used, for example, by another clothes manufacturer. To be resold, it needs to be in a bigger volume, which requires planning, logistics, and prearrangement with the buyer. This indicates that such crime cannot be carried out by a lone perpetrator, but only by an organized group that is able to organize and perform the action.

The classification of value also depends on the volume. Basically, big volumes of primary value become secondary value because executing a theft of big volumes requires planning and logistics. For example, several bottles of wine are primary value whereas a whole truck of wine is secondary value. Stealing a truckload of wine requires an organization, a buyer, logistics, storage space big enough to contain such an amount of items, and so forth.

The type and volume of the protected value, matched with the level of security measures, also indicate the probability of an action and the modus operandi of perpetrators. For instance, in the example of wine bottles, a lone perpetrator is unlikely to target a well-secured warehouse that contains large volumes of packed wine bottles to steal one or two of them. We call this phenomenon the ratio between effort (or risk) and reward.

Another aspect of value is the justified cost of security measures compared with the cost of loss. Basically, the investment in security measures must not exceed the cost of incidents over a reasonable period of time. Organizations prefer not to lose money regardless of where the money is going. Security does not generate profit and its mission is to protect the profit and save costs. If your security measures are more expensive than the incidents, your organizations will opt to accept the risk and lose less.

Crime Triangle

By analyzing the concept of value, we basically analyzed one of the three elements necessary to commit a crime—motive. Motive, opportunity, and means together create the triangle of crime.

A successful security strategy concentrates on understanding the motive, limiting the opportunity, and obstructing the means in the earliest possible stage of an incident by incorporating all of the security elements that we have previously discussed. As an example, to conduct an action, a perpetrator must collect information (means) to execute an action successfully. Obstructing the collection of information is basically obstructing the means, therefore limiting the opportunity in the earliest possible stage (preparation phase) and preventing an incident from occurring.

Understanding Incident Phases

When we plan a protection strategy, we do not assess only the possible risk by assessing the probability of successful attack but also the probability of a successful execution of all three phases of an attack:

- Arrival
- Action
- Escape

Because a perpetrator needs to plan all phases of an attack, a successful protection strategy concentrates on making all three phases harder for the perpetrator.

Basically, the only situation in which a perpetrator executes an action and escapes at the same time is in the case of a suicide bomber.

Probability

Another basic principle of security and an essential element of security planning and strategy is probability. Although possibility is an immeasurable concept (everything is possible), probability helps us concentrate on the real issues and be cost-effective. Apart from determining the probability of an action against our asset in terms of motive, we also anticipate the probable course of action (PCA) against it. To determine the PCA, we assess the value and nature of what we are protecting, the physical position of the asset, our security measures, historical data such as previous actions, and finally, common sense.

BASIC PRINCIPLES OF SECURITY
Security Is Active and Proactive

First, let us start with what is not a security model. Regardless of what model of security we are using, one of the basic principles of security is that it is always active and proactive. In security, as well as in nature, the active will always defeat the passive regardless of strength. For example, water will shape a stronger but passive rock whereas the roots of a growing tree will break static concrete and bend metal, simply because of their persistent activity and movement.

Routine

Routine has two sides: positive and negative. In both ways, routine is one of the most important aspects of security. Performing according to a pattern (routine) is a negative aspect of routine. Breaking the routine is a golden rule of security. We know that our objective is to stop an attack in the earliest possible stage—in the stage of collecting information. An attacker will need as much information about our routine as possible to be able to plan an attack. Not being able to collect information will be a large turnoff for a potential perpetrator and an efficient target-hardening method. Ways to break the routine can go as far as our imagination, but we must keep in mind that we should not exaggerate in a way that could confuse us and interfere with our performing tasks and vital processes. However, knowing the routine of our environment is a must and a positive aspect of routine. Knowing the routine is crucial for being able to single out anything that does not fit into the routine. We will generally classify something as suspicious if it does not fit the routine of the place. Also, knowing a routine is being familiar with the necessary emergency infrastructure in our area and the fastest ways to get there.

Security Is Everybody's Responsibility

The role of security professionals is to assess, design, implement, direct, manage, and control. Still, no security system can function if security professionals are perceived as the only ones responsible for security without all of the people in the system being involved and doing their part.

Information Is Essential

Information is essential for security both as a tool for security professionals and as a crucial piece of the puzzle perpetrators require to plan an action. As security professionals, we are required to have as much information as we can, ranging from global issues such as the international and local political climate and risks, for example, to information directly concerning our place of work. At the same time, we are required to protect information in terms of protecting value and of blocking a tool that can be used for an action against us.

Security Is a Process, Not a Product

With the development of security companies offering services and solutions, security started to be perceived increasingly as a product and not the process it is. For example, manned guarding companies, or companies that are dealing with security equipment, are selling products by making their clients believe that they are selling them security. Security consists of many interactive elements and phases and is a circular, never-ending process.

Worst-Case Scenario

The human brain has the ability to look for reasons or justify certain obvious situations. It is usually referred to as the "It will not happen to me" security strategy. One of the iron security principles is to design protection strategies by taking into account the worst possible scenario and to handle incidents while keeping in mind their worst possible outcome.

Good Relations

The success of any security system greatly depends on its ability to recruit helpers, collect information, and have as many eyes and ears as possible. To achieve that goal, it is crucial to have motivated collaborators with a personal interest to assist. Although motivating people with fear and punishment or compliments and rewards will provide some results, the best performance is achieved when people perceive the goal as their personal issue. We will have the best result in our security processes if we recruit people by making them understand that security is their personal issue as well. Good relations with people in our surroundings and good communication will motivate people to cooperate and provide assistance and information voluntarily.

Think Like a Perpetrator

To fully understand our vulnerabilities, gaps in our systems, and probable courses of actions, we must place ourselves in the shoes of a potential perpetrator. For example, actually performing the exercise of collecting information about our own installation will tell us about good models for collecting information and places from which to collect it. It will also give us clear indications about how easy or difficult is it to "read" us. We would learn what our weaknesses are and what the good spots are to collect information. By simulating an attack, we will find the best preparation points for an attack and understand the probable courses of action, including starting an attack, performing it, and escaping. Of, course, the elements we incorporate in our exercise should match the probable threat. It is different if we are threatened by terrorism or by employees' theft.

Use Layered Defense

Layered defense is the model of combining multiple security controls for protection. Although it is often considered by scholars to be a model, layered defense is one of the basic principles of security. Even though we often think of security layers as manned guarding systems divided into circles, we need to understand the layers on all levels of a protection system.

Layers include not only the security staff, but all protection elements such as collected intelligence that is processed and implemented in the right way, sets of procedures, physical barriers, the people, and technical systems.

GLOSSARY OF CORPORATE SECURITY TERMS AND ABBREVIATIONS

ABCP Associate Business Continuity Planner.

Account takeover A fraudster changes the personal identification number or address so that the account owner can no longer access the account.

Advance fee fraud A victim is promised a large sum of money as reward for a small investment.

Affinity fraud Targeting victims who share the same race/religion/culture/politics as the fraudster.

Akwukwo A fake check used by Nigerian letter scammers.

ALF Animal Liberation Front.

Altered card A payment card whose genuine magnetic stripe is removed and replaced with fraudulently obtained information.

Arbitrator An independent person or body officially appointed to settle a dispute.

Arson Malicious burning to destroy property.

ASP Accredited Security Professional.

ATM attachments Numerous attachments that are mounted on automatic teller machines for fraudulent purposes.

Audit trail The path or series of procedures and records by which any single transaction or inquiry can be traced through a system, computer, or other facility.

AV Antivirus, a common abbreviation referring to virus protection software or services for computer and Internet use.

AVS Address Verification System. The system used to determine whether the billing address on an account matches the mailing address on a credit card.

Background screening An inquiry into the history and behaviors of an individual who is considered for employment, credit, or access to sensitive assets or for other reasons.

BCCE Business Continuity Certified Expert.

BCCP Business Continuity Certified Planner.

BCCS Business Continuity Certified Specialist.

Big store A fake shop, betting house, office, or similar environment set up by the con artist.

Bribery Corrupt payment, receipt, or solicitation of a private favor for official action.

Business continuity Organizational effort to plan and execute mitigation strategies to ensure effective and efficient organizational response to the challenges that threaten its processes during and after a crisis.

Business continuity plan An ongoing process aimed at ensuring that the necessary steps are taken to identify the impact of potential losses and ensure recovery.

Business impact analysis Process of analyzing all operational functions and the effect that an operational interruption might have on them.

Bust-out fraud Amount of available credit fraudulently raised on otherwise legitimate credit cards.

Cackle bladder Death faked for the purposes of a scam.

Card-not-present (CNP) A transaction in which the credit card is not physically present at the time of purchase, such as for Internet, mail, or telephone orders.

CBCP Certified Business Continuity Professional.

CCFP Certified Cyber Forensics Professional.

CCSK Certificate of Cloud Security Knowledge.

CEH Certified Ethical Hacker.

CFE Certified Fraud Examiner.

CFID Certified Forensic Interviewer Designation.

Chain letter A pyramid scheme in which new recipients of a letter pay old recipients.

Chargeback The reversal of the currency value, in whole or in part, of a particular transaction by the card issuer to the acquirer.

CIA Certified Internal Auditor.

CISM Certified Information Security Manager.

CISO Chief Information Security Officer.

CISSP Certified Information Systems Professional.

Clean desk policy A standard corporate directive that arranges how employees should leave their working space, especially valuable office equipment, items, and documents, before they leave the office.

CLSD Certified Lodging Security Director.

CM Crisis management.

Conflict of interest A factor in which an organization, group, or individual is subject to incompatible demands, opportunities, incentives, or responsibilities.

Contraband Goods prohibited by law from being exported or imported. Smuggling.

Copyright Exclusive legal rights to make copies, publish, broadcast, or sell a piece of work such as a book, a film, music, or a picture.

Corporate fraud The dishonest abuse of position, usually by senior members of staff.

Corporate identity theft Misappropriation of the identity of a company or business without that entity's knowledge or consent.

Corruption Illegal behavior, such as bribery, by people in positions of authority, e.g., politicians.

Counterfeiting The forging, copying, or imitating of something (usually money) without the right to do so and with the purpose of deceiving or defrauding.

CPISM Certified Professional in Information Security Management.

CPO Certified Protection Officer.

CPP Certified Protection Professional.

Credit card fraud Fraud committed using or involving a payment credit or debit card.

Crisis management Management process that identifies potential impacts that threaten an organization and provides a framework for building resilience.

Crisis management team A management-level group responsible for managing the development and execution of the response to a crisis and leading the organization during the recovery phase.

CSO Chief Security Officer.

CSP Certified Surveillance Professional.

CSPM Certified Security Project Manager.

CSSLP Certified Secure Software Lifecycle Professional.

CST Certified Security Trainer.

C-TPAT Customs Trade Partnership Against Terrorism.

Cybercrime Criminal activities carried out by means of computers or the Internet.

Cyber squatting The illegal activity of buying and registering a domain name that is a well-known brand or someone's name, with the intent of selling it.

Cyber stalking The act of threatening, harassing, or annoying someone through multiple e-mail messages.

Cyber theft The act of using an online computer service, such as one on the Internet, to steal someone else's property.

Damage limitation The process of trying to limit the amount of damage, bad results, or loss caused by a particular situation or event.

Deadbeat A person or company that tries to avoid paying debts.

Disaster recovery Action taken by an organization to minimize further damage after a disaster and to begin the process of recovery.

Disaster recovery site Secondary location that contains backup systems and applications that are critical for the business.

Double-dipping The practice, usually regarded as unethical, of receiving two incomes or benefits from the same source: for example, receiving a pension and consultancy income from the same employer.

DRCE Disaster Recovery Certificate Expert.

DRCS Disaster Recovery Certified Specialist.

Due diligence The attention and care exercised to avoid foreseeable harm to other persons or their property. Lack of due diligence may be considered negligence.

Dumpster diving The act of rummaging through someone's trash to obtain personal information used to commit identity theft.

ECSA Certified Security Analyst.

ELF Earth Liberation Front.

E-mail interception The act of reading, storing, or intercepting e-mail intended for another person without that person's permission.

Embezzlement Dishonestly appropriating goods or money from one's employer, thus abusing a position.

Encryption Method of making information secret by transforming plain text into ciphered text.

Financial fraud Fraud that involves a financial account or transaction such as a bank account including a consumer loan or a credit card account.

Firewall A system in a computer that prevents unwanted or unauthorized access but allows the authorized user to receive information.

Flash mob A secretly planned, quickly formed, organized group of people.

Forensic accounting The use of accounting, corporate, and criminal investigation techniques in legal proceedings.

Fourrée Fake currency.

Front A legitimate business or person used to cover illegal dealings.

Fraud ring A group of individuals who scheme together to commit fraud.

GIAC Global Information Assurance Certification.

Gray market Supply of official goods through unofficial channels.

High-tech crime Generally understood to mean the use of high technology to facilitate criminal activity.

Identity theft A crime in which someone obtains another person's personal information.

Insurance claims fraud The making of a claim(s) under one or more insurance policies with one or more material falsehoods or by presenting a false or forged document.

Intangible assets Includes such assets as reputation, customer confidence, client confidence, trade secrets, intellectual property, and goodwill.

Internal audit Systematic, independent, and documented process for obtaining audit evidence and evaluating it objectively to determine the extent to which the management system audit criteria set by the organization are fulfilled.

ISO 28000 A supply chain security management system.

Lebanese loop The piece of equipment inserted into automatic teller machines to steal cards or cash.

Loss event An occurrence that produces a financial loss or negative impact on assets.

LPC Loss Prevention Certified.

LPQ Loss Prevention Qualified.

LPT Licensed Penetration Tester.

Mail redirect Post can be fraudulently redirected to another address. The fraudster then receives any important documents intended for the victim, possibly to facilitate identity fraud.

Malware Any software or computer program that is designed to intentionally damage or disable computers or computer systems. Malware examples are computer viruses, Trojan horses, and spyware.

Man in the middle attack An attack in which a third party is able to read and change computer messages between two parties without either party knowing that the link between them has been compromised.

MBCP Master Business Continuity Professional.

Medical fraud A fraudster steals someone's personal information to obtain medical care, buy prescription drugs, or submit fake billings.

Mobbing Workplace emotional assaults or bullying.

Money laundering The process by which criminals attempt to conceal the true origin of the financial proceeds of crime.

Mortgage fraud Any attempt by an applicant to obtain a mortgage by deliberately providing false details.

Negligent hiring The failure to use reasonable care in the employee selection process.

Noncompliance Failure or refusal to obey or comply with a rule, regulation, or standard, which can commonly result in serious action by an inspector or ombudsman.

Nonconformity Nonfulfillment of a requirement.

Nondisclosure agreement (NDA) A legal contract between at least two parties that outlines confidential materials or knowledge.

Occupational hazard Aspects of a job that can be dangerous or pose a high risk of injury.

Organizational resilience An ongoing management and governance process supported by top management; resourced to ensure that necessary steps are taken to identify and mitigate the impact of potential losses.

OSSTMM Professional Security Analyst certification.

Paper hanging Presenting fake or bad checks.

PCI Professional Certified Investigator.

PCIP Professional in Critical Infrastructure Protection.

PCISAG Professional Certificate in Information Systems Security, Auditing, and Governance.

Penetration testing A method of evaluating computer and network security by simulating an attack on a computer system or network from external and internal threats.

PFSO Port Facility Security Officer.

Pharming Stealing a victim's personal information via spyware.

Phishing A fraudulent attempt to acquire sensitive information through e-mail in which the fraudster sends out a legitimate-looking e-mail in an attempt to gather personal and financial information from recipients.

Phreaking Hacking into or exploiting telephone systems to obtain communications services at no cost.

PIN Personal Identification Number. A number given by a bank to a customer so the customer can access a bank account using an automatic teller machine or point of sale terminal in retail outlets.

PIP Partners in Protection.

Ponzi scheme Named after Charles Ponzi; a fraudulent investment scheme similar to a pyramid scheme.

Professional liability The legal liability of a professional such as a doctor, accountant, or lawyer, who causes loss, harm, or injury to clients while performing professional duties.

PSP Physical Security Professional.

Q/ISP Qualified Information Security Professional.

Rag A stock market scam.

Risk acceptance Informed decision to take a particular risk.

Risk management Identifying, assessing, managing, and controlling potential events or situations, and then taking measures to control or reduce them.

Sexting Sending sexually explicit messages and/or pictures by mobile phone.

Sextortion A form of sexual exploitation that employs nonphysical forms of coercion to extort sexual favors from the victim.

Shark A dishonest businessperson who cheats and swindles others.

Shoulder surfing The act of sneakily looking over the shoulder of someone using a PIN or password to use it to commit a fraud.

Skimming A method that fraudsters use to obtain credit card information illegally. This is done using a small electronic device called a skimmer, to swipe and store hundreds of victims' credit card numbers.

Smishing A variation on phishing in which the criminal fishes for personal data over a cell phone. Instead of receiving an e-mail, the person receives a text message that tells him or her to call a toll-free number, which is answered by a bogus interactive voice-response system that tries to fool the person into providing his or her account number and password.

Social engineering Nontechnical intrusion that relies heavily on human interaction and often involves tricking other people to break normal security procedures.

Spam Unsolicited e-mail sent to numerous recipients.

Spear phishing Phishing e-mail that looks as if it came from someone you know.

Spoofs An attempt to harvest personal information direct from potential victims, to facilitate identity fraud.

SSCP Systems Security Certification Practitioner.

Strike Work stoppage caused by a disagreement between employees and management.

Synthetic fraud A type of identification fraud in which fraudsters combine real and fake identifying information to create new identities.

TAPA Transported Assets Protection Agency.

Trojan virus A destructive program that masquerades as a benign application.

Virus A computer program that replicates itself to infect computers. Viruses are typically spread from one computer to another through executable code in an infected file.

Vishing A variation of phishing in which the criminal fishes for personal information or attempts to install malicious software on a computer through a video file.

Whistle-blower A person who informs the public and/or relevant authorities about wrongdoings, failings, corruption, or other illegal activities within an organization.

White collar crime An illegal act such as fraud, embezzlement, or bribery committed by a worker in business or an administrative function.

Worm A worm is similar to a virus but is self-contained; as such, it does not require a host to spread. A worm may destroy, modify, or copy data for a third party.

CHAPTER 2

Corporations and the Place of Corporate Security

CORPORATIONS

Corporations and Corporate Structure

Although in theory a corporation can be nonprofit, most corporations are legal, for-profit entities created through the laws of their state of incorporation. The laws basically treat corporations as legally independent persons who can sue and be sued, separate from their stockholders. This independence of corporations prevents shareholders from being held personally financially responsible for corporate debts. A corporation consists of various departments that work together to achieve company goals. There were four essential departments in traditional corporations: operations, human resources, finances and sales, and marketing; but with the development of information and communication technologies and their crucial role in conducting business, information and communication technologies (ICT) became the fifth key corporate department. However, depending on the size of the company, the types of products and services and their variety and complexity, geographical structure, and the legal, compliance, and risk specifics of the corporation, there could be other key departments in a corporation.

A corporate structure is run by top management composed of a chief executive officer (CEO) and a board of directors who represent each department. In large, especially multisite corporations, there is a CEO and a board of directors in each affiliate (e.g., country or market) and a president (chairman, group CEO) in the headquarters of the corporation, with vice presidents responsible for parts of the business and/or certain geographical areas. The president is obligated to represent the interests of the owners of the company (its shareholders) and is usually appointed by them from the board of directors. Decision making is usually divided between the board of directors and the shareholders.

The president and vice presidents are on the top of the decision-making pyramid and delegate power down through the organizations. For example, the top management will appoint a CEO in a certain market, the CEO will appoint department heads (department directors), department heads will appoint managers for certain parts of their departments, and so on. Apart from their responsibility toward the local management of the company, some expert positions in terms of expertise report to their global functions in the headquarters of the company. This relationship is usually called the "dotted line" or "competence line." For example, a national chief security officer reports to the local CEO but also to the global chief security officer who is responsible for the security of the entire corporation.

There are four common models of corporate structures:

- Functional structure—Functional structure is the simplest corporate structure because it is based on departments (functions). This type of corporate structure usually exists in smaller corporations with a single and simple product or service.
- Product structure—This structure exists mostly in multiproduct companies where parallel structures exist for each product and/or service.
- Combined structure—This is the most common structure in large, multiproduct, multisite corporations. Because complexity, large volumes, and market specifics require greater control, it is basically a multiple-dimension structure based on the product as well as on the functions.
- Multisite structure—This structure exists in corporations covering a wide geographical area with parallel structures for each area or market.

A business division refers to the parts into which a corporation is divided. The divisions are distinct parts of the business that may be part of the same legal entity, or in large corporations, they may be divided into separate legal entities owned by the corporation. For example, a corporation that is producing and selling a product may own two companies, one of which produces the product (operations) and the other which markets and sells the product (sales). These legally distinct companies and their parts perform services for each other. For example, one company produces for the second one, which sells the product for the first one. In general, the two companies will not have completely parallel structures. For example, the legal, compliance, and internal audit units may officially be in sales but will still give service to operations. The security department, which could be officially located in operations, will be responsible for the whole lifecycle of the product, including parts of processes delegated to sales.

Companies have the freedom to organize their internal structure as they wish. The most common starts with divisions (or sectors) that are the crucial departments in the corporation and their heads. Together with the CEO, these heads form the management team. Those sectors are key business sectors such as sales, marketing, finance, human resources, operations, and ICT, usually with the addition of the legal department and internal controls department, which are not sectors but departments or units owing to their usually smaller size but are still represented in the management team because of their importance to the company and its decisions.

Each of the divisions or sectors is usually divided into departments. For example, the operations sector in an industrial company can consist of various departments such as procurement, production, logistics, operations planning, quality assurance, and so forth. Together, heads of these departments form the management team of their sector. In the case of operations, it would be the operations management team.

Departments are further divided into units. For example, the procurement department can be divided into a unit dealing with procurement of raw materials and one dealing with the procurement of services. The units can be further divided into teams dealing with specific issues.

Corporate Security Organizations

Security organizations in big corporations are usually headed by a group global security director (CSO) who usually reports to a member of the board of directors of the corporation, often to a vice president in charge of operations. Sometimes in industrial corporations, where security is often united with environment, health, and safety (EHS, HS, and HSE), a global security director reports to the director in charge of global environment, health, safety, and security (EHSS).

The number of people and functions that report to the group CSO and together form the security management team differ from company to company depending on a company's size and complexity, but mostly on its perceptions of the importance of security. Security management teams can vary from small teams consisting of a couple of experts to serious security organizations consisting of tens of experts. Functions represented in global security teams consist of managers, each of whom is responsible for a field of expertise: for example, security of facilities (physical and technical security), executive protection, security governance, security trainings, anti-fraud, business continuity management, and special situations.

Global security teams often contract external consulting companies that provide specialized services such as intelligence (and sometimes they contract several companies, each for a different geographical area in which they specialize) and special situations (such as evacuations from hostile environments, hostage rescue, etc.).

Apart from division in terms of expertise, global security teams are geographically represented by regional security managers who are in charge of certain large geographical areas. The most common division of geographical areas for which regional security managers are responsible are: Europe, the Middle East, and Africa; Asia and the Pacific; South and Central America and Mexico; and the United States and Canada.

Regional security managers supervise national security directors (national CSOs, security managers) who are in charge of heading the security on a national or market level. National security directors (managers) report to their local management board and report in the professional sense (dotted line/competence line) to the regional security manager who manages the security of a wider geographical area.

Corporate Governance

Corporate governance on the level that affects security is a system of internal rules and regulations by which all processes in a company are directed and controlled. Basically, corporate governance is the official management of a corporation through internal regulations. Every company can grade its internal documents as it wishes. However, in many cases, policies are the highest-level internal regulations that regulate issues in the entire organization; procedures are based on policies and regulate a specific issue of the policy between two or more organizational units. Procedures do not have to be based on policy but could be standalone regulations between two or more departments. Working instruction is an internal regulation of a single organizational unit that can be based on a procedure. Technical instruction is usually an annex to a policy that explains technical details associated with a certain policy or procedure. For example, a technical instruction will list technical requirements of closed-circuit television (CCTV) as an annex to a procedure that regulates the security of an office.

Centralized corporate governance is a system in which rules and regulations (policies, procedures, working instructions, etc.) are created by the highest level of power and then sent to relevant parts of the corporations to be approved and implemented. On the example of security, the group security team creates policies and procedures that regulate specific security processes and then sends them to all of the affiliates (countries). In every affiliate, country security directors are obligated to receive the approval/commitment of the local management for the document and implement it locally. When it is not possible to implement the rule owing to, for example, local legal constraints, the local security will request from the body that issued the rule (in this case, the global security team) a nonbinding agreement—official acceptance from the issuer that a decision does not have to be obeyed.

Federal (decentralized) corporate governance is a system in which the high level of power sets general standards without creating documents that are ready to be implemented. Instead, the lower levels are responsible for creating regulating documents based on general standards while taking into account local particulars. Only after the regulating documents are created and approved by the local management will they be sent to the higher level of power, as commitment of compliance with the standards.

Corporate Communication

Logically, there are two communication models: official and unofficial. Official business communication occurs through official organizational channels such as meetings, presentations, e-mails, notice boards, newsletters, and official requests. Official communication is a tool to achieve company strategy and is imposed by company executives as part of corporate culture. The better the communication is, the better employees and staff will understand the expectations of the supervisor. The culture of the company also arranges appropriate models of communication such as the maximum time allowed to answer to a superior's or peer's e-mail, which function can freely write to which function and when, when a direct superior should be carbon copied in an e-mail, how unanswered communication should be escalated, and so forth. The usual type of official communication is downward (management) communication. It is initiated by higher functions and passed downward.

With the development of change management, continuous improvement, and other business philosophies aimed at increasing the involvement of employees in suggesting improvements, corporations started encouraging upward communication. This communication climbs upward from lower levels of the corporate hierarchy toward management functions. Upward communication can help upper management to learn immediately about a potential or existing problem and assist in solving it.

However, unofficial communication between colleagues spreads quickly because it has no restrictions and requires no approvals or appropriate forms. It is impossible and unnecessary to stop or control informal communication, but it is possible to manage it and direct it through good, frequent, and effective official communication, especially when organizations are going through changes and employees feel threatened. Still, we should not forget that unofficial communication is the most influential model of communication and that we should work on identifying existing influential channels of unofficial communication and use them as our tool and to our advantage.

KEY CORPORATE PARTNERS OF SECURITY

Key Corporate Organizational Units

Earlier, we mentioned functions that are crucial for a corporation; now, we will list and explain functions that are the key partners of security. Security aligns with core business to have a supporting strategy and common goals and works closely with its partners to achieve the best results. Security is a control function in a corporation, together with internal audit (internal controls), compliance, and operational risk, especially concerning combating fraud and particularly in the banking industry. These functions form the second and third levels of control, whereas all organizational units that are in charge of processes (or parts of processes) form the first level of control. We will now explain the key organizational units; we will thoroughly analyze the control levels further on in this book.

Internal Audit

The role of internal audit in an organization is to ensure a systematic and disciplined approach to processes with a commitment to integrity and accountability. The scope of internal audit activities is wide and often includes compliance with internal and external rules and procedures (governance), effectiveness of operations, and reliability of financial and management reporting. After an audit, internal audit will issue a report consisting of findings and obligatory measures aimed at improving the audited processes. Internal audit also conducts anti-fraud audits to identify potential frauds. It participates in fraud investigations, together with professional investigators, and conducts post-investigation audits to identify control breakdowns, establish financial loss, and impose measures aimed at closing gaps. Although internal auditors are employed by the company, independence and objectivity are the basis of internal audit. This requires organizational independence from the management of the company, which enables unrestricted control of management activities. In most cases, chief internal audit executives report to the audit committee, which is a subcommittee of the board of directors.

Compliance

The compliance unit ensures that a company complies with laws, regulations, and rules. It has a crucial role in preserving the integrity and reputation of the company, especially in the industry of financial services. The goal of the unit is for the company to comply with rules set by legislators, regulators, and its board of directors. In financial institutions, anti-money laundering, which combats the transformation of crime money into legitimate money and/or assets through regulations and controls, is usually part of the compliance unit. Anti-money laundering also complies with international and national regulations aimed at detecting and disabling the financing of terrorism.

Operational Risk

The role of operational risk is to focus on risks arising from assets (people, systems, etc.) with which the company operates and to quantify those risks. Basically, operational risk manages the risk tolerance of an organization and the loss it is prepared to accept owing to the imperfection of its assets. It balances between the cost of errors, the cost of correcting the errors, and the financial benefit of the improvements. Operational risk is different from credit risk, whose main goal is to ensure profit, and from market risk, which ensures the profitability of an investment in a certain market, such as preventing poor strategic business decisions. Operational risk in financial institutions is regulated by the Basel Accords, which are issued by the Basel Committee on Banking Supervision and recommend banking laws and regulations. The Basel definition of operational risk includes, for example, reputational risk (damage to an organization through loss of its reputation or standing) or impact of operational failures, as well as from other events including fraud, employment practices and work safety, damage to physical assets, business disruption and systems failure, and so forth.

Credit Risk

In financial institutions, security also cooperates closely with credit risk, especially by performing investigations concerning fraudulent credit applications (external fraud) and approved bad credits that have the elements of internal or internal–external (external–internal) fraud.

Market Risk

Security provides assistance to market risk by assessing the security and political violence risks associated with the potential investment.

Human Resources

Apart from control functions, security cooperates closely with human resources, especially in fields related to employee relations, user profiles (availability of tools, benefits, access rights, and right to know and see, based on an employee's function), employment (background screening), job termination (strategy and risks of job termination, including security strategies for massive redundancies), and disciplinary measures and sanctions. Human resources is also a partner of security when it comes to designing and delivering trainings for employees and fitting the security training into the overall training matrix of the organization. Human resources and security also work together in designing strategies for travel security and protecting top executives. Human resources deals with the employee relations aspect of business continuity management and basically designs a strategy to ensure sufficient workforce during a holiday season, for example. Human resources is also responsible for negotiations with trade unions to ensure common goals and strategies and during crisis situations such as strikes and demonstrations.

Legal Department

The legal department (unit) is a crucial partner of security when it comes to the legality of measures which security is planning to implement, contracts and contractor management, and assistance in official communications with the criminal justice system and law enforcement. Together, the legal department, human resources, and security assess potential legal risks associated with sanctions against employees. Security creates the default security clause that is inserted into all legal contracts between the company and its contractors, and together with the legal department creates the nondisclosure agreement as one of the crucial agreements between the company and its internal and external employees and contracted companies.

Information and Communication Technologies

Information and communication technologies is a key partner of security in several dimensions. Apart from the fact that ICT hosts and operates the core infrastructure, it is also the central technology partner of security for some of its crucial technical systems such as access control, CCTV, alarms, and more. Also, ICT infrastructure has a central role in internal investigations, especially when it comes to, for example, information technology (IT) forensics, analysis of employees' correspondence and communication, and time and attendance. Because of its sensitivity and importance, security is the second-level control of IT, especially in terms of ICT security governance. Whereas IT is physically responsible for the security of the network, systems, and applications, security is in charge of its protection philosophy and performance. They also share the actual responsibility of protecting information: ICT in terms of electronically stored and transmitted information and security in terms of spoken, written, and visual information.

Security is responsible for leading business continuity management and disaster recovery, owing to the monopoly of ICT over systems that are crucial for the functioning of a business such as the network, systems, and applications, but it works closely with ICT to ensure that all the crucial systems are identified and working properly and are disaster-proof or easily recoverable.

Accounting

The financial/accounting department is important not only as a budgeting partner but also during fraud investigations that include forensic accounting.

Environment, Health, and Safety

In industrial systems, security is often united with EHS. Even if it is not officially organizationally integrated, security and EHS together share certain responsibilities, the most important of which is fire safety, in which security, EHS, and the engineering department have a shared responsibility. A fire safety system consists of technical systems (engineering), procedures aimed at limiting the possibility of fire (EHS), compliance with those procedures (security), and people (a fire brigade is usually part of the security department). Environment, Health, and Safety is also responsible for the health aspect of business continuity management, and together with security, it provides a solution for health threats to employees and their impact on the business.

Engineering

The engineering department (facility management) is responsible for the physical and technical (non-ICT) aspects of the business and for business continuity associated with critical infrastructure (electricity, water, etc.). Engineering is also the main partner of security in the domain of physical and technical security. In many companies, security is logically and operationally responsible for security equipment whereas engineering is responsible for budgeting, purchasing, installing, and maintaining the equipment. Security is responsible for imposing security guidelines and standards on engineering for any construction work and ensuring that they are implemented.

Procurement

The procurement department organizes and conducts bidding for the purchase of equipment and external services. If we are talking about security equipment and services, procurement negotiates the best prices based on security requests. However, security assists procurement with the protection of information during bidding processes, ensures that there are no internal conflicts of interest, and, upon request, performs investigations to evaluate participating companies and bidding documentation to prevent fraud.

The best practice of communicating with key internal clients is organizing recurring weekly meetings to go through all of the current projects and processes.

ABOUT CORPORATE SECURITY: THE PROFESSION AND ITS CHALLENGES

Defining Corporate Security

Corporate security is responsible for coordinating the overall security of a corporation in close coordination with the business management and all the functions that are concerned with security, safety, business continuity, and compliance to safeguard business interests, people, profits, and reputation and mitigate risks. It is also responsible for guiding all employees into doing their part in the security system through their everyday actions and judgments. Apart from dealing with traditional security areas such as physical, technical, and human elements of securing people and property, corporate security incorporates information security, business continuity, and disaster recovery through the entire lifecycle of products and business processes to provide actual support in achieving business goals. Corporate security is in charge of analyzing and quantifying risks; inventing, planning, setting, and controlling security measures; and measuring the performance and success of security measures to predict and notice trends, prevent and stop incidents, and understand their correlation in diverse parts of the corporation and in different phases of business processes. Apart from knowledge and experience in security, key competencies required for a successful corporate security gig are integrity, business acumen, people orientation, management skills, and the ability to effectively communicate and convince.

Traditional business approaches perceived security as an obstacle to business. Security is partly to blame for that. With the mindset of preventing all risks, it was indeed an obstacle to business that actually must take risks to stay ahead of competition and survive. There is certainly an association between risk and profit (reward). Only recently did security managers realize that their role is not to prevent companies from taking risks but actually to help them lessen the risks they are taking to profit.

Core security elements of corporate security are:
- Physical and technical security of people, processes, products, and assets
- Safeguarding the reputation of the company and the brands
- Information security
- Security governance
- Crime prevention and detection
- Anti-fraud
- Investigations
- Nonfinancial risk management
- Business continuity management and disaster recovery
- Crisis management

Chief Security Officer

The CSO is a corporate security management position in charge of the overall security of a corporation or one of its affiliates (national CSO or market CSO). The CSO is responsible for the security of people, processes, products, and assets. A CSO is in charge of the design, implementation, and management of the company's security strategy, vision, and programs, as well as of the coordination of all security elements to notice vulnerabilities and gaps, develop sustainable and cost-effective strategies, and lower the exposure of a corporation to financial, physical, reputation, and human risks, prevent incidents, and manage crisis and recovery to reduce its effects on the company and ensure business continuity.

A CSO is not only a security professional but is also a business manager with security expertise. Successfully managing security of a corporation includes managing teams with people who may often be spread over diverse geographical locations, planning and budgeting, proactively identifying risks, controlling and improving performance (financial, operational, strategical, and human), and interacting with all of the vertical and horizontal corporate players (corporate diplomacy) as well as with external contractors and national security, police, and justice systems.

The complexity of corporate security requires both strategic analysis and planning and a reactive (responsive) tactical approach to solving problems. In reality, the biggest part of daily tasks executed by security managers is responsive rather than strategic. However, further on in this book, we will analyze the differences between the tactical and responsive approaches and examine their success potentials.

Corporate Security Challenges

Although not long ago security risks mostly came down to traditional types of crime such as robberies, thefts, and fraud, in recent years, apart from the growth of those risks, the development of business and its transition toward new areas and new technologies brought new risks and the use of contemporary means for committing crime. Crime is not only able to follow changing business models closely but is often a few steps ahead with a sophistication that reaches the limits of human creativity and uses the newest cutting-edge technology. This has also led to the transition of security from a defensive approach to a more proactive role.

The transnational nature of corporations brought another risk to corporate security: terrorism. Terrorism suddenly became a serious threat for corporations on all levels, including diverse types of terrorism as well as threats such as direct threat against the corporation and also the threat of being used to facilitate terrorism: for example, through the supply chain or financial transactions.

The focus on cost savings such as reducing human resources to an operational minimum, the orientation toward technological solutions for processes, the trend of outsourcing all support functions and the tendency to get the maximum from resources (human as well as physical), and the reduction of stock to a minimal operational amount managed to cut operational costs but also increased the vulnerability of organizations and the impact of incidents and decreased the ability of companies to ensure business continuity and recovery after a disaster. If we take the example of reduction of stock, for companies operating according to the "just in time" principle, the loss of cargo with materials needed for production would cause severe problems in production and delay the arrival of a product to customers.

The concept of outsourcing provides companies with the freedom to concentrate on core business and directly cut costs and gives them the feeling that they are protected, but it indirectly negatively influences the actual security of a company and increases its loses. A classic example of this is the outsourcing of financial risk: insurance. Companies are outsourcing the potential loss, which gives them a false feeling of security. This approach often leads to decreasing security measures and cutting security costs. On the one hand, insurance will cover the losses; however, the lack of security measures will most likely increase the number of incidents, resulting in a weakening of the reputation of the company and brand. Repeated incidents will also result in more expensive insurance. In many cases, companies are required by insurance agencies to implement some security measures. However, these measures are usually implemented just pro forma with no added value. This kind of arrangement often ends up being more expensive than investing in security would have been.

Still, because of the spread of costs over different cost centers, functional divisions of corporations into independent sectors and separate key performance indicators (KPIs), companies are often unable to identify the connections between incidents and costs that occur in different phases of processes or the product lifecycle as well the indirect losses that the incidents are causing. Even if they are collecting data about direct and visible losses, companies often fail to calculate the complete losses and predict risks and future incidents and their influence on the reputation of the company and of the brand.

Key Terms and Their Diverse Perceptions

Although we listed some key corporate terms and abbreviations, it is not only the business terms that form corporate language but also the way in which common terms are used in corporate jargon. One challenge that every security professional faces when entering the corporate world is the different perceptions and uses of some of the key terms.

The first and the most obvious is the word "security," which in business language is a financial term for a document that proves ownership of stocks, shares, bonds, or other investments. More loosely, the term "securities" refers to investments in general. This obvious difference illustrates the financial connotation that is the main difference between the corporate language and security language. Although "security" is probably the first example that comes to mind, the evident difference in uses of the term is not as problematic as the slightly different understanding of terms that seem the same but come with a financial twist in corporate language.

For example, one such word is "efficiency," which is traditionally understood by security as achieving a goal regardless of costs. However, in a business sense, for something to be efficient, it must be cost-effective as well.

Some terms became so strongly associated with financial language that they are by default understood financially. A good example is "risk," which is used in corporate language to explain financial and investment risks. Moreover, "risk" became so strongly associated with financial risk that it became its default connotation. Basically, to describe risks in their traditional (security) sense, we use the term "nonfinancial risk." In the same way, "security" is being used more and more as an IT term, so that it is sometimes even necessary to call security "traditional" (or physical) security to distinguish it from its IT counterpart.

Another example of diverse understandings is the term "protection," which is mostly used to describe legal (contract) and financial (insurance) protection. A false sense of protection certainly negatively influences the intangible assets of an organization, such as reputation and client confidence, but also indirectly has a negative impact on security processes.

The concept of value is an extremely important element of security assessments and analyses. As for different perceptions of the term, business counts the value of its product in terms of cost and profit whereas security counts the value of a product in terms of its usability as a motive to commit crime, and calculates the risks based on that value.

GLOSSARY OF CORPORATE TERMS AND ABBREVIATIONS

ABS Always be selling.
Accrual The accumulation of payments or benefits over time.
Added value An amount added to the value of a product or service, equal to the difference between its cost and the amount received when it is sold.
AML Anti-money laundering.
Appraisal A review of performance and capability, typically of an employee.
ASAP As soon as possible.
Assets Anything of value that is owned by an individual, company, organization, etc.
B2B Business-to-business.
BAU Business as usual.
BCM & DR Business continuity management and disaster recovery.
BD Business development.
Benchmark A standard or point of reference against which things may be compared.
BI Brand integrity.
BIA Business impact analysis.
Bidding A formal presentation of offer based on the request from the procurement of a company and based on a tender.
Board of directors A body of elected or appointed members who jointly oversee the activities of a company or organization.
Bonus An extra sum of money given to an employee on top of the salary, often for achieving targets.

Brand loyalty When a consumer repeatedly buys a particular brand of product and is reluctant to switch to another brand.

Brownfield Previously developed land, either commercial or industrial, that has been cleared for redevelopment.

Budgeting Reserving (a sum of money) for a particular purpose.

Business plan A written document that sets out a business's plans and objectives and how it will achieve them.

BYOD Bring your own device.

CAO Chief accounting officer.

CAPEX Capital expenditure.

CEO Chief executive officer.

CFO Chief financial officer.

Chamber of commerce A group of business owners who form a network to promote business.

CIA Certified internal auditor.

CIO Chief information officer or chief investment officer.

CISA Certified information systems auditor.

CMA Certified management accountant.

CMO Chief marketing officer.

CMR Customer relationship management.

Competitive advantage A condition or circumstance that puts a company in a favorable or superior business position.

Compliance To ensure that a company is complying with regulations.

Compliance officer A corporate official whose job is to ensure that a company is complying with regulations, and that its employees are complying with internal policies and procedures.

Conference call A telephone or Internet call that allows three or more people to take part at the same time.

Consultant An expert who is paid by a company, individual, and so forth, to give advice on developing plans and achieving goals.

Consumer An individual who uses goods and services but who may not have been the purchaser.

Continuous improvement An ongoing effort to improve products, services, or processes.

Contractor A person or firm that undertakes a contract to provide materials or labor to perform a service or do a job.

COO Chief operating officer.

Copyright A legal right to make copies of, broadcast, publish, or sell a piece of work.

Core business The primary area or activity on which a company was founded or on which it focuses in its business operations.

Core workers Employees performing the main activity of the company.

Corporate governance Visible, transparent, and published policies and practices by which an organization is directed and managed.

Corporate objectives A company's goals.

Cost avoidance Action taken to reduce future costs.

Cost–center Part of an organization to which costs may be charged for accounting purposes.

Cost–effective Producing a product or performing a process in the most economical way to the benefit of the company.

Cost saving A reduction in expenses.

CPA Certified public accountant.

CTO Chief technology officer.

Decentralization The process of redistributing or dispersing functions, powers, people, or things away from a central location or authority.

Delayering Reducing the size of a business hierarchy, especially in terms of a reduction in management.

Dividend A portion of profits paid by a company to its shareholders.

Downsizing Making a company smaller by shedding staff as a way to save costs.

e-Business Using the Internet to conduct business.

e-Commerce Electronic commerce. The buying and selling of products and services over the Internet.

EHS Environment, health, and safety.

Emerging market A country that has some characteristics of a developed market but is not yet a developed market.

e-Procurement Using the Internet to purchase or sell goods and services.

Exit strategy A plan by an investor to dispose of an investment.

EXP Export.

Expatriate A person who lives outside his or her native country.

Factory floor The production part of a factory and the collective name for ordinary workers.

Fast-moving consumer goods (FMCG) Products (and the related industry) that are sold in large volumes by big retailers at low profit margins, traditionally foods and groceries, household consumables, and so forth.

Feasibility study Assessment of a new project to determine whether it will be successful and practical.

Feasible Doable.

FIFO First in, first out.

Fixed assets Assets that are purchased for long-term use and are not likely to be converted quickly into cash, such as land, buildings, and equipment.

FME Fixed manufacturing expense.

FOB Freight onboard.

FYI For your information.

Gap analysis The comparison of actual performance with potential performance.

GDP Gross domestic product, generally considered an indicator of a national standard of living.

Glass wall An imaginary barrier in the workplace that prevents women and minority groups from being employed in other sectors of business or industry.

GM General manager.

Gone to the wall Describes a business that has failed.

GP Gross profit.

Grace A period of time given to debtors to enable them to pay an overdue bill or loan, or extra time given in a contract for a piece of work to be finished.

Grassroots The ordinary people in a business or organization, rather than the management.

Greenfield A form of foreign direct investment in which a parent company starts a new venture in a foreign country by constructing new operational facilities from the ground up.

Headcount Total number of people, especially the number of people employed in a particular organization.

Headhunt To find people who are specialized in a particular job, usually for a senior position in a company, and then persuade them to leave their present employment.

Health and safety Concerned with the protection of employees from risks and dangers in the workplace.

HO Head office.

Holding company A company formed for owning and holding controlling shares in other companies.

HQ Headquarters.

HR Human resources.

HRM Human resource management.

Human capital The skills, knowledge, and experience possessed by an individual or population, viewed in terms of their value or cost to an organization.

IA Internal audit.

ICT Information and communication technologies.

IMP Import.

Incentive A thing that motivates or encourages someone to do something.

Induction The introduction and training of a member of staff in a new job or position in a company.

Intellectual property (IP) An idea or creation, e.g., artwork or writing, that belongs to an individual or organization, which has commercial value and therefore cannot be copied or sold without the owner's permission.

Internal controls A process for ensuring achievement of an organization's objectives in operational effectiveness and efficiency, reliable financial reporting, and compliance with laws, regulations, and policies.

IS Information systems.

ISO Information security officer.

IT Information technologies.

JIT "Just in time" manufacturing system in which materials and components are delivered immediately before they are required, to increase efficiency, reduce waste, and minimize storage costs.

Job costing A system of calculating the cost of each individual job or project carried out by a business, including time, labor, materials, etc.

K Abbreviation for 1,000.

Kaizen Japanese for "improvement." When implemented in the workplace, *kaizen* activities help to improve the running of a business.

Key account In business, a company's main client or customer.

Knowledge base In a computer system, a database with a store of information, facts, and rules that can be used for problem solving.

KPI Key performance indicators: a type of performance measurement. An organization may use KPIs to evaluate its success or evaluate the success of a particular activity in which it is engaged.

KYC Know your customer.

Laid-off In industry, for example, when workers lose their jobs, sometimes temporarily, because there is no work for them.

Lean Also known as the Toyota production system or "just in time" production. A system used in management, production, manufacturing, and so forth, to decrease waste and increase efficiency, especially with the use of automated assembly lines.

Legal entity An individual or organization that has the legal right to enter into a contract or agreement.

Liabilities Debts that are owed to someone, obligations, or responsibilities that are legally binding.

LIFO Last in, first out.

Lightning strike A sudden strike by workers, with little or no warning. These strikes are often short in duration and usually without official union backing.

LLC Limited liability company.

Lockout A term used during an industrial dispute, when management closes down a workplace and bars employees from entering until they agree to certain terms and conditions.

Ltd Limited company.

LTI Lost time injury.

Macromanagement Management style that allows employees to do their jobs with minimal supervision.

Management team A team of individuals at the highest level of organizational management who have the day-to-day responsibilities of managing a company or corporation.

Market penetration The extent to which a product is recognized and bought by customers in a particular market.

Market share The portion of a market controlled by a particular company or product.

MD Managing director.

Merchandising The practice of promoting and selling goods.

Meta/meta-tags/metadata "Meta" means an additional useful part of the whole thing, usually data or communication of some sort, and usually hidden or underlying and coded.

Micromanagement A management style whereby a manager closely observes or controls the work of subordinates. Micromanagement generally has a negative connotation.

Middle management In organizations and business, managers who are in charge of small departments and groups of people while reporting to upper management.

Milestone A significant stage or event in the development of something.

Mitigate To make something less severe or dangerous, e.g., using "mitigating circumstances" as an excuse to try to make an offense seem less serious than it appears.

MTD Month-to-date.

Mystery shopper A person hired by market research companies or manufacturers to visit shops or service providers anonymously to assess the quality of goods and service.

Niche market A specialized market in which a specific product is sold to a particular type or group of customers. A product or service for which there is sometimes little demand and often little or no competition.

NOA Net operating assets.

NTE Not to exceed.

Occupational hazard An aspect of a job that can be dangerous or pose a high risk of injury.

Offshoring The practice of basing some of a company's processes or services overseas so as to take advantage of lower costs.

Optimize To get the most out of something. To use something in the best possible way.

Outsourcing An arrangement in which a company produces goods or provides services for another company.

Overtime Time worked in addition to normal working hours. The pay received, usually charged at a higher rate, for working outside regular working hours.

Overtrading A term in financial statement analysis. Overtrading often occurs when companies expand their own operations too quickly.

P&L Profit and loss.

P2P Peer-to-peer: a model for computer connectivity and file sharing.

P4P Pay for performance.

PAT Profit after tax.

PBT Profit before tax

PEST analysis Political, economical, social, and technological analysis: a business tool used in strategic planning that helps in understanding environmental influences on a business.

Primary distribution Distribution toward distribution centers and warehouses.

Primary production Preparation of raw materials or parts of a product that can be used later in secondary production to manufacture the actual product.

Production floor The part of a factory housing the machines and workers directly involved in production.

Project manager A person responsible for planning and delivering a large standalone task, objective, venture, and so forth (a large and complex project) or a professional who is skilled in doing this.

Project sponsor A person in an organization who instigates or proposes a project and creates/establishes/agrees to the necessary executive approval, funding, resourcing, etc.

Puff In advertising, to exaggerate the qualities of a product, etc., without actually breaking the law.

QA Quality assurance.

QC Quality control.

Quick win Result that can be achieved with minimal effort.

R&D Research and development.

Raw materials Basic material from which a product is made.

Recall Asking customers to return a product they have bought because it has been found to be faulty or dangerous.

Redundancy The state of being no longer needed. Usually refers to employees' layoffs as a way to cut costs.

RFP Request for proposal.

Risk In business, especially insurance, the amount of money a company stands to lose or the threat of an action or event that will have an adverse effect on a business.

ROI Return of investment.

ROS Return on sales.

Salary grade A step within a compensation system that defines the salary range based on position.

Sales forecasting Projection of achievable sales revenue, based on historical sales data, analysis of market surveys and trends, and salespersons.

Scam Means of making money by deceit or fraud.

SCM Supply chain management.

Screening interview A brief, first job interview, sometimes conducted over the phone.

Secondary distribution Distribution toward clients.

Secondary production Production of the final product.

Security/securities The strict financial meaning of a security is a document that proves ownership of stocks, shares, bonds, and so forth, or other investments or financial derivatives.

Server A computer that provides services to other computers connected to the network.

Six sigma A business strategy developed by Motorola that strives for perfection in production and quality.

SMART objectives (also ASMART) Tasks that are feasible by being specific, measurable, achievable, realistic, and timely.

SME Small and medium enterprises.

Spam Unsolicited e-mail sent to numerous recipients.

Spin doctor A public relations official or press/media spokesperson in government or corporate work.

Spin The presentation of information in a way designed to support a particular position.

Stakeholder A person or group, such as shareholders, customers, employees, suppliers, etc., with a vested interest in a company or organization, or successful completion of a project.

Stealth marketing A method of advertising a product in which customers do not realize they are being persuaded to buy something.

Strike-breaker A person who continues to work, or is employed to work, during a strike.

SWOT Strengths, weaknesses, opportunities, and threats.

Talent Advancement potential of an employee.

Targets Financial performance goals.

Task force A group of people formed to work on a particular project or assignment.

TBD To be defined.

Threshold The magnitude or intensity that must be exceeded, or the lowest acceptable result.

Uptime Time during which a machine is in operation.

VAT Value-added tax.

Win–win Describes a situation or arrangement in which all parties benefit or profit.

YTD Year-to-date.

Who: Arrange

CHAPTER 3

The People

CHIEF SECURITY OFFICER COMPETENCES

We know that the difference between homeland security and corporate security is enormous in terms of philosophies, priorities, strategies, models, and threats. Also, corporate security engagements require different competences that usually make the difference between a security professional in a corporation and a professional corporate security manager. Apart from default competences such as security skills and knowledge, integrity and commitment, flexibility, and the ability to acquire new skills, corporate roles require certain business competences such as:

- Understanding corporate culture
- Business acumen
- Management skills
- Communication and presentation skills

Understanding Corporate Culture

Aside from giving a short definition and explanation of corporate culture, in this part we will not research corporate culture in a scientific sense but more on the level at which it affects the working atmosphere, interpersonal interactions, daily tasks, privacy, and morale and ethics. Corporate security managers must have the ability to feel and understand the culture of the company and blend in successfully. This also means understanding peer-to-peer relations and applying the right level of distance and intimacy to prevent and manage conflicts and achieve goals.

The term "corporate culture" refers to the specific models of behavior, people and process management, and peer interactions that a corporation management is communicating and imposing throughout the organization.

These models include values, visions, language, management and communication techniques and models, change management, and involvement of workforce in proposing business decisions. They also define how the company interacts and communicates with partners, clients, and consumers and its involvement in the community and social responsibility. Some factors that influence corporate culture are the geographical location and structure of the workforce, the level of risk a company is willing to take in its business decisions, and how close to the edge of legality a company is willing to go to market the product, especially for business fields experiencing legal limitations, such as tobacco or alcohol manufacturers.

On a more personal level, corporate culture defines the preferred model of management, such as micro- or macromanagement, including the level of trust in employees and how they are controlled, regarding, for example, strict control of time and attendance compared with focus on achievements or the matter of respect of the privacy of employees, such as random routine control of e-mail correspondence. The openness or distance throughout the organizational hierarchy is also derived from corporate culture as well as the way ethics and morale are practically exercised in a company. Corporate culture also defines the accepted level of competiveness between employees. Unfortunately, in many corporations employees prefer to invest time and energy in discrediting their colleagues instead of focusing on their own achievements as a way to gain more professional respect. This "bear" philosophy is best explained in an old hoary saying: "You don't have to run faster than the bear to get away. You just have to run faster than the guy next to you." Basically, in every corporation there are employees who will devote the same amount of time to completing their assignments as to making sure that they will receive credit for its success or "run faster than a colleague" in case of failure. Moreover, in many cases concerns about responsibility slow down sensitive business processes. For example, it is important to know that every e-mail you send, as insignificant as it may seem at that moment, could be archived by the receiver and eventually be pulled out against you as a way for your colleague to escape responsibility. Your counterpart might present out-of-context pieces of e-mail correspondence while hoping that you, on the other hand, did not archive the e-mails.

There are several indications concerning the corporate culture for which a potential employee would look: reward and benefits, accessibility of tools, advancement and training possibilities, management styles, peer-to-peer communication, and workforce fluctuation.

Business Acumen

Literally, business acumen is the ability to understand business and make successful business decisions. It is certainly one of the crucial chief security officer (CSO) competences. In terms of CSO competence, we can divide business acumen into three main components:

- Understanding business
- Understanding the company's specifics and its core processes
- Being financially literate

Understanding Business

Understanding the concept of business is the first component of business acumen. A corporation is a limited liability for-profit organization created by its shareholders and run by a board of directors who appoint and oversee the management of the corporation. Corporations apply business strategies to grow and expand in terms of variety of services and products and by spreading out to new markets, as well as in the ways they market their products and save costs to make a profit, gain wider audiences, and stay ahead of their competition. To be successful, security strategies must be designed with business strategies in mind. Security must support the business vision of the corporation and its direction, which requires the CSO to be able to understand the essence of business and see the wider picture.

Understanding the Company's Specifics and Its Core Processes

Apart from understanding business as a phenomenon, a CSO must know and understand the specifics of the industry and the particular corporation, the company's core business processes, and the particulars of the product or service, including its lifecycle. Understanding the core business means understanding how it influences security as well as how security influences the core business. Not only is there no corporate security model applicable to all the industries, but often, even in companies belonging to the same industry and having a similar product, security strategies might have to be opposite each other to be successful.

Being Financially Literate

Financial literacy is a must in the corporate world. First, to protect profit, we must be able to understand how it is generated. On a more hands-on level, security planning requires budgeting. Moreover, a key indicator of successful management is successful budgeting and budget management. Chief security officers are required not only to produce solid security results but also to achieve cost savings and cost avoidance. Financial literacy is also crucial during negotiations with contractors and contractor management.

Management Skills versus Technical Expertise

The traditional approach tells us that we should be more technically expert than the people we are managing, but this is absolutely not true. Basically, it is unlikely that you know everything better than your employees. If you do, you have a problem. You will end up trying to do their job for them or micromanage instead of managing the system as a whole. You will certainly not be able to successfully take over the tasks from all people in your organization and produce solid results. The goal of expertise on a management level is to put the pieces together into a successful and sustainable security system. The purpose of management and leadership is to direct all elements toward producing the best results that correspond with the security strategy and overall business goals of the organization. One important element of management is the development of subordinates by coaching, providing honest and constructive feedback and empowering the team by encouraging teamwork. The reputation and success of managers depend on their ability to lead and coach their team into producing relevant results.

On a more personal level, management also means helping employees with career development. Contrary to the opinion that development of subordinates will jeopardize a position owing to competition, developed subordinates are a sign of successful management and add to the managerial reputation. Second, for a manager to move on and take over a position with greater responsibility, the organization must have a potential candidate in mind who is able to replace him in his current role.

Communication and Presentation Skills

The success of CSOs and their goals depend greatly on their ability to communicate effectively with superiors, peers, subordinates, and partners (contractors). This communication consists of educating, selling security to the management, engaging peers, and motivating subordinates and partners. Communication and presentation skills consist of two sides: the "what" and the "how." The "what" element is basically clear, but the true challenge and the element that could make the difference lies in the "how." Communication not only depends on the charisma of the CSO; it requires the CSO to be familiar with the corporate culture and accepted models of communication, including e-mail correspondence and presentation templates. It also calls for relevance, level of simplicity, complexity, and terminology tailored to the audience, and the ability to listen and observe.

Effective communication, as well as presentation, can be summarized as four principles:

1. *Knowledgeable speaker*—a knowledgeable, passionate, enthusiastic, motivated, reliable, and credible communicator
2. *Interesting presentation*—an enthusiastic, ethical, and attention-grabbing presentation
3. *Relevance*—a well-structured, realistic, relevant, meaningful, and applicable message tailored to the audience
4. *Call for action*—The aim of communication and a presentation is not to communicate and present, but to achieve a goal. This basically means that the audience will know exactly what to do after you finish your presentation.

SECURITY TEAM

Building a Team

Building a security team is a far more complex task than simply gathering security professionals who specialize in various fields of security. First, an engine (a team) is much more than many independent parts (members), regardless of their quality. Second, no security team formula can work in every situation, ranging from variations in the size and hierarchical structure of the team to professional profiles of individual team members and their compatibility. However, the structure and size of a security team and the profiles of its members depend on many factors such as the budget, the industry, the nature of the business (product, service, or mixed orientation), the type of business, and the business's product, core processes, vulnerabilities, and location and whether the business is a single or multisite operation. As we have discussed, every investment needs to be financially justifiable. This is especially true for the investment in human resources, which is believed by companies to be the most expensive one, especially in parts of the company that do not generate profit, such as security. Basically, as we have already mentioned, investment in security measures, including people, has to correlate logically with the cost of incidents. To be more specific, the cost of security measures must not exceed the cost of incidents over a reasonable period (return of investment). As we mentioned, the main objective of the business is not to lose money, regardless of where the money is going. If your security organization is more expensive than the cost of not having it, your company will opt to accept the risk and lose less.

Second, even in the unlikely situation where you are given the freedom to employ as many expensive professionals as you want, professional expertise and the size of the organization are not necessarily crucial factors when it comes to producing results. However, it is more important to have a coherent team that is working toward a common goal than a group of excellent individuals who are working independently. When building a team, we usually concentrate on several features that are crucial for team dynamics:

- Performance (right position at a right time doing right things in the right way)—It basically means that you have the person with relevant skills for the position, at the right moment in his career, who is appropriately instructed concerning his tasks and has the ability to execute them.
- Best for the team—You want a person who will fit in the team like a piece of a puzzle but at the same time motivate the team. It is not unusual or wrong to involve the other team members in assessing a potential newcomer to the team.
- A communicator—Good communication is essential for the team and the management and for dealing with issues at an early stage.
- Character—You are employing not only a professional but also a person with whom you are going to interact.

A typical division of professional security pillars in a security organization is based on specific skills and experience required for a certain field of security. The most common pillars in a security organization are:

- Physical security and manned guarding
- Security technology
- Anti-fraud
- Information and information communications technologies (ICT) security
- Business continuity management (BCM) and disaster recovery (DR)

Certainly, what parts of the organization will be reserved for a certain pillar, as well as required experience, seniority, knowledge, and specific expectations from the person in charge, depend on the importance of that segment in the particular company. Basically, there is a big difference between expertise, job descriptions, importance, and attention given to an ICT security professional in a retail chain and in a bank, including the number of professionals required to manage the process successfully.

A simple system that can help you understand your employment (team-building) requirements and help you decide if you will merge certain positions, have more professionals in other positions, or create separate teams is grading the importance of each pillar in your security organization by awarding it percentages. Therefore, if the entire team is worth 100%, award percentages to each pillar based on its importance and complexity, for example:

- Physical security and manned guarding (10%)
- Security technology (10%)
- Anti-fraud (30%)
- Information and ICT security (30%)
- BCM and DR (20%)

You may decide to have one person dealing with physical and technical security instead of two, have one BCM and DR manager, and create an ICT security and anti-fraud team consisting of a team head and two executives. Based on the complexity of a certain function, you may decide to split it in two. For example, if your ICT security part of the team is responsible for the technical aspect of ICT security as well as for information security and ICT security governance, you may want to divide that pillar between two executives, each covering a particular segment of information and ICT security.

As security managers, it is unlikely that we have experience and sufficient knowledge of all the segments of security. Unfortunately, this sometimes leads to a wrong judgment when building a security team. Many times, instead of building a team based on the requirements of the business, security managers tend to exaggerate by over-focusing on the positions in which they do not specialize. Opposite that approach but also wrong, some security managers focus on their comfort zone and gather professionals who have expertise in fields with which they are familiar (clones), which gives them the false feeling that they are successfully managing the team.

Professional Pillars in a Security Team

To assist you in identifying the right professional expertise, I will analyze the basic job requirements for the most common positions in a security team.

Physical Security and Manned Guarding

In most corporate systems, manned guarding is outsourced. Physical security managers mostly deal with the organization of the outsourced workforce in terms of the quality and quantity of performed services. Manned guarding systems usually perform the following tasks:

- Reception and hostess—directing visitors, handling postal mail, and answering calls
- Access control—keeping out everything and anyone who should not enter and keeping in everything that should stay
- Patrolling—trying to single out any suspicious behavior, object, or event

- Operation of security and fire safety equipment—any technical equipment that can assist in detecting, preventing, and mitigating incidents
- Cash in transit (CIT) and/or security escort of goods—security measures aimed at protecting the transported items.

The physical security manager is in charge of:

- Maintaining regular contact with the management of the outsourced company
- Receiving and checking invoices for the delivered service and matching them with actual performance
- Constantly working on ensuring and improving the performance of the manned guarding system by performing drills, tests, and trainings
- Measuring performance (key performance indicators)
- Creating procedures and working instructions for security officers and ensuring that they are being followed
- Creating the systems of physical checks of employees during entering and exiting
- Ensuring that all the employees comply with procedures (including those dealing with some other aspects of security, such as a clean desk policy)
- Creating routes and systematically breaking the routine of CIT and transport
- Physical key management and procedures
- Making sure that all physical security elements (fences, walls, doors, windows, lighting, etc.) are maintained and working properly
- Keeping a record of incidents
- Creating and following the budget for manned guarding services and physical security
- Keeping track of dates, anniversaries, and information that could affect the security of the facility
- Creating and maintaining emergency plans in terms of evacuation and response
- Dealing with employee theft (of personal items and company assets)

Physical security managers often have a military, police, or national security background.

Technical Security Engineer

Security engineering is a field of security (and engineering) that deals with security technology used by the company (in the facilities, vehicles, homes of top executives, and so forth). The security engineer works closely with the physical security manager and is in charge of budgeting, designing, engineering, controlling, and maintaining security equipment (not ICT security technology). Security technology includes, but is not limited to:

- Closed-circuit television
- Alarms
- Access control

- Global positioning systems
- Retail security equipment
- Electronic locks
- Weapon detection equipment (metal detection gates and devices, X-rays, etc.)
- Fire detection, fire prevention, and firefighting equipment
- Emergency alarming and evacuation technology (alerting and directing systems)

The security engineer is also responsible for creating facility files that list all of the technical equipment and its location, use, and age, maintenance requirements, and basically all technical information concerning the secured perimeter and the area that could be useful during a special situation.

Security engineers are usually required to have an academic background in electrical engineering or related fields and experience in working with security technology.

Information and ICT

Basically, the ICT security function can be divided into two processes. The first one (ICT security analyst) deals with technical ICT security such as:
- Determining security violations and insufficiencies
- Recommending setting enhancements and purchases
- Performing risk assessments and testing of data-processing systems
- Creating, testing, and implementing network disaster recovery plans
- Performing periodic penetration tests

Information security analysts are usually required to have an academic background in computer science or related fields and experience in ICT security and to have professional certification such as CISS or PCISM and/or vendor credentials such as the ones offered by Cisco or Microsoft.

The second part of ICT security deals with information security and ICT security governance and audits (information security specialist) such as:
- Defining access privileges, user profiles and control structures, and resources
- Assessing the situation, evaluating trends, and anticipating requirements
- Conducting periodic audits
- Implementing and maintaining security controls
- Preparing performance reports
- Educating users
- Following organizational standards
- Creating and implementing procedures
- Ensuring compliance with procedures, rules, and standards

Information security specialists are usually required to have an academic background in computer science or related fields and experience in ICT security, and to have professional certification such as CISA and CISM.

Business Continuity and DR Manager

The BCM manager is responsible for developing, maintaining, and managing the company's business continuity program. He or she supports all activities necessary to enable the company to respond to a business interruption. Main tasks performed by a BCM manager include:

- Developing and maintaining a corporate-wide business continuity program that addresses disaster recovery, business recovery, and emergency response management
- Developing, producing, and updating business continuity plan (BCP)/DR materials and documentation, such as plans and emergency response procedures
- Planning and coordinating all business continuity technical and user tests
- Anticipating business interruptions
- Creating and periodically updating business impact analysis
- Working closely with the ICT department to develop/maintain DR plans for critical systems and applications and to ensure that internal recovery sites are updated and functioning properly
- Liaising with business continuity coordinators in all departments to develop effective working relationships
- Performing risk analyses for functional areas to identify points of vulnerability and single points of failure and to identify risk avoidance and mitigation strategies
- Leading crisis management efforts in the event of a business interruption
- Developing status reports on departmental continuity plans and preparing management reports as necessary
- Checking and approving BCPs of suppliers and service providers

Business continuity managers are usually required to have a background in economics, business administration, finances, or related fields, with strong IT skills and experience in business continuity.

Fraud Prevention and Detection Specialist

The fraud prevention and detection specialist job description greatly depends on the industry and the type of company, its products and services, and the way it conducts its processes. Here are some of the main fraud prevention and detection processes:

- Using intelligence and analytics to identify emerging fraud
- Detecting additional people involved in detected fraud
- Analyzing transactional anomalies
- Establishing plans and tests to identify fraudulent activity proactively
- Checking fraud vulnerability for new products, services, and processes and advising on improvements
- Gathering information and understanding new fraudulent trends in the industry.
- Performing investigations and investigative interviews

- Coordinating ICT forensics and accounting forensics as part of fraud investigations
- Leading cross-departmental teams focused on fraud prevention

Fraud prevention and detection specialists are usually required to have a background in accounting, finance, computer science, or related fields with experience in investigations or internal audits, for example, and to have strong IT skills.

PRIVATE SECURITY INDUSTRY
About Private Security Industry

According to the number of people it employs, the private security industry is one of the largest industries in the world and is rapidly growing. If we were to count the private and state security/military sectors together, we would see that security is definitely the industry with the largest number of employees worldwide, with countless numbers of people around the globe who have been engaged in security in one way or another at some point in their careers.

Private security companies are enterprises that provide armed and/or unarmed security service and/or knowledge to clients. The largest part of the private security industry belongs to companies providing manned guarding services by deploying security guards (security officers) at their clients' facilities for the purpose of protecting people and assets. Manned guarding companies mostly deal with entry control, receptionist services, patrolling and stewarding, protection of cash in transit, operation of technical systems, fire protection, and prevention and detection of theft. Manned guarding companies often also provide bodyguard services, bouncer services, and guard dog services. Whereas manned guarding jobs were traditionally reserved for male guards, in recent years female security officers have become the necessity and privilege of every modern manned guarding system. One reason is the ability of female officers to perform physical checks on females, as well as their assumed advantage over male officers when it comes to noticing details, spotting suspicious behavior, and questioning (performing a security interview).

Use of firearms by security guards in corporate security greatly has decreased in recent years as security systems are concentrating more on prevention than on reaction. Apart from the shift in the nature and perception of security, one reason is the lack of skill. The low cost of security services and the workforce fluctuation makes it hard for security companies to invest in proper firearms training for employees. Unfortunately, cases of successful use of firearms by security guards during an incident are incomparably lower than cases of accidental deaths and injuries caused by their incorrect and unsafe use.

Apart from manned guarding companies, the private security industry consists mostly of companies dealing with technical systems (engineering, selling, and installing), security consulting companies, companies delivering specialized trainings, private military companies (often referred to as security contractors), investigation agencies, and ICT security providers.

Private Security Industry Challenges

In the time of a global economy crisis, we are witnessing two major industries that are experiencing significant growth: the private security industry, which is considered one of the fastest growing industries in the world, and crime, which is probably the most profitable industry worldwide. Unskilled workers who have lost their jobs owing to cuts and layoffs are often left to choose one of the two. Employment in the private security sector has long been a matter of necessity, not of choice, but it seems that the situation is becoming even worse. In this part, we will analyze the challenges that the manned guarding part of the security industry, as its largest piece, is experiencing.

Private security companies are facing the problem of having to employ staff quickly, to meet the headcount requirements of their clients, so that it often exceeds their background screening, training, and proper people management capacities. More and more companies are deciding to replace their in-house security service with a contracted workforce to lower expenses and often outsource not only the guarding services but the entire security organization.

Security companies often submit the lowest bids possible to win contracts from a client; this reflects on the salaries of the guards. Such contracts also mean lower profits and less money for training and equipment. The only way security companies are able to survive is to employ cheaper unskilled workers and immediately dress them in a uniform that, together with a radio station, is sometimes the only equipment the guards will get. Also, they work long shifts, sometimes without being provided with basic comfort and appropriate working conditions. Low pay rates influence job retention, which is somewhere between medium and low. For example, according to the January 2006 report by the Service Employees International Union (SEIU.org) [1], private security is one of the fastest growing occupations in the United States, with turnover rates comparable to the fast-food industry but with little oversight and regulations.

What should be the scope of service of private security companies, which are contracted to provide a complete security solution for their clients? In a perfect world, private security companies would be well-informed, understand the impact that the global and local climate, such as politics and economy, can have on security, be able to process data, predict events, and implement timely adjustments by combining physical and technical security, develop procedures, perform trainings, and collect and protect information and developing communication channels. Unfortunately, many private security companies are based on day-to-day service and are mostly concentrated on routine activities and emergency response without spending resources and energy on understanding the causes and observing trends, predicting unfavorable developments, and adjusting accordingly. Of course, according to the employment criteria mentioned previously, it would be unrealistic to expect it.

The private security sector often tends to forget that security does not exist to serve itself but to serve and assist the business, and that its performance depends on contacts and relations with the clients. The reality is that private security companies' managements often do not seem interested in learning the specifics of the business to which they are providing a service. What about the popular statement that "Services are tailored according to the specific needs of the client," which we can find on almost every private security company's Web site? It probably became lost somewhere between the clients' preoccupation with core business, cuts in the budget, and complete outsourcing of almost all supporting services, including security, thus placing security out of sight and creating the inability of the security industry to become a business partner by getting to know the business it is protecting and being able to negotiate more favorable contracts. Even more so, in some companies, field employees are instructed to keep a low profile in communication with the client and are isolating themselves completely. Lack of communication in no way contributes to a better understanding of security by the clients and often leads to security guards being given tasks that have nothing to do with security, thus shifting them even further from providing professional security services. Some private security companies seem to be no more than manpower agencies that supply unskilled personnel to clients to act as security guards. Sometimes the only contact between the security company and its employees and with the client is via a bank account.

But are the increased demand for security services that exceed the capacity of some private security companies, unfavorable contracts, lack of business knowledge, and unskilled personnel the only causes of the decrease in the quality of service that the private security industry is experiencing?

Outsourcing of Manned Guarding

The outsourcing of manned guarding services is a trend that is gaining popularity among companies everywhere. For companies it seems to be the perfect way to cut expenses, not waste time and resources on nonprofit activities, and distant themselves from processes about which they know nothing. As security providers gained more contracts while their clients managed to cut on expenses, the concept of outsourcing has encountered little opposition. But is it that perfect? I would like to explore two opposed opinions concerning outsourcing by two senior security professionals and let you come to your own conclusions.

In Favor of Outsourcing

Security outsourcing is an unavoidable joint project performed by the security service provider and the company in which security is not a core business process, to achieve three main benefits: cost savings, quality improvement, and increased motivation of outsourced security staff. The financial benefit is clear. Taking into account that every employee is entitled to have a vacation and go on sick leave, it is clear that on these occasions there is a need for additional staff to occupy positions that are temporarily unattended. If the company has extra headcount to fill in the gaps, it would have a surplus once everyone is back on their positions. This means decreased functionality of security and higher expenses. Professional security companies are able to fill in the blanks from their own resources and keep the number of present staff steady and the expenses unchanged. In the case that there is misconduct or negligence by outsourced security staff that results in financial loss to the company, the damage is reimbursed by the security services provider or, in the case of great damage, by an insurance company.

All expenses such as training uniforms, communication equipment, and so forth are dealt with by the security service provider. If a company has numerous operations and premises and requires additional staff anywhere, large security service providers that are present all over the country can provide staff and high-quality service on short notice and with minimal cost. As for the improvement of the quality of service, the fact that security is a core business for security providers inevitably means that these companies are following all of the security trends and constantly working on innovations and improvement of service that they provide. A big part of the improved quality of service is procedures dealing with selecting and employing new staff. The procedures are adapted to match all of the specifics of the security industry and are being developed according to the highest international security industry standards. By contracting professional security service providers, the quick and efficient replacement of security personnel who have not performed according to requirements is done easily and without complicated processes and human resources procedures. Security personnel who are transferred from a company in which they were employed to an outsourcing security company will be more motivated to perform their task in surroundings that are concentrated on their field of work and understand all of the specifics of the job. Security companies know how to value security; apart from providing trainings and courses, they facilitate career moves based on results. According to the requirements of the client, staff can stay on the same positions they were occupying before the takeover and preserve the same income for the agreed-upon period of time.

Opposed to Outsourcing

Outsourcing of security staff is usually performed by companies that do not understand the concept of professional security and the concept of cost avoidance as opposed to cost savings. It is certain that for those companies security is not a core business process, but preserving their interests, such as effective loss prevention and control over processes that are designed to protect the profit, product, all processes, business continuity, and well-being of staff according to the specifics of the company, is definitely a core interest.

Is outsourcing really another name for cost savings? How can a company save money if it has to pay the company's fee on top of the salaries of security officers? It is clear that officers go on vacations and sick leave, but the blanks can be solved by temporarily reorganizing the setup. Of course, there can be still a need for additional officers, but that can be resolved by having on-call security officers or then using the services of a security services provider. Because of the familiarity with work, the on-call security officers will also be able to join the security team permanently once there is a vacancy. If a loss happens owing to misconduct or negligence by contracted security officers, insurance companies will pay the damage, but only to a certain extent and only for a directly visible loss. For example, secondary loss such as damage to the reputation of the company that would result in a decrease in profit or loss as a result of leakage of valuable business information will not be dealt with. Of course, if you do not employ security officers directly, this means that you cannot control their performance sufficiently to be in control and have the security officers adopt your company's core values. Another issue is that the large staff turnover in security companies widens the population that is familiar with your security setup; keeping in mind the high percentage of crimes committed by current or ex-security employees, this enormously increases the risk of crimes being committed against your company. Service providers can supply staff quickly, but there is a big question about the quality of staff they can provide, especially if we know that a large number of people become security officers after losing their jobs as unqualified laborers on construction sites. On the other hand, even the best officers need sufficient time to adapt to the new environment and learn the specifics of the job to become efficient. What about the improvement of performance? How can a company apply change management and continuous improvement or other business philosophies to contracted employees?

How is it possible to promote unity, teamwork, and common goals when you have a whole department in your company working for another company? Does the selection process really make a difference? Employment in the private security sector has long been a matter of necessity, not choice. Private security companies are facing a problem of having to employ staff quickly to meet the headcount requirements of their clients, which often exceeds their background screening, training, and proper people management capacities. Let us also mention that a company that uses contracted security services can often unofficially (legally) influence the employment criteria of its security contractor. Security is not a core business but every security department is different and the way it works depends on the core business and the knowledge of the staff about core business processes. Security companies provide some sort of general training, but only in the actual place of work can officers really start learning the job, which will require time and money but will not be covered by the security company. Of course, because security companies have a high personnel turnover, this investment is likely to become a loss within a short time. It is known that motivation cannot be increased by increasing salaries, but when it comes to salaries becoming lower, this will definitely have a negative impact on employee motivation.

After takeover, salaries can stay the same if this is the agreement between the company and the service provider, but the fee of the security provider is added, which does not really make sense. It is naive to believe that a drastic difference between salaries of staff employed directly and outsourced staff will not have a negative impact on motivation and ownership. Anyway, why not ask security officers who are working for a respected company whether they wish it to be taken over by a security provider?

How to Choose a Provider of Manned Guarding Services

The company has chosen the option of not burdening the core business with the organization of security services within the company or the existing security service does not work the way in which it is expected. The company searches for a security provider that will respond to all requests and needs in the field of security while confirming the financial justification of the whole project.

The first step toward introducing security companies operating in the market can be to search an open source (Internet, media, etc.), ask for a recommendation from someone who had experience with a similar project, or open a public announcement of procurement. In all three cases, it is likely that the choice will be wrong.

Searching for a security provider through an open source such as the Internet will result in a large quantity of mostly useless and even false information. It is common for companies to advertise enormous staff capacity, knowledge, experience, and state-of-the-art equipment and to list hundreds of respectful clients and then prove to be no more than one-man-show companies with no real abilities. Moreover, tens and sometimes even hundreds of companies call themselves market leaders.

Firsthand recommendations can be the basis for selecting a service provider. However, security risks, threats, and consequently security needs vary not only within different industries, but also within the same industry and similar processes. Depending on the micro-locations, social circumstances, the complexity of facilities, and so forth, a successful security provider in one company can prove to be a completely wrong choice for another company. For instance, in addition to capacity and professional capabilities, a security service provider must have sufficient presence (for example, staff, technology, and infrastructure) in the specific geographical area to respond in a timely and successful manner to incidents and special requests. A large respectful security company will be useless if it has no significant operations in the required location. Another aspect is the level of attention the security service provider gives to its clients. Large companies certainly have a higher potential to respond to the needs of their clients. However, large companies with numerous clients will not devote the same level of attention to all of their clients, but will, mostly based on profit (and not on the level of risk), classify clients into categories and certainly take more care of their key accounts than other companies which they regard as less important. Sometimes, choosing a smaller service provider will generate better result in terms of care, attention, and response time.

Open public advertising of procurement is usually a waste of valuable time because of the numerous companies that apply for it. In many cases, companies will apply even if they do not meet the required criteria. Worse, some companies will even provide false information regardless of the consequences.

Companies should definitely look for a security provider that offers a broad range of multiple security services and has a capacity beyond immediate requirements. Although some companies prefer to have several service providers to ensure business continuity, I believe that having multiple security service providers adds unnecessary complexity and makes security management more difficult and less controllable.

Like when hiring new employees, references are important. A company should definitely contact them for feedback. A good sign for service providers could be high customer retention and customers who have extended their contracts multiple times. This gives some level of quality assurance that the security service provider can really deliver.

The advantage should be given to a security provider who is profitable and reinvests most profits back into growing its operational capabilities. However, finding a profitable security service provider could prove to be challenging with so many security service providers that depend on constant venture capital.

Security officers are often the weakest link in the security company. Knowing that the staff has relevant capabilities, training, and security clearances and that these criteria are taken into account during the recruitment process is important. A security service provider should have experience in the particular industry and assign staff who are experienced in specific environments and in performing specific tasks. Expectations and penalties should be well-defined and clearly stated in the service agreement. For the expectations to be met and flaws sanctioned, the entire process should be described in detail, as well as time frames within which the company can expect a response.

Contracting Specialized Services

For global operations, companies often use the services of specialized security companies. These services usually include special tasks such as assistance in emergency and evacuation from hostile situations, hostage rescue operations, due diligence, and intelligence.

On a more local level, security departments often decide to contract external investigators. The financial reason is that professional investigators are an expensive asset that is usually not needed on a daily basis. From the operational side, security departments prefer to have an external expert conducting internal investigations and interviews with employees and to maintain good contact with the investigated colleagues once the investigations are over.

Another type of outsourced service is news reports. News agencies provide reports concerning announced and predicted events, such as planned strikes and demonstrations, commemoration dates, anniversaries, and problematic upcoming sports events, which are useful tools for short-term security planning.

Subcontracted Security Services

Often there are situations when a company contracts a service provider that then subcontracts security. One such example is party-like events sponsored by companies to promote their brand. Companies outsource the entire organization of the event, including security, and in this way transfer legal risks to another company. This basically means that the contracted company is officially the owner of the event whereas the first company is only the sponsor, so that if something goes wrong at the event, the outsourced company will be legally responsible.

However, there is a problem, or actually a few problems. First, although the event is officially organized by a no-name company, the event is promoting the brand of your company. The brand, whether it is Coca-Cola, Carlsberg, Marlboro, Levi's, or you name it, is what everybody will remember, because that is the point of marketing. Moreover, if anything goes wrong at the event, the outsourced company could be legally responsible but the brand will get negative publicity and its reputation will be jeopardized.

Second, most of your company's employees will be at the event, so basically, at your company's event, you have a contracted event-organizing company that has contracted a security company that is in charge of the security of your people.

These are just two of many reasons not to allow security process, contracted or subcontracted, to run without your involvement, starting with identifying the company and continuing with assessing its capacity, designing its protection strategy, briefing it, and directly supervising it during deployment.

PEOPLE MANAGEMENT AND LEADERSHIP
Basic Principles of Effective Leadership

Management is a two-way street. As a manager, you are not only managing processes, but you are also managing people as well as managing professionals who are executing processes. Whereas managing processes requires people skills as well as professional expertise, managing people is a step above pure management because it requires leadership. Leaders are not afraid to make the difficult decisions and establish the constantly improving standards of performance. Many managers never become leaders because leadership requires effort and time to understand people and to learn how to motivate and direct them. Leadership also means knowing each member of the team, how each member individually contributes to the team, and how to create a team in which all individual personal qualities are used for the benefit of the team.

Most companies have well-established principles, systems, and templates for managing and appraising performance. Still, these principles are mostly used as administrative tools and not as real leadership tools. There are numerous free sources and available literature aimed at developing leadership skills. I strongly suggest that you invest your time in improving your leadership abilities. Here, I would like to briefly mention some ground rules of effective leadership.

Be Your Own Boss
Be accountable for your actions and manage the organization with ownership, personal commitment, and an entrepreneurship mindset.

Be an Example

Be an example in terms of integrity, morale, communication, devotion, and execution of tasks.

Be an Authority

Sustainable authority is not achieved only through professional expertise or hierarchy. You need to set the rules that should be followed by everyone, including yourself.

Know Your Team

Knowing your team members and their strengths and weaknesses is crucial for the further development of the individual in your team and also for creating an efficient team in which every individual fits like a piece of a puzzle.

Be Transparent

Be transparent when defining rules, communicating expectations, and giving feedback. Be fair and avoid having double standards.

Give Timely Feedback

Feedback is effective only if it is given immediately, when the reason for the feedback is still fresh. This will make your message clear, understood, and applicable.

Acknowledge

Acknowledge failure as well as success. Your subordinates should know that you care about the results and that you notice both the good and the bad.

Reward Success

Reward success even if success means just correctly executing a task. Success does not have to be financial. Even a congratulation e-mail for a team member sent to the entire team could do the job.

Support Your Team

Your team must know that you are a part of the team as much as they are. Always support them if you believe that they are right.

Get Your Subordinates to Manage You

Lead your subordinates toward being proactive and not waiting for tasks but proposing their own. Do not impose tasks, but instead guide and direct your subordinates.

REFERENCE

[1] Service Employees International Union (SEIU.org). "Our Industry." 2006. http://www.seiu.org/a/standforsecurity/about-the-ind.php.

How: Organize

CHAPTER 4

Managing a Security Organization

SECURITY MODELS ACCORDING TO INDUSTRY
Industry Specifics

Corporate security in the production industry and corporate security in the industry of financial services feature opposite philosophies, mostly owing to completely different models of doing business and the nature of the products and risks.

Whereas the production industry is physical, the industry of financial services functions mostly in the virtual world. Although the product in the banking industry is money, actual physical handling of cash occurs for a limited period of time before it is virtualized, during which it is completely insured. Insurance of cash is simple because it is based on the allowed maximum of cash a branch can have and it is easily quantifiable. However, it is impossible to quantify the cost of a hacking incident against the bank, whose impact could be enormous. Naturally, the focus and modus operandi of criminals have shifted from physical robberies and thefts to hacking and fraud. Therefore, the focus of security is on information and communication technology (ICT) security and fraud prevention instead of physical (traditional) security.

The risks are not only external, but also internal, and they also differ in the same way. For example, in the production industry, the focus in preventing employee-related crime is on the product. To prevent a product from being smuggled out of the production facility, we concentrate on the physical exit points in the facility. Because of its virtual nature, it is possible to remove the product from a financial institution during almost every phase of core processes that involve numerous departments in the front office and back office and many employees, in which each link in that chain could be the exit point. This specific risk in the industry of financial services has led to the development of much stronger internal control functions such as internal audits, compliance and operational risk, and the development of more levels of control for employees and processes.

Security is also perceived completely differently regarding its impact on the reputation of the company and the impact that jeopardized reputation resulting from security flaws has on profit. Basically, to simplify, security flaws in the banking industry have an immediate impact on the reputation and the confidence of clients, and thus on profit. In the production industry, the biggest jeopardies for reputation are brand integrity and timely delivery. The appearance of a product on the black market or of counterfeit products will jeopardize the reputation of the brand over a relatively longer time. Another risk to reputation is the delay of products delivered to consumers, as a result of supply chain security incidents, for example.

Another large difference is the impact of business discontinuity on consumers. Whereas in the production industry the impact of business discontinuity is mostly felt by the company and not as much by the consumer, owing to its nature, the disruption of business in the industry of financial services can have catastrophic consequences for both the company and the client. Basically, with the exception of the pharmaceutical industry, and only in certain cases, the antimonopoly system usually gives consumers the ability to acquire the product from another source. In the industry of financial services, a client who was completing a transaction at the moment the service became unavailable cannot suddenly turn to another provider.

The work environment is also completely dissimilar in the two models we are comparing. In the production industry, environment, health, and safety (EHS) is an issue of utmost importance. An integral part, fire safety, is one of the most important issues in the production industry. Environment, health, and safety is also crucial in terms of compliance with local laws and regulations as well as to ensure production continuity and avoid costs such as lost time injury, which is basically the cost of work time lost owing to an injury of an employee. Naturally, the office workspace in the banking industry with a virtualized production environment reduces the need for EHS to simple pro forma and is usually under the supervision of human resources or general services. We should also not forget the incomparably stronger presence and influence of trade unions in the production industry, in which the safety of employees is a top issue on the agenda.

Industry specifics and diverse priorities are responsible for completely different approaches to corporate security, the fields it covers, its focus, and its relationship with other departments.

The general philosophy of physical security in industrial facilities and financial institutions is also different. The basic idea of physical security in industrial facilities is to keep out anything and anyone who is not wanted to come in and to prevent anything valuable from illegally leaving the facility. In financial institutions such as bank branches, the task of physical security is mostly to deter (target hardening) and prevent a problem from entering the branch. However, once the perpetrator has entered the facility and the problem, such as a robbery, has occurred, the idea is to limit damage to financial loss without human casualties (although cash is completely insured) and to have the perpetrator leave the facility with his stolen goods as quickly as possible.

Production Industry

In the production industry, security is usually affiliated with EHS. Sometimes it is even merged into one environment, health, safety, and security department. The ICT security function is usually not affiliated with security, although advocates of information technology (IT) security and traditional security convergence in corporate security have become louder over the past few years. The lack of efficient cooperation between security and ICT security creates a vacuum for certain crucial aspects of security, especially information security. The development of ICT technologies has led to the perception of information as being purely electronic. This has caused ICT security and information security to be perceived as the same. Unfortunately, ICT security experts often concentrate on electronically stored and transferred information and neglect information in the traditional sense, such as written, spoken, and visual information. On the other hand, traditional security departments are convinced that the other guys have information security covered, which creates a huge gap in protecting information.

Business continuity is often separated into two systems: one ensuring business continuity from a physical side (such as the water supply and electricity needed for production), in which security closely cooperates with the engineering department; and IT business continuity (which concentrates on the necessary IT infrastructure, availability of systems, and applications required for production), which is functionally placed in the ICT department. There are rare occasions when these two parts of business continuity come together, usually in times of crisis as parts of a crisis management team.

Because of the different models of business, especially the maturity and development of business processes depending on the geographical location, security governance functions according to a different model compared with financial institutions. Basically, in terms of the standards, policies, and procedures, many industrial production organizations opt for the federal model of corporate governance. Instead of imposing group policies and procedures featuring detailed requirements to the affiliates, they prefer to impose only the standards and leave to affiliates the freedom to find out how to achieve them (basically concentrating on the final outcome and not on the process itself—the "what" instead of the "how"). On some occasions, this loose involvement of group security leads to procedures concentrating mostly on physical, technical, and human elements of security, the immediate concerns of local security management. Sometimes, the group will classify the affiliates into clusters according to geographical proximity, similar business models, and similar security issues and impose detailed policies and procedures on clusters.

A frequent weakness is the position of security in the production industry. Its position greatly depends on the focus of the industry and its division. To optimize the way in which they conduct business, corporations sometimes choose to separate productions and sales officially by registering separate companies. In such cases, it is rare that security be placed under the chief executive officer who is responsible for both companies. Security is placed where the focus is in the company, usually linked to production and reporting to the operations director. This division shifts the focus of security mostly to processes and parts of processes that are linked to operations, and less on other processes. The separate companies conduct business for each other and are responsible for parts of processes that together create the full product lifecycle. If we take the supply chain as an example, operations are responsible for the arrival of raw materials for production, the warehouse storage of the final product within the production facility, and the primary distribution to distribution centers. Sales are responsible for storage in distribution centers and for secondary distribution to clients. Sales are also responsible for marketing the product: for example, through marketing venues. Unfortunately, sometimes security managers are forced to concentrate on parts of processes that are the responsibility of their department (company) and are unable to oversee entire processes.

Financial Institutions: Banking Industry

In financial institutions, ICT is the closest partner to security. However, security serves as the second level control of ICT security, and whereas actual technical ICT security is in the ICT department, ICT security governance and control are part of the security department. Its activities include ensuring compliance with IT regulations and security policies and procedures, penetration testing, queries, and performance controls. Information security is also managed by the security department, including the processes of data classification and user profiles (need-to-know basis access to information, tools, and equipment for all employees). Information security must be well-managed because of numerous highly classified hardcopy documents and forms used by institutions.

Although business continuity management (BCM)–disaster recovery (DR) is part of corporate security, it is usually perceived as a completely ICT-related issue with BCM and DR paying almost no attention to other factors that could cause business discontinuity, such as natural disasters and pandemics (the term "pandemic" is by default used to describe IT virus-related issues). Whereas security is in charge of guiding the entire organization in creating business continuity plans and managing disaster recovery, ICT is responsible for maintaining the technical infrastructure of BCM and DR.

Because banking infrastructures and security issues are similar regardless of the location, financial institutions usually opt for the centralized system of security governance. Instead of sending general security standards to affiliates, the group sends turnkey policies and procedures to be officially accepted by the local management and implemented as such, perhaps with some minor adjustments.

Compared with the production industry, corporate security in financial institutions is in a better position to supervise entire processes. It is not rare in financial institutions for security to report directly to the group security unit instead of local management. This is similar to, for example, internal audit, which reports to the group internal audit or audit committee instead of the local management. This gives security more freedom to control frauds regardless of where in the hierarchy they occur.

Security in financial institutions is in charge of preventing, combating, and investigating fraud. Whereas fraud and investigations are integral parts of the security job description in industrial productions, the number of investigations performed in financial institutions is incomparably higher.

The physical, technical, and manned guarding part of corporate security concentrates on access control, protects the technical and ICT infrastructure of the institution, and is in charge of the security of cash manipulation points such as cash in transit, tellers, vaults, and automatic teller machines (ATMs). It also deals with executive protection to a certain degree.

Identifying Company-Specific Issues (Company's Security Identification)

As we know, there are no two identical security models. Designing a successful security setup, strategy, and model depends on knowing company-specific issues. It starts with industry specifics but continues with numerous other aspects such as the scope of services, type and value of the product, processes, size, location, employees' structure, geographical diversification, national identity, agenda, risk appetite and strategy, brand recognizability, and so forth. Another line (or pattern) that is an important element of every company's fingerprint is its corporate culture, which we have previously analyzed.

Scope of Services

The scope of services is basically the complexity of the business regardless of the product. Two companies that produce the same type of product can have completely different scopes of service. For example, company A is focused on manufacturing a single simple product that it wholesales to clients that are picking it up directly from the production facility. Company A does not have a supply chain or retail. On the other hand, production company B has numerous complex products manufactured and assembled from raw materials and parts coming from numerous suppliers. Apart from wholesale, it has primary distribution to distribution centers all over the country, from where it distributes the product directly to clients and to its own retail chain.

Type and Value of the Product

The type and value of the product make up the crime potential against it. As we know, the value in the security sense is the motive to commit crime. The type and value of the product determine the level of probability of crime, type of threat, and types of perpetrators and their modus operandi.

Company C manufactures shipping containers that have high value in terms of cost but almost no value as a motive to steal them. Stealing a shipping container could be performed only by an organized group because of its size and weight and the logistics required, but a shipping container is a robust item that is difficult to transport unnoticed and hide, and it would probably not generate profit on the black market to justify the expenses.

Company D produces bread, which is a fast-moving consumer goods (FMCG) item. The value for an organized group of criminals is minimal because it requires significant logistics to steal a sufficient amount of items to generate profit. Moreover, the bread will be fresh for only a short time. This all makes it unattractive to criminals. However, bread is attractive for a lone poverty-motivated perpetrator. Still, bread is a sensitive product and securing it requires attention during the entire production and supply chain processes to protect it from tampering and sabotage.

Company E manufactures cigarettes, which are also FMCG products. Because of its type and value, the product is attractive to both organized criminal groups that target large amounts and lone perpetrators who target small amounts for personal use.

Company F is a pharmaceutical active ingredient manufacturer that produces ingredients for pharmaceutical companies that produce and sell medications. Its product is absolutely not attractive for a lone perpetrator because it has no personal use potential, it must be in large quantities to be sold, and it requires a sales channel and a buyer or buyers. Such a product is attractive only to an organized group. Just like the product of company D, the product of company F is sensitive and securing it requires attention during the entire production and supply chain process to protect it from tampering and sabotage. Also, although the product may not be attractive to single perpetrators, tools used in production could be valuable and usable and subject to employee theft.

Processes

Two companies could have a similar scope and similar product but still have different processes that greatly influence security requirements and setup for the companies. For example, companies G and H produce jeans and other clothing items. But whereas company G is a traditional family-owned company that produces jeans in a traditional way, using human skills and simple tools, company H uses highly automated processes including various systems, software, and applications in production as well as in other processes. Although the product is similarly vulnerable, there is a large difference in the vulnerabilities of the two companies concerning ICT security, the impact of the unavailability of ICT systems on core processes, and the philosophy and scope of BCM and DR.

Size

Size refers to production volumes, the number of employees, and the size of the facility.

The physical size of a company mostly influences the physical security setup required to control the area and ensure the security of people and product in its production, movements, and storage around the facility. If we take the product as the example of a motive to commit crime, larger volumes certainly influence probability. As for the size of the workforce, because we know that people are always the executors of crime, but they can also be the target of crime, a larger workforce increases the probability of crimes being committed by or against employees.

Location

The location of the company, both on a macro-level and a micro-level, has an important role in the security identification of the company. If we analyze the location on a macro-level, we can analyze the region and the country and its political and economical climate, and the way it can influence the security of the company. On a middle level, we can analyze the area of the country, city, and neighborhood and all of the security specifics, such as the social structure of people living in the area, poverty figures, education, crime rates, and so forth. On a micro-level, we can analyze the exact location of the facility, physical terrain, arrival and evacuation routes, proximity of emergency services and response times, and so forth. Another important parameter is the extent to which the company, including the profiles of its employees, fits in the area. Basically, does the company stand out in any way that could jeopardize the company or its employees?

Employees' Structure

The structure of employees depends on the industry as well as the location of the company. For example, we have completely different structures of employees in a bank and a steel mill. This includes the background, levels of education, male–female ratio, and so forth. Also, the workforce tends to be different depending on the location of the company, its rural or urban structure, crime rates, job availability in the area, etc. Every particular concerning the configuration of the employees has an important part in security strategies, but also in accepted models of communication and people management.

Geographical Diversification

Most multinational corporations have operations around the globe to increase profits and reduce expenses by opening plants in lower-cost emerging markets. From a security point of view, the higher the geographical diversification, the more complex it is to assess and to manage security in terms of all of the specifics we have already mentioned. First, we are talking about the challenge of managing multiple locations from a distance. Also, security specifics, requirements, and available infrastructures may be poles apart. Every location can have completely different laws that regulate security and supporting processes but also have the entirely different potential of cooperation with authorities, including the risks of corruption and bribery. Another possible challenge and hardship may be the unavailability of a quality workforce to manage and execute security for the site.

National Identity and Brand Recognizability

Most corporations proudly link their brand to a national identity. However, even if they do not use it as a marketing tool, corporations act as symbols of the economies of their founding countries. In that sense, they are a serious potential target of terror and political violence. There are numerous known cases in which demonstrators trashed McDonald's restaurants to demonstrate their dissatisfaction with United States foreign policy. There are also known cases of environmentalists demonstrating in front of Japanese embassies and headquarters of industrial companies against the Japanese slaughter of whales in the Japanese Sea.

Agenda

Almost no corporations have programs that are not opposed by individuals or groups. As for individuals, it is impossible to mention all possible motives that could result in dissatisfaction and incidents. They range from loss of jobs to dissatisfaction with the quality of products and services. As an example, a regional sales manager of Bulbank in Bulgaria (part of UniCredit Bank) was shot and killed in 2013 on her way to work by a client who was refused credit by the bank several days earlier. If we talk about organized groups, we must start by mentioning anti-globalization groups, but not forget environmental protection groups, animal protection groups, and so forth.

Risk Appetite and Strategy

Risk appetite is an important element in identifying the security identification of a company. Risk appetite determines the level of risk a company is willing to take to achieve its goals. High-risk appetite includes investing in politically, economically, and security-risky locations. Risk appetite also includes walking on the edge of compliance with legal regulations and sometimes crossing the line of good taste and morale when marketing the product, for example.

SECURITY MANAGEMENT STYLES

The number of variations that exist in contemporary corporate security is equal to the number of security professionals who manage corporate security. Basically, every security manager has a unique understanding of security, focus, and goals and ways to achieve them, some with more success and some with less. Security management styles mostly depend on the industry, company specifics, and knowledge and experience of security managers and their background, character, and support of their organizations. We previously analyzed industry and company specifics, corporate security management philosophies, and chief security office competences required to gain peer and management support.

Most Common Models of Security Management

To provide illustrative examples that will help us explore the four main security management styles, we will intentionally use stereotypes that rarely exist in practice as completely distinct models of management.

Ex-Military/Law Enforcement Style

Corporate security management is a contemporary security discipline although security has been performed in corporations since their beginnings. The once prevalent, and still present, ex-law enforcement style of management had nothing to do with corporate security management apart from the fact that it was security management physically performed in a corporation. Basically, the security department is isolated from the rest of the corporation and mostly concentrates on managing access control (guards and technology), on occasions dealing with executive protection, but mostly focused on preventing and detecting internal fraud and employees' dishonesty and theft. One main feature of the ex-law enforcement style is exaggerated control of employees by constant surveillance and overuse of internally recruited informants. Such control has a natural tendency to expand and shift focus from fraud prevention and detection to checking the work performance of employees. Such an iron fist security management style certainly does not help improve the image of security that was, until recently, perceived as a corporate cop with little value for the business. However, with the development of corporate security, ex-law enforcement and ex-military newcomers to corporations soon realized that they had to adapt their focus, management styles, accessibility, communication, and transparency to the business, as well as receive the support and commitment of employees if they wanted to achieve optimal results.

Information Technology Security Style

A new trend in corporate security management, especially in industries with strong IT orientation, such as the banking industry, is to have an IT security professional in charge of the overall security of the company, including its physical side. Although not necessarily an unsuccessful trend, it tends to have certain weaknesses. One of the often-mentioned weaknesses associated with IT security professionals who deal with other security aspects is the tendency to address security issues using technological solutions. One key success factor of every security strategy is sustainability. Unfortunately, in the time of vertiginous development of technology, it is unlikely that using any solely technological solution can be called a sustainable strategy. Another deficiency associated with the IT mindset and the main difference between the IT and physical security strategic approach is the difference in the perception and use of routine. Whereas breaking routine is a crucial protection principle in physical security, the concept of breaking routine almost does not exist in IT security.

Non-Security Background Style (Lateral Move)

In some corporations, security managers originated from other support functions and were moved laterally to a security management function based on position availability and on their assessed performance and advancement potential (talent pool). If we were to generalize, apart from evident knowledge of the company and its processes, which is certainly a precondition to successfully managing corporate security, the other precondition, knowledge of security, is usually missing. The systematic approach to addressing security issues but without real predisposition and knowledge of security is often referred to as the checklist style of security management. Using such a systematic approach is beneficial in dealing with daily issues, and checklists can certainly be helpful when appropriate, but they are ineffective for dealing with emergencies and managing unplanned events. This approach to security management usually produces good results when it comes to security governance and analytics. Although this style of management is often perceived by stakeholders as successful, it usually does not produce results when it comes to core security processes.

Progressive Responsibility (Vertical Move)

Another common model of taking over a security management position in a corporation is starting on lower positions and climbing up the hierarchy leader. The philosophy behind it is that a good secretary would make a good chief executive officer. Although it is generally a concept that seems proper, there are traps associated with it. First, as we have mentioned, it is a tricky management situation to know the job of your subordinate better than he does. It requires a lot of care not to become a professional with more responsibility but instead be a manager who leads professionals and processes. It also takes effort to resist the temptation of micromanaging instead of macromanaging the system.

KEY SUCCESS FACTORS IN MANAGING SECURITY PROCESSES

Incorporate All Security System Elements

To manage security successfully, we must incorporate all elements that make up a security system: human, physical, technical, information, procedures, communication, and control.

Quantify

For security management to be applicable and assist the business, apart from knowing the deficiencies and goals and being able to design successful protection strategies, we need to quantify (calculate) the security risk and vulnerabilities and compare them with the cost of security measures.

Efficiency Equals Cost Efficiency

Basically, quantifying the incidents and the measures guides us in being cost-effective when managing security. In business, efficiency equals cost efficiency.

Using Simplicity and Logic to Solve Complex Issues

We are often caught in a trap to believe falsely that our security measures have to be as complicated as the problem. When solving a high-tech crime issue, we try to use the same or a higher level of technology to address the issue.

Automatic Teller Machine Skimming: Case Study

Skimmers are credit card–reading and copying devices used by criminals to copy the magnetic code of a credit card so that it can be duplicated later and used for fraudulent activities. A skimmer looks like an original part of the ATM and is placed over the credit card slot on an ATM in a way that, when a card is inserted, it goes through the skimmer where it is copied before entering the genuine credit card slot. Apart from just copying the magnetic code on the card, there is usually a micro camera that records the video of a personal identification number (PIN) being typed on the ATM keyboard. The PIN is sometimes recorded by a camera placed elsewhere on the ATM, or by a thin unnotice-able recording keyboard placed over the original one. What all skimmer parts have in common is that they look like genuine parts of the ATM. They are made from the same material and are the same color, and often are actually original parts of an ATM that were adapted by criminals. Bank U used the same ATMs (maker, type, and color) as roughly 90% of all banks in the country. Because bank U was small in terms of retail, it had a small number of ATMs compared with other banks in the local market. Of course, other banks that had the same type of ATM were also victims of skimming and were struggling to find ways to combat it successfully.

As well as other banks, bank U has been trying out different, often expensive, tech-nology solutions to tackle skimming. Some were unsuccessful from the start but some managed to lower the number of skimming with limited success and only for a while.

Instead of continuing the technology race that the bank was evidently losing to the criminals, the bank's chief security officer (CSO) decided to try another, much less technical approach to solving the skimming problem. Because the skimmers were gray like most ATMs, the criminals had close to unlimited choice as to where to install the devices. Because bank U had a small number of ATMs, the CSO assumed that if he were to change something in the physical appearance of the ATMs, the criminals would be better off continuing to use the skimmers on other banks' ATMs that stayed the same rather than adapting the skimmers to the bank U's ATMs and then being able to use them on only a small number of ATMs and losing the majority. The CSO managed to convince the management of the bank and the marketing department to paint the ATMs red, which is the corporate color of the bank. More-over, during negotiations with the vendor, the bank managed to get the manufacturer of ATMs to manufacture the ATMs and spare parts in the new color at no additional charge.

Not only did the strategy work, as it managed to stop the skimming incidents, but the change received overwhelming support from the business management of the bank because it supported the visibility of the brand.

Striving toward Sustainability

In fast-moving corporate environments, we are often required to achieve quick-win results to meet short-term goals, be visible, and excel in appraisals. This is a necessity in the corporate world, but we must remember that only sustainable security strategies make a difference. We have the best chance to create successful security models if our quick-win projects are actually pieces of a sustainable strategic puzzle.

Difference between Strategic and Responsive Models

In reality, most security management work is merely reactive, such as peer-to-peer communication, consulting upon request, responding to current issues, and performing investigations. Many corporate security practitioners believe that whereas strategy and leadership are somewhat necessary, the daily tasks should account for the largest portion of a security manager's daily routine. Building working partnerships and consulting are certainly significant tasks of a security manager. Still, although a security department should primarily deal with current issues, the good segregation of duties in a security department should enable the security manager to lead, design, create, and implement strategies instead of allocating most of the time to physically managing issues that will take him or her away from strategic management to a purely executive role.

First, a management position is far more than just a position with great technical expertise. Also, over-involvement in day-to-day issues has a tendency to lead to patching instead of strategically addressing issues and creating sustainable protection systems. Moreover, we should look at the three periods that together form an incident: preparation, action, and aftermath (consequences). Security systems in companies are usually not structured so as to be able to stop an incident successfully when action begins. If we take an armed robbery as an example, the outsourced unarmed and often unskilled guards have little to offer once a robbery has started. On the other hand, companies concentrate on preventing an incident and minimizing damage, which is a concept that requires precise planning and strategy.

Sustainability versus Quick-Win Strategy

Quick-win has become a popular corporate concept for many reasons. For instance, a top manager will most likely hold a current position for a short period, maybe a few years, before moving to another position. The move will be horizontal or vertical depending on the successes. Strategies that could take a longer time to generate results are unlikely to be approved by top management. One reason is that the vast majority of strategies, even cost-avoidance strategies, require an initial investment. Having a long-term strategy will practically mean that, for instance, money was invested in a project during the term of one manager who could only report expenditure, whereas his successor claims the results with no spending. The only way for a current manager to show good results is to have quick-win strategies.

The second reason, which is linked to the first, is that security managers must link their goals to the goals of their superiors for the whole organization to follow a common strategy.

Another reason is the appraisal systems that evaluate the performance of employees on a yearly basis, with control assessment often being performed even on a quarterly basis. Security managers who are also being evaluated by their superiors often need to produce solid results based on short-term goals and appraisal periods, which makes it challenging to create long-term strategies.

The reality is that the only way to plan and execute long-term strategic projects successfully is to segment them into short-term, quick-win projects.

CORPORATE SECURITY SETUP

Corporate security setups are not security models but actually ways in which companies coordinate different security-related issues in an organization that are organizationally assigned to different process owners or are spread over a large geographical area.

Physical (Traditional) and ICT Security Convergence

The outdated question of "Which is older, the chicken or the egg?" has been replaced by "If your USB flash memory was stolen, is it a matter of physical security or IT security?" Who is responsible if someone stole the piece of paper on which you have written your password? That one is easy: you! The real questions are how these issues are officially regulated and practiced, how they should be practiced, and how they will be regulated and practiced a few years from now.

In some organizations, IT security and physical security are handled by different parts of the company. How do the lack of cooperation and simplified understanding of physical security affect information security in a company? First, "information" could be a key word. Physical security is certain that IT security has this covered whereas IT security often fails to understand that information does not necessarily have to be electronic. This leaves actual information unprotected regardless of its form. Also, the fact that IT security and physical security are not cooperating puts both securities at jeopardy.

The way we do business has greatly improved with the development of information and communication technologies. Unfortunately, they also created a completely new set of risks which, like in the benign example at the beginning of this text, do not form a separate isolated group of ICT risks but actually incorporate and affect both ICT and physical security and require a joint effort to be addressed properly. Basically, to address the problem completely, we must not look at incidents as isolated happenings in our part, but actually see how the problems affect all aspects of security and solve them in a coordinated manner. This understanding of the complexity of security initiated the trend of incorporating two historically distinct security functions—physical security and ICT security—under one leadership and working together toward a common goal.

The need for joint efforts is much more complex than just addressing the physical risk aspects of information security and the need for physical security to protect the IT infrastructure and systems and control the physical access to hardware that leads to system intrusion. Basically, IT security and physical security complement each other in almost all processes. Physical security protects physical access to systems whereas IT security helps physical security by managing systems such as, for example, access control systems. Security technology that assists physical security runs on the IT systems and is hosted by IT and protected by IT security. It is impossible to perform investigations without involving both sides of security. It is also unthinkable to have BCM and DR without having both securities participating: one dealing with potential physical risks and the other with the unavailability of the network, systems, and applications.

It is actually almost impossible to have one professional who is equally proficient in physical and IT security in charge of both sides of security; this is not what security convergence is about. Security convergence is about having both sides of security managed jointly instead of separately.

Security Committee

A security committee is another way to coordinate various functions that form the security system of a company. Instead of joining all security-like functions into one department, companies often choose the model of having each department responsible for its narrow field of expertise and its routine daily management. Many companies have several functions that deal with a certain aspect of security, such as a security department that deals with traditional security, information and ICT security, fraud prevention, compliance and Anti-Money Laundering (AML), internal controls, brand integrity, and so forth. The division of functions also depends on the core security issues. Although by default fraud prevention is usually an integral part of the security department, in companies with a focus on fraud, such as, for instance, a mobile phone network operator or an insurance company, fraud prevention and detection could be separated from the security department.

To have full coordination of security issues, overall security is managed by a security committee, attended by all security functions, that makes joint strategic decisions during its weekly meetings, e-mail groups, and authorization and approval systems.

Combined Model

In most cases, companies choose to have a combination of several security setups to achieve the best performance and highest level of control.

Managing Security from a Distance

Any management from a distance is challenging. The need for corporations to successfully manage parts of the business that are operating in different parts of the world, under different political and economic circumstances, and encountering different problems led to the creation of cluster structures. A cluster structure enables companies to group affiliates according to politics, economics, products, processes, and other similarities. A corporation may decide to group its parts into clusters based on similar geopolitical issues. For example, one cluster formed by a company operating around Europe may consist of affiliates in Bulgaria, Romania, Hungary, and Turkey owing to economic and political similarities. On the other hand, it can form clusters according to similar processes. For instance, if the company's factories in Europe are located in Turkey, Hungary, Sweden, and Portugal, those countries could be the production cluster, whereas Bulgaria, Romania, France, and Austria, which are only selling the product but not manufacturing it, could be the market cluster. A company can also have a cluster matrix consisting of different clusters created by different divisions of the company. For example, production can have its own cluster system that gathers affiliates in a certain area that are producing the product while sales and marketing can have their own cluster system, which would gather sales-oriented affiliates in a certain area. On the other hand, security can have its own system of clustering based on similar security problems and not on the geographical area. Basically, according to the matrix system of clusters, one affiliate could belong to several clusters.

The criteria for security clusters are often a combination of similar security issues, parallel security organizations in affiliates, and geographical proximity. Security clusters are created for several reasons.

The first reason is to be able to have a combination of centralized and federal governance approaches. Basically, the headquarters of the company would not impose the same security policies on all of its affiliates and also would not allow every affiliate to create its own policies, but would instead create policies according to cluster specifics.

The second reason is to have concentrated security expertise that would help to manage security practically. In that way, all of the CSOs in a cluster would be able to contribute and share their expertise and even be the official cluster leaders for certain fields of security. We can take as an example a security cluster whose members are Bulgaria, Romania, Hungary, and Turkey, where each of the CSOs has a different security background, experience, and knowledge. Whereas the CSO in Turkey is an expert in BCM, the Bulgarian CSO is an experienced fraud prevention specialist and investigator, the Romanian CSO has notable achievements in supply chain security, and the CSO in Hungary is an information and ICT security professional. According to our example, Turkey would be the official cluster BCM manager, Bulgaria would manage fraud prevention, and so forth.

In some cases, the cluster managers would also be responsible for governance on the cluster level concerning the subjects of their expertise.

CHAPTER 5

Incorporating Security Elements

INFORMATION AND INTELLIGENCE

Importance of Information

If we were to compare a security system with a human organism, the muscles and its strength would be physical security; the ability to hear, see, smell, and sense would be security technology; the skeleton would be the human factor of security; the bloodstream would represent communication; the brain would be the management; coordination of the body would be procedures; and air, water, and food would be information.

Having information is absolutely essential for a security system to be able to survive. Just as a living organism continuously searches for new sources of food and water by using its brain, senses, and strength, a security system uses all of its elements to collect and process information.

The variety and levels of information that we are collecting range from macro-information about the international political climate down to the immediate microenvironment concerning our place of work. We certainly have to collect and process information methodically to make sure that the information that we have is relevant and correctly used. We also need to have strict boundaries when collecting information to be sure that we are using ethical methodologies as well as not crossing the line of privacy intrusion and exaggerated control.

For information to be usable, it needs to be:
- Leading
- Relevant
- Meaningful
- Understandable
- Reasonably precise

For information to be complete and for us to be able to use the information to, for instance, design a response or use it for a strategy, we need to have the answers to the following questions:
- What? (What is happening? What will happen?)
- Who? (Who are the actors?)
- Where? (Where did/will it happen or where is it happening?)
- Where from? (Who/what is the source and is it reliable?)
- What way? (How was it done/will it be done?)
- When? (When did/will it happen?)

- Why? (What are the reasons/background?)
- What could it do to us? (How could it affect us?)

Global Information

Global (macro) information concerns the international political and economic climate that has the potential to affect our processes and our security. We are usually interested in:

- Information about the wider geographical area (region) in which we are located
- Information about our industry and what affects it worldwide and whether it has the potential to become a trend
- Global security industry best practices
- Information concerning the founding state of our company and whether, for instance, its foreign policy could have an impact on the local security of our company

Relevant information can be collected from various sources: through media; through specialized reports from contracted intelligence providers, as either general country profiles or specialized reports targeting a certain area and/or certain type of risk; from a company's affiliates in other countries via regular and irregular reports such as, for example, the company's security bulletin, upon request, or through incident reports sent to all affiliates; or through specialized security newsletters, specific industry security forums, and participation in seminars and congresses.

National Information

We are especially concerned about information on happenings that could influence the security of our processes and people and basically influence daily routine. We are mostly interested in information such as announced and predicted events that have a security potential as well any local information about our industry, such as:

- Security happenings and trends targeting our industry on a local level
- The political, economic, and social climate (including poverty, crime rates, and crime statistics) and its direction
- Events that could influence our daily routine, such as high-risk sports events, massive sports and music events, predicted and announced strikes and demonstrations, weather, and the unavailability of infrastructure such as water and power cuts and main road construction works
- Significant dates such as anniversaries, commemorations, national and religious holidays, etc.

We collect such information from the media via press clipping reports and from special reports from contracted press agencies that generate reports based on our specific requests.

Importance of Reading the Dates

What we all know is that terrorism is far from being a pure act of destruction; its main purpose is to promote a cause through media reports. Basically, terrorists believe that for an activity to be successful, it needs to be shocking and have significance and relevance, and as such be attractive enough to grab the attention of the media and hold it for a while. Moreover, over the years, terrorists have realized that a bit of irony, if we can call it that, adds to the feeling of victory. The failure of American intelligence in the terrible tragic events that hit the United States (US) in 2001 and shocked the world seems even graver if we know that the particular date, along with some other dates, had been marked as extremely risky by US security agencies. One reason is the significance of the number 911 (September 11), which is the US telephone number for emergency services. Over the years, the numbers lost their importance but the date certainly did not. Every year, we see that terrorists all over the world mark this anniversary by performing new terrorist attacks. In fact, every year on this date, the number of terrorist attacks is much higher than usual. Of course, dates and anniversaries are important not only for Islamic terrorism but for all sorts of ideology-driven acts of terror, such as the extreme left and right, animal rights extremists, and so forth. The causes are numerous and can range from the date of arrest of an activist to incidents against nature or animals, and, of course, terrorist attacks.

Micro-Information

Micro-information concerns our immediate environment. It can be basically divided into two types of information:
- Business processes insight
- Information on abnormal events

Having detailed information concerning business processes is essential for security. For example, any new or changed process or project can have the potential to pose certain risks as well security gaps that could negatively influence it. Every corporate security management system must have functional access to business-relevant information in a systematic manner. This includes the active involvement of security in, for instance, project management committees that approve new projects, and is one of the functions that approve new projects and processes and their modification.

Apart from official information concerning incidents, such as incident reports that are sent to security, security must have the potential to collect information independently and proactively. In the same way in which we analyzed official and unofficial corporate communication, the collection of information concerning abnormal events needs to be both official and unofficial and certainly proactive. If we are talking about information received through unofficial communication channels, it is not enough to wait for information to be overheard during a coffee break. Although it sometimes may seem unethical, the reality is that security must recruit and use internal sources of information (informers) to have timely and relevant information.

Recruitment of Internal Intelligence Sources

Recruiting internal informers is a method of corporate intelligence that is often disputed but is certainly necessary. Without a doubt, there is a thin line between the ethical and unethical use of informers, and even illegal conduct. The first precondition is to have top management support to engage in such models of intelligence, and their understanding and acceptance that you keep the identity of the informers to yourself. The second precondition is an agreement with the management that informers are used only to warn about potential and actual internal crime and security issues, such as embezzlement and fraud, and not to report the bad work performance of their colleagues. The third precondition is the close cooperation of security with the human resources department and a joint strategy regarding the recruitment of internal informers. Ethical or not, the following is the most common approach to recruiting internal informers used by many corporate security managers.

In practice, potential informers are usually identified in the first stages of the job recruitment process and are recruited during the final stages (interview with the chief security officer (CSO)) of the job recruitment process. As we mentioned, recruitment of informers requires proficiency with local laws to make sure that there are no legal obstacles (such as, for example, illegal or unethical interview questions) that would make the process of recruitment of internal intelligence sources more complicated.

Basically, future employees are approached with the request to cooperate based on their eagerness to be employed, matched with minor mismatches in background. Potential employees are presented with mismatches or flaws in their resume or background check results and are made aware that these particulars can negatively influence the hiring decision. The candidates are then asked to compensate for the flaws, if hired. The employees are told that, apart from providing good results, to show loyalty, they would be expected to provide periodical information (incident and request based) concerning potential or actual crimes and security risks and occurrences. In any case, recruited informers are usually told that they are not expected to provide information concerning the work performance of their colleagues but only about illegal activities, that their role will be confidential, and that the fact that they are cooperating with security will not affect (positively or negatively) their work performance appraisal. Informers are also usually told that there are other informers and that the reports will be cross-referenced. Another moment in which recruitment occurs is during the CSO interview with an employee after a minor disciplinary misbehavior.

However, many CSOs will also opt not to recruit informers because of ethical concerns. There are many cases of employees volunteering information even if they have not been recruited, either because they simply want to do the right thing, because they are motivated by good peer relations with the CSO, or as a way to compensate bad performance. Still, it is important that every source of information be aware that although cooperation is highly appreciated, it will not compensate for bad performance and that a certain level of function and hierarchy distance will continue to exist.

Another situation which we must avoid is paying for information, especially if it means giving information in return. Giving information in return practically makes us informers and puts the employee in charge.

Internal Whistleblowing System

A good way to collect information about internal misconduct, crime, employee dishonesty, and other illegal activities is to create a system that employees can use anonymously to report it. The most common and easiest method is to use suggestion boxes.

Knowledge as Information

Apart from collecting new information, we must be able to collect and use information on recurring events. There are many recurring events that we should take into consideration. For example, knowing about changes in the density of traffic during various periods of the day can make an enormous difference during the massive transport to a hospital of employees injured in a fire.

Significant dates and anniversaries recur every year, and instead of collecting information every year, we should have information about default significant dates and their potential influence.

Another significant parameter is the period of the year and its security specifics. For example, summer is characterized by higher criminality and increased criminal violence, autumn is usually the period of political turbulence, and so forth. Although we need to know specific information about upcoming risky events, we can anticipate certain risks by knowing when they could occur. For instance, although we need information about an upcoming soccer game that could be risky in terms of hooliganism and violence, we know when the soccer season starts and ends, during which the problematic event could occur.

Information on Default Risks as Business Continuity Management Tool

In the same way that we use knowledge as information, this knowledge is a useful tool for business continuity management. As we already know, business continuity is not only about the information technology infrastructure, but about all situations that have the potential to cause business discontinuity. Unfortunately, I have often stumbled upon security systems that see business continuity management and disaster recovery purely as a technical system with the potential to respond to risks but without correctly anticipating the risks. Basically, many risks that can influence the continuity of business have the tendency to recur. For instance, every period of the year has a default set of risks. If we talk about the human resources segment of business continuity, summer is the vacation season during which, unless we anticipate problems and plan properly, we can have a potential lack of workforce owing to vacations, which could affect business processes. We know that, for instance, during Christmas holidays, there are traditionally more malicious e-mails and viruses than usual. Also, in winter we can anticipate harsh weather conditions that can influence our supply chain.

Management Intelligence Reports

As mentioned, the information we collect must be relevant and useful. For management to have useful intelligence reports, we must process and present information in a way that it is relevant to the business. For instance, apart from informing about an upcoming high-risk soccer match, we need to establish whether our offices are close to the predicted hooligans' routes, what the probability of incidents is, and how to minimize the risk.

I suggest making regular weekly intelligence reports for management, which would contain a list of upcoming risks by days, classified according to risk categories (e.g., political violence, hooliganism, natural disasters, traffic disruptions) and with an awarded severity index (insignificant, low, medium, high, or extreme), with each risk containing a security suggestion. A good report should also contain an executive summary, which is a textual section of the report that gives an overview of the overall projected security situation in the coming period. Apart from regular reports, you will need to send irregular reports based on new information and incidents that were unavailable at the time the regular report was sent out.

SECURITY GOVERNANCE

Governance is essential for management. Security governance is an internal framework with which an organization proactively addresses security issues by systematically arranging and explaining the roles, responsibilities, and actions of all its elements and their coordination. Governance is a system of principles, rules, standards, policies, procedures, technical instructions, and working instructions.

- A principle is abstract general guidance
- A rule is a general criterion based on a principle
- A standard is a decided general model of applying a rule
- A policy is a high-level commitment of the whole organization to comply with a standard
- A procedure is a detailed document that practically explains and arranges how a standard is applied. It usually involves several departments and arranges their interaction in applying the standard
- A technical instruction is the part of the procedure that arranges technical details
- A working instruction is a detailed practical document that arranges a specific part of the procedure. It usually targets one department or function and explains in detail how this part of the organization performs the part of the procedure that is its direct responsibility
- Guidelines are pieces of advice comprising governance documents

We can take as an example company A, which has affiliates in several countries and entrance control as the subject:

- The principle is that every facility must have entrance control
- The rule is that entrance control is performed by combining people (manned guarding) and technology
- The standard requires that each entrance be attended by both a male and a female officer, that the entrance be covered by closed-circuit television (CCTV), and that an electronic access control system be used

Centralized Model of Governance

The security department of company A will send to all the national CSOs in the affiliates (A1, A2, A3, etc.) the global policy of the company concerning entrance control. This policy will contain a detailed explanation of the standard and a turnkey implementation, management, and performance methodology, including a list of involved departments and their general roles in the entrance control system. A policy sent to affiliates is the product of high-level agreement between the global security function and other functions mentioned in the policy.

Basically, if the policy allocates responsibilities to the facility management department (such as the responsibility to purchase and install the access control system), involvement of the local facility management departments in the affiliates must have been previously agreed upon (and signed) with the global facility management function in the headquarters of company A. The policy is sent to a department in the affiliates that is responsible for distributing the policy to all departments mentioned in it. All mentioned departments have the responsibility of analyzing the policy and determining whether it is applicable locally (legally, practically, etc.).

Although usually several departments are required to implement the policy, the subject of the policy determines which department is responsible for managing it. In the case of entrance control, it is a security policy and therefore the security department is responsible for managing it. For a policy to become an official internal document in the affiliate, it must be approved by the management board, based on the recommendation of the security department and with the input and approval of other involved departments.

A governance system of an organization has a defined period of time during which a policy has to be approved by the affiliate, starting from the moment it was received. Apart from being officially approved, a policy has to be implemented during a certain time frame from the moment it was approved.

Based on the policy, the affiliate will create a set of local regulations such as procedures and working instructions to be more efficient in implementing the policy. For the regulations, procedures and working instructions are modified annually to match actual conditions.

If the local affiliate determines that it is impossible to approve or implement the policy owing to, for instance, local legal restrictions or special local conditions, it would return the policy to its issuers with a nonbinding opinion, requesting not be obliged to approve or implement the policy or modify certain parts.

Federal Model of Governance

Company A will not send to its affiliates a turnkey policy, but will instead send a rule or a standard. All affiliates will be then obligated to create local policies, procedures, and working instructions that will be most appropriate for local conditions. Even though procedures are created locally and not imposed by headquarters, the responsibilities and approval and implementation method would remain the same.

PEOPLE

People Are Security

Security is basically a process during which people protect people from other people. Security is not the exclusive responsibility of the security department and the people tasked to perform security. This means that the security department initiates, leads, and manages all security subjects in an organization, of which employees are the most important subjects.

For security to be successful, each person in the organization has to be a part of the security system, regardless of how seemingly small or large that part may be. A common reason for the failure of a security system is the famous traditionally introverted nature of security and the failure, or lack of effort, to receive support and initiate cooperation from all people in the organization. Moreover, it takes true effort and lots of magic to change the default opinion of people about security as a burden, to get everybody to do their constructive part, and still to be in control and have authority.

Still, as much as we would like to believe that just by presenting security as a common goal we can get where we want by doing nothing else, that is not true. Receiving commitment and performance from people requires a blend of:

- Personal example
- Classification of people
- Training
- Governance
- Communication
- Control
- Sanctions and reward

Personal Example

To motivate people, the precondition for your message to be taken seriously and perceived as a desirable model of behavior is that you yourself are an example. A good personal image (and thus a good example) is achieved through zealously obeying your own rules. It also requires visible personal commitment, devotion, belief, and integrity.

Classification of People

Communication, trainings, and basically every information flow requires that you know which horizontal and vertical groups of people exist in your organization and exactly what will be communicated to whom, as well as what level of training is suitable for which group.

The first step is the orderly use of the need-to-know principle in your communication. Apart from this principle, which is one of the key principles of the protection of information and data classification, effective trainings and communication rely on balanced information. Not providing enough vital information is as bad as providing too much. Also, you will not send the same message to a production floor worker and a member of the management board. Basically, as much as they are both parts of the security system, each is supposed to do a specific part and exercise a different model of behavior. Second, you will not be able to use the same communication means. For instance, a production floor employee will probably not have an official e-mail address or a company-issued cell phone.

Training

We have touched on the key principles of effective training; further in this book, we will perform a detailed analysis of different training needs and models in an organization. Here, we will go over the basics. An effective training consists of "what" and "how." "What" is the message that you are communicating whereas "how" is the way in which you are communicating it. Basically, your training has to be relevant, clear, and tailored to the audience.

Governance

When we talk about people, governance is an organized systematic model of imposing desired behavior through official internal documents that are supported by management.

Communication

Communication connects people and makes the difference between a group of individuals and an organization. We shall analyze communication in the following chapters.

Control

Apart from purely managing and leading, we are required to control if measures are being implemented and everyone is doing his part. Control requires balance to be effective. Too much control (micromanagement) will usually do more harm than good.

Sanctions and Reward

Sanctions and reward speak for themselves. As much as we would like to think that we can get people to cooperate by just communicating, rewarding desired behavior and sanctioning misbehavior are key elements of managing people.

PHYSICAL ELEMENTS

Physical Security

To distinguish between two terms, before listing the physical elements of a security system, we will first explain physical security. Physical security is a field of security that incorporates physical and mechanical barriers, security technology, guards, and security procedures into a system designed to prevent damage or harm to people and property. The philosophy of physical security is to prevent or stop a physical attack at the earliest possible stage.

There are numerous physical security methods and strategies; in this chapter, we will briefly analyze the three most common physical security approaches to crime prevention. Until recently, security scholars were mostly advocates of one method and criticized the other two; however, scholars are increasingly realizing that effective crime prevention can be achieved only by combining all three methods.

Crime Prevention through Environmental Design

The main purposes and main ideas behind crime prevention through environmental design (CPTED) are the architectural design, modification, and setup of the environment in urban areas, which have the ability to shape the landscape in a way that deters criminal activity by reducing opportunities for crime to occur. CPTED not only addresses environmental design so as to make the environment less accessible physically; it is also uninviting. The difference between the approach to being uninviting between CPTED and situational crime prevention (SCP) is that SCP uses the target-hardening system (visible security measures) to deter criminals whereas CPTED shapes the environment through, for instance, building wide, open, well-lit spaces that are not likely to attract criminals and would deter problematic groups from gathering. This method was often criticized as being elitist and basically not preventing crime but shifting it to poorer areas.

Although the purpose of this method was originally to address crime on a national, city, or municipality level and not as a security tool that could be used by a physical security system—for instance, a factory—even smaller security systems started applying CPTED as part of the strategies to prevent crime from occurring in or around their facilities.

Situational Crime Prevention

SCP is the traditional and most used method of crime prevention. When we think about physical security we think of SCP. Whereas CPTED addresses the situation in terms of environmental design, SCP addressed it as a set of measures designed to practically prevent or stop criminal acts. SCP methodology incorporates physical, mechanical, and technical means to prevent, detect, and stop an attack in the earliest possible stage. One classic method used by SCP is target hardening, which is basically a system of informing a potential perpetrator that executing an action would be extremely difficult. It includes posting warning signs and visible physical, technical, and mechanical security measures and the presence of guards aimed at deterring perpetrators. In the same way that CPTED is criticized as being elitist, SCP is often criticized as being a system whose aim is not to address crime but only shift it elsewhere. Although it may not be true on a more global level such as a state, city, or municipality, the idea behind physical security in a corporation is exactly that—not to stop crime globally but to send it elsewhere. Critics also criticize the often over-controlling "Big Brother" nature of SCP.

Crime Prevention through Social Development

The idea behind crime prevention through social development (CPTSD) is to tackle crime by developing communities and addressing the social and economic causes of crime. CPTSD is believed to be the lengthiest but most sustainable crime prevention method. Practically, CPTSD involves improving basic services or resources to individuals, families, schools, or communities to minimize the impact of social and economic factors on the development of criminal behavior. Owing to its nature and resources required, CPTSD is not a method applied by corporate security apart from some elements. Basically, one method of CPTSD is to get the members of a community to work together to stop crime: for instance, through a voluntary, organized neighborhood watch. Although CPTSD is often seen as an unorthodox method of performing security, there are cases when companies apply some CPTSD methods, such as recruiting local sports hooligans, who pose a security risk, to assist in securing the facility or helping secure events organized by the company.

Physical Security Elements

Physical security elements are physical, mechanical, and electrical barriers that are parts of the layered defense system of a facility. Layers include the security staff but are also a system of interactive security elements such as collected intelligence that is processed and implemented in the right way, a set of procedures, physical barriers, all people in the system, and technical elements.

Physical security elements usually consist of two main groups of barriers:
- Physical
- Visual

Physical Barriers

Physical barriers include physical and mechanical and elements that should physically prevent an action from being carried out, such as walls, fences, doors, windows, access ramps, locks, safes, vaults, illumination, and so forth.

Visual Barriers

The aims of visual barriers are to limit the ability of a perpetrator to collect visual information and plan an action, and to prevent a perpetrator from executing an attack. For example, executive protection systems use visual barriers to prevent an assassin from being able to perform an attack successfully. Visual barriers include physical barriers such as walls, fences, doors, lights, and such, but also curtains, vegetation, blinds, etc.

TECHNOLOGY (ELECTRONIC SYSTEMS)

As we mentioned at the beginning of this book, what changed over time is not the essence of security but its technology. Still, as much as technology is a key element of a security system, it is also a weakness if not used properly. Although we usually use the term "technology solutions" for technology elements, it is impossible to have a "solution" without having people operate the technology while complying with procedures that regulate its use.

Although technology is an important part of security, we will not attempt to list and explain all types of available security technology because it would be a never-ending process. Second, even if we managed to list and explain all existing technology, because of the speedy development of technology, as soon as we completed the list, it would be outdated. Still, we will mention the main groups of security technology used by private security systems.

The main groups of electronic security systems are:

- Access control (electronic access control, gates, alarms, etc.)
- Surveillance (e.g., CCTV)
- Positioning (e.g., global positioning satellite)
- Detection (metal detector; X-ray; fire detectors; chemical tests for explosives, alcohol tests, etc.)
- Evacuation (speaker systems, electronic evacuation sign systems, etc.)

Basically, I believe that the correct philosophy concerning incorporating technology is to concentrate on effective planning, which consists of understanding the threats and vulnerabilities and addressing them by applying common sense, simplicity, and logic. It also calls for combining all other security elements and then planning technology to assist (and not take over) in covering the gaps.

COMMUNICATION

The Importance of Communication

Communication is the bloodstream of a security system. Like a bloodstream in a complex living organism, communication works on many levels, according to different models and with different intensities, but it still has predefined channels and is systematic and continuous. Communication is simply a transportation system that distributes information throughout the structure according to a predefined matrix. Communication can be:

- Verbal
- Nonverbal
- Signal

Furthermore, it can be routine and emergency; downward and upward; official and unofficial; or direct and indirect, which we have already explained in the chapter on corporate communication.

Key success factors for effective communication are to identify proper models of communication according to situation, hierarchy, need-to-know basis, and specifics of the audience and the goal we are trying to achieve. Second, the person who is communicating needs to be officially entitled and recognized by others as eligible. Basically, a commander in a military unit is able to communicate to soldiers effectively and pass on a message both routinely and in an emergency, because of the commander's predefined position and understanding and acceptance by soldiers that he is the primary communicator. Moreover, the way the sound of an emergency siren is able to reach people to evacuate is not because of its abstract nature but because of its predefined role and the knowledge and acceptance of people that it is an eligible model of communication.

Verbal Communication

Verbal communication (using words in communication) is further divided into oral and written communication.

Oral communication uses spoken words. Its advantage is that it is the most efficient way to pass on a message (but not necessarily the quickest); its disadvantage is that it cannot be edited and corrected. One more disadvantage if we talk about corporations is the lack of weight and official commitment potential that it has compared with recorded written communication. Written communication uses written words in the form of e-mails, signs, procedures, and so forth. In business environments, it is the most common form of communication. Even more so, oral communication is often transformed into a written form so as to be legitimate, such as meeting minutes, formalization of tasks, and reports. Written communication can be directed and general. Directed communication such as e-mails sent to a specific person or group has a much greater impact than, for instance, general e-mails sent to the entire organization or posters calling for, for example, security awareness. That does not mean that we will not use posters or mass e-mails, but those will certainly not be our only methods of communicating but rather reminders of messages that we have previously communicated directly.

We also use verbal communication both written and oral, in emergencies, to direct an evacuation, for example.

Nonverbal Communication

Nonverbal communication is about sending a message without using words. It includes body language, tone of voice, facial expressions, and the appearance of the communicator. Effective communication requires verbal and nonverbal aspects of communication to match each other. When we talk about the nonverbal aspects of written communication, we refer to the design, using, for example, colors, underline, bold letters, and capitals in an e-mail to emphasize its parts. Apart from paying attention to the nonverbal message that accompanies our verbal message, during questioning and interrogation, we look for nonverbal signals in the communication. We also use nonverbal communication in many ways during emergency communication. Our nonverbal communication will often make the difference between an orderly evacuation and a panic stampede.

Also, we use nonverbal communication to establish legitimacy. For instance, a security uniform (as well as almost any uniform) is a form of nonverbal communication whose aim is to establish authority. Moreover, a tidy appearance, including a tidy uniform, is likely to be more effective in nonverbal communication than an untidy appearance.

Signal Communication

We all often use signals for communication, which are a shorter form of passing on a message instead of communicating it verbally. Used correctly, such as, for instance, alarms and sirens, signals only replace basic messages. Many security systems use sirens to announce an evacuation as well as inform people to shelter. Whereas the simple action of sheltering (for example, locking the office and staying inside) can indeed be communicated with a siren, an evacuation whose efficiency depends on several factors such as direction (evacuating away from the danger and using a safe exit) cannot be efficiently announced with a siren without the threat of people evacuating toward the danger instead away from it.

Incident Communication

What proved to be a challenge for many organizations and where many fail is establishing proper models of incident communication. Security is not only a process; it is a process based on learning from experience and probability that derives from experience. Establishing proper incident communication channels is essential to be able to receive and distribute timely information and react efficiently.

CONTROL

Control versus Controls

Control and coordination are the basic tasks of the security department and the CSO as its head. However, first, we have to know the difference between control and controls.

Control is a system of numerous controls aimed at checking and improving the capabilities of the system and compliance with the security procedures, and detecting flaws and incidents.

If we talk about people, it is the task of a CSO to be on the top of the control pyramid, which is a system of controls aimed at checking and improving the efficiency of security and compliance with security measures in an organization. It is the responsibility of all managing positions to control and ensure compliance in their organizational units and to continuously communicate and promote security measures, requirements, and expectations.

Certainly, security controls are not only about controlling people. Controls are used by all fields of security to check all elements of a security system. Moreover, in the planning phases of any action and system which we want to implement, it is absolutely essential to plan and formalize (in procedures and working instructions) their controls.

Controls can be classified according to their timing and means. According to timing, security controls are classified into:

- **Preventive (routine) controls**—controls are aimed at checking that the security setup is working properly
- **Detective controls**—intended to detect an incident while it is happening or after it has happened
- **Corrective controls**—intended to check whether corrective actions are being implemented properly
  According to means, controls can be classified into:
- **Electronic controls**—controls performed electronically, either by a person operating technology per each control, or independently through a system with predefined values that reports on anomalies
- **Human controls**—visual control, investigations, patrols, etc.
- **Analytics**—controls aimed at controlling the efficiency of a system, such as metrics (key performance indicators) that control whether the measures we have implemented are giving results

Why: Understand

CHAPTER 6

Internal Risks

OVERVIEW OF INTERNAL RISKS

In the past, internal risks were often mistakenly considered secondary to external ones. One of the reasons could be the mainly military and police background of security managers in companies and their previous professional preoccupation with external risks. However, corporate security practitioners are increasingly realizing that to mitigate risks successfully, they should devote the same amount of time and resources to both external and internal risks. Moreover, it is often difficult to draw a clear line between internal and external crimes. In many cases, corporate investigators stumble upon the involvement of employees during investigations of externally committed crimes. Internal risks are composed not only of property crime risks but of numerous other risks, the most significant of which are:

- Reputation risks
- Acts of protest
- Inadequate organizational resilience
- Sexual harassment and mobbing
- Employee screening (bad hires)
- Substance abuse

If we divide risks into two groups, they would be "the risk of doing" and "the risk of not doing" (the risk of doing nothing). Basically, the "doing" group would consist of risks from intentional acts whereas the second group would consist of negligence risks.

For instance, risks from intentional acts (doing) include all actions performed by an employee or group of employees, either as planned or unplanned acts, such as embezzlement, larceny, fraud, strikes, workplace violence, information technology (IT) and compliance violations, sexual harassment, mobbing, and substance (alcohol and drug) abuse.

The second ("not doing") group consists of risks that are a product of the imperfection of internal processes, without the addition of intentional action aimed at improving them: for example, reputation risks as a product of oversight, inadequate organizational resilience such as misses in planning and execution of business continuity management and disaster recovery, and bad hires as a product of an inadequate pre-employment screening process.

However, in reality, apart from the need to address both groups of risks, we cannot draw a straight line to clearly distinguish between them. For instance, the reputation of an organization could be jeopardized by intentional acts as well as by oversight. Moreover, a bad hire could occur even after we have performed perfect background screening.

Still, what should be universal is the need to be preventive and proactive to address the risks adequately.

In this chapter, we will analyze different internal security and security-related risks. However, we will not deal with business risks such as investment risks and risks from making a bad strategic business decision.

REPUTATIONAL RISKS

Reputational risks are considered a part of financial risk. Basically, the ruined reputation of a company would certainly result in financial loss. However, we will not analyze reputation risks from the viewpoint of quality of product, corporate ethics, and risks associated with research and development (for instance, research methods that could jeopardize public perception about the company, such as testing performed on animals). We will analyze reputational risks that include loss of reputation owing to security incidents, reputation risks as derivates of risk outsourcing, and reputation risks associated with misbehavior of employees. Also, because reputation and security influence each other, we will analyze not only how security influences reputation or how a jeopardized reputation can influence security, but also what security can do to enhance the reputation of a company.

Security-Initiated Risks to Reputation

Security protects an organization from risks, but owing to its nature it can cause reputation risks. We can explain such risks by starting with the most common one. In most cases, manned guarding services in companies are outsourced as part of cost-saving initiatives. However, blinded by savings, companies often fail to realize that the first person a client will meet when he visits the company, and basically his first impression about the company, will be the outsourced security guard at the gate. Unfortunately, judging by private security industry trends, guards are often underpaid; in that sense, because they are not motivated and there may be high staff turnover, they may not stick around long enough to be properly instructed and trained.

Regardless of the quality and devotion of security guards, it is often difficult to achieve a good balance between security orientation and service (client-friendly) orientation, and in most cases one of the requirements will suffer.

It is also common for companies to experience a lot of negative media publicity because of the bad judgment and misbehavior of security guards who, for instance, denied entrance to a facility to someone based on his or her ethnicity or invalidity. Decisions that could cause bad publicity and reputation risks do not have to be malicious; on the contrary, they are intended to protect or assist the person. Take the example of a pregnant woman who is denied access to a crowded music event by a security officer who is concerned about her safety, or the opposite example of an underage person who is allowed to enter a venue organized to promote alcohol or cigarettes.

On the other hand, the same level of security measures can be perceived differently by different people. For some, high-level security measures can add up to the reputation of the company and its perceived value; for others, they can be the sign of a lack of respect for clients. For instance, a bank can face a reputational dilemma if it keeps security guards in its branches. Security guards have no real security value for the security of bank branches because they are mostly instructed not to react in cases of incidents, apart from handling smaller incidents and misunderstandings. On the other hand, as mentioned earlier, they can jeopardize reputation. However, banks are often perceived by clients as more serious if security guards are present in their branches.

A sensitive group that deserves special attention and careful treatment are members of the press. Security systems often have special entrance procedures for groups that deserve special attention, such as VIP and certainly members of the press.

"Soft Target" Reputation Risk

As much as security measures can pose a threat to reputation, the lack of security measures can endanger the reputation of a company. By "soft target" reputation risks, we do not mean only the perception of criminals regarding whether the company is an easy target owing to numerous successful actions against the company, but also the perception of clients. For instance, a client of a bank can feel threatened both physically and financially because of numerous successful robberies of the branch that he frequently visits.

Reputational Risks from Outsourced Risk

Companies are able and often opt to outsource as many risks as possible and in that sense be protected from financial risks and liability, but they sometimes fail to understand that even if they manage to outsource the immediate financial risk, the risks to reputation remain. However, by outsourcing risks, companies tend to put their own reputation in someone else's hands. A good example is marketing events organized by a famous cigarette manufacturer, "company P." A part of its marketing strategy is to promote its brands, especially the company's most famous brand, through party-like massive music events. To outsource the legal responsibility in case something goes wrong during an event, a service provider would be the official organizer of the event while company "P" would officially be just the sponsor of the event. Not only would it transfer the responsibility legally, but the service provider would actually be entirely in charge of organizing and executing the event, including the security of the event, with limited supervision by company P's marketing executives. If a serious incident occurred during the event, apart from legal responsibility, no one would remember the name of the official organizer of the event, but the brand would experience negative publicity.

EMBEZZLEMENT, THEFT, AND FRAUD

Some security practitioners do not divide employees' crimes into these three groups, but rather classify them all under "employee dishonesty," which can be defined as "any dishonest act performed by an employee that causes a loss to the employer." However, because they are indeed three different types of dishonest behavior by employees performed by different types of employees, using different techniques and causing different consequences, it is important that we explain the differences and analyze each one separately.

Embezzlement

Embezzlement is the most common and costly type of employee crime. Although embezzlement is both a type of theft and a type of fraud, not every theft or fraud is embezzlement. For a crime to be categorized as embezzlement, it has to be a theft committed by an employee who is entitled to be in possession of (have access and manipulate) the property that was stolen. For instance, if a bank employee who has access to clients' accounts transfers funds to his personal account, this type of fraud is embezzlement. The same goes for a salesperson in a store who steals an item from the store. Embezzlement does not have to be committed against a company. For example, a person who collects "charity" money from colleagues for an existing cause but who uses the money for personal gain is also embezzling. However, if he is collecting money for a nonexistent cause, he is committing fraud.

Many studies revealed that embezzlers are usually not career criminals, but in most cases are people with no criminal background or prior convictions.

Like any crime, embezzlement needs to have three elements to be committed successfully: motive, opportunity, and means. When looking at the crime triangle, it is obvious why embezzlement is so widespread. An employee entrusted with assets has both the opportunity and the means. If we take the example of a bank clerk, he has been given the means (authority, software applications, etc.) by the bank to manipulate the accounts of clients. He also does not have to create an opportunity because he already has it with the work position. As for the motive, because most embezzlers are first-time offenders, it is difficult to notice it during, for example, pre-employment background screening. Motive can also appear later with aggravation of the financial situation, for numerous reasons. Other factors that can influence motive are the two other elements of the crime triangle. Basically, a bank clerk who has access to money and the opportunity to take it is more likely to attempt a fraud just because it is easy.

Let us look at the figures:

- According to the highlights of the 2012 Report to the Nations published on the Web site of the Association of Certified Fraud Examiners (ACFE.com) [1], a typical organization loses 5% of its annual revenue to embezzlement. Applied to the estimated 2011 gross world product, this figure translates to a potential global loss of more than $3.5 trillion.

- According to the United States (US) Department of Justice [2], nearly 30% of all employees commit some sort of embezzlement.
- Employee Theft Solutions, a division of the Shulman Center for Compulsive Theft and Spending [3], estimates that one-third of all US corporate bankruptcies are directly caused by embezzlement.
- The US Chamber of Commerce [4] estimates that 75% of employees steal from the workplace, and that most do so repeatedly.

If we look at embezzlement in a broader sense, the figures are much worse. A survey conducted by the forensic accounting firm Kessler [5] found that as much as 95% of employees steal from their employers. This survey included not only physical property and money, but also intellectual property such as client lists, projects which they or other employees have performed for the company, and so forth. According to a 2007 study by the Data Management Institute [6], 70% of companies go out of business after a major data loss.

Theft

Employee theft is similar to embezzlement, but unlike embezzlement, it does not involve stealing entrusted assets. For example, if an employee of a certain section in a department store steals an item from his department, he has committed embezzlement. However, if he steals an item from another section of the same department store, he has committed theft. In theory, it is easier to spot theft than embezzlement, because to commit theft, a perpetrator does not have immediate access to opportunity and means, but has to create it and must have a stronger, more easily detectible motive. Although it might be true in some cases, the reality is that it is often more difficult to solve cases of embezzlement than cases of fraud. The reason is simple: If an item is missing, an investigator will first consider the person to whom the item was entrusted. If the investigation shows that it was not a case of embezzlement, a theft could have been committed by practically anyone. Opportunity is not just being able to perform a crime, but performing a crime without being detected. We can take the example of a production floor in a factory where numerous production workers work alongside each other using the same types of tools. If one worker decides to steal a tool, he would more likely perform theft instead of embezzlement and steal a tool belonging to his colleague instead of the one he is using, to limit the possibility of being discovered. In that way, he is basically dividing the probability of being discovered by the number of colleagues.

One of the models of performing theft is through identity theft. For example, an employee in the bank would use the log-in and password of his colleague, or his access control card, to enter a restricted area or access restricted applications. That is an interesting example because it can help explain the difference between theft and fraud. Theft has to be an act against tangible assets that have a material value. Thus, theft of identity (identity being intangible) is not theft but fraud. Basically, the employee in our example has committed fraud to commit theft. For instance, an employee can falsify time and attendance records and in that way steal time. Although time in a company has a value, it would still be fraud and not theft.

Theft in a company is basically any theft of tangible assets that is not embezzlement, whether it is performed against the company or against a client or another employee (e.g., stealing personal belongings or cash).

Fraud

We have analyzed embezzlement and theft, which are types of fraud with material consequences. Although internal fraud is dishonest behavior exercised by an employee or employees to secure unfair or unlawful gain, it does not necessarily have to cause material damage to the employer. The most common and most benign internal frauds in companies are probably falsification of time and attendance records, misrepresentation of background data in a resume, falsification of medical records for the purpose of medical leave, and tampering with e-mail content. Like embezzlement and theft, fraud is not exclusively reserved for the bottom of the company hierarchy. Actually, senior executives are not immune to employee dishonesty. Common types of senior executive fraud that do not cause material damage are falsification of achievements and creating false payment and financial information to mask the losses temporarily. Other common types of fraud include:

- Procurement fraud—when the tender (bidding) process has not been followed, so that fraud can be committed. Procurement fraud can be committed by one or more employees. It can occur in many forms, such as favoring one bidder over another because of bribes or friendship, or for other reasons. Procurement fraud can also happen when an employee knowingly approves payment claims for goods or services that were not delivered.
- Travel and subsistence fraud—This type of fraud includes claims for fake journeys or fake client entertainment claims, claims for amounts higher than those spent, and forged receipts and signatures authorizing payment.
- Personnel management fraud—employee working elsewhere while on sick leave, abuse of flexible working time systems, using a company's computer for private purposes, etc.
- Exploiting information—e.g., employee supplying information to outsiders for personal gain.

ACTS OF PROTEST

Acts of protest are usually initiated by decisions made by the company or its managers and can range from massive protests organized by trade unions such as work stoppage (strike) and demonstrations, to personal protests such as sabotage, self-mutilations, suicide, and assault, caused by the loss of a job, mobbing, sexual harassment, and so forth. What is common to all acts of protest is that they are usually announced, communicated either openly or hinted at, or anticipated.

Strikes

Strike is work stoppage caused by the mass refusal of employees to work. It is usually organized by trade unions or, if there are no trade unions, by employees unofficially grouping together to protest against a certain decision by the company or parts of the company. Because most strikes are organized by trade unions, to prevent strikes from happening, in many cases, companies try to include a no-strike clause in the collective agreement with trade unions to prevent strikes. Even when allowed, strikes are rare and usually occur only after the failure to reach an agreement. In cases when unsatisfied workers are not unionized or trade unions are not present in a company, workers may decide to strike without the involvement and approval of trade unions. Such strikes are called wildcat strikes; in most countries, they do not have the same legal protection as official trade union strikes.

Strikes usually imply the refusal of workers to work. In some cases, strikers can continue to work by performing tasks to a certain level. For example, employees striking in a hospital can continue to deal with emergencies but refuse to engage in anything else. Such strikes are often referred to as partial strikes or slowdowns. Less frequently, strikes can also have a reverse form such as the refusal of workers to stop working and leave, for instance, after a massive redundancy announcement. This type of strike is called a "work-in." Also rare is the "sit-down strike," in which workers occupy the workplace but refuse to do their jobs or leave. "Hunger strikes" are an extremely unusual type of protest and usually are the last resort when an agreement is not reached during negotiations and conventional strikes.

Strikes are sensitive not only because they cause losses for the company, but because, if not addressed properly by the company, they can lead to violence, vandalism, and even hostage situations.

Involvement of Security

Negotiations with employees are the responsibility of the company management. To mitigate additional risks and properly plan for the crisis, security must be informed from the moment a decision has been made that could trigger protests, and before it has been communicated to employees. Because strikes are not only initiated by business decisions but also by, for example, mistreatment of employees by their manager, security should be able to notice early warning signs either through the complaints of employees or through its internal sources of information and alert the management.

The role of security is to design and implement a strategy with the aims of minimizing damage and preventing the situation from becoming aggravated. The security strategy for dealing with strikes consists of several elements: understanding the motive, anticipating, preparing how to minimize the impact (for example, preventively evacuating management), and creating strategies in case the security situation becomes aggravated during the strike.

Demonstrations

Demonstrations are another way of protesting. They can occur independently or be part of a strike. Dealing with a demonstration is sensitive because it is a "political" issue as well as a security issue, not only because of its media potential (reputation hazard) but because of the potential for the crowd to turn violent and pose a security threat. We have to understand that even the most violent demonstrations start as peaceful ones and that the smallest wrong step can initiate the switch. Although negotiations with demonstrators are reserved for management functions in the corporation, security must be involved in every step of negotiations to make sure the situation does not get out of hand.

Involvement of Security

The role of security is also proactive. Apart from anticipating demonstrations and protests, together with management, security should design a strategy that would enable it to be in control of the situation, minimize the impact of the protest if it turns violent, and react effectively in case of a threat. Prevention includes negotiating with people who are organizing the demonstration and openly presenting security concerns and asking for cooperation and their commitment to security and safety. One strategy is to offer to assist in organizing the demonstration to ensure the safety of all by, for example, offering the organizers of the demonstration a safer place for the demonstration. However, the organizers of the demonstration are not always the people with the best ability to motivate the crowd. It is important to identify the "leaders" and to have a way to keep them under control. Prevention also includes preventively evacuating the management and removing objects that could be used for violence as well as those that could initiate violence, such as, for instance, cars belonging to company executives. It is advisable to have a "low-profile" person who will, from the inside of the demonstration, keep an eye on developments and inform security about any plans or changes in the situation. Police must be informed about a planned demonstration, but should be asked not to react if the demonstration remains peaceful and to communicate and cooperate with the chief security officer to have a common strategy. A trigger for the police to react should be aggravation of the situation such as threats by demonstrators, violence, and crossing of the "red line." If a demonstration starts turning violent, demonstrators should be informed about the "red line," which is an imaginary line that distinguishes the perimeter protected by security. Demonstrators must know that they are allowed to demonstrate but would be considered intruders if they cross the "red line," which would make the security and police react.

Sabotage

Sabotage is a way of protesting. Although sabotage performed by groups of employees is rare, sabotage performed by a lone employee or ex-employee is a real threat. The most common situation in which sabotage occurs is after job termination. Sabotage can be performed in many ways, such as physically vandalizing tools and machines, tampering with a product, or deleting crucial data from the IT system. The key to addressing the issue of sabotage proactively is to have a system in place that would limit the exposure of vital data and infrastructure before job termination. This also includes making an assessment, anticipating problems, and making a preventive decision on how to deal with the employee. Basically it means deciding whether it is safe to keep the employee in the company until his or her contract expires or to reach a different agreement. The strategy should include the denial of certain access rights to the employee and control during entry to and exits from the facility, but also a decision and communication with the employee regarding when and under what conditions he or she would receive severance pay, a recommendation letter, and so forth.

Assault

As an extreme way to protest, assault could occur against a superior, from the level of a direct supervisor to the top executive of a company. It could be triggered by numerous reasons ranging from real or perceived unfair conduct by a superior, mobbing, sexual harassment, job termination (single job termination or massive redundancy), and so forth. It could occur at work or away from work. The strategy for preventing an assault is to take seriously any information concerning possible motives and address the issue proactively, such as conducting misconduct investigations and advising the employee regarding how and to whom to legally and officially report the issue. In cases in which the probability of assault against a manager or managers is higher, such as when a manager has been receiving threats, or during massive redundancies, security must implement preventive security measures that include security awareness trainings and, for instance, advice to managers to vary arrival and departure times and break daily routines.

Self-Mutilation/Suicide

Together with assault, self-mutilation and suicide are the most extreme types of protest. As with assault, reasons could be numerous. It is important to notice warning signals, such as signs in appearance and behavior, and to act proactively: for example, by consulting a professional psychological counselor and increasing surveillance on the particular employee.

SEXUAL HARASSMENT AND MOBBING

Sexual harassment and mobbing are not classic security issues; when reported, they are mostly dealt with by human resources in companies or by other appointed functions. However, many times, sexual harassment and mobbing are not reported; as such, they often depend on security to notice and report them. Although both are issues that have to be properly and addressed in a timely manner to protect the well-being of employees, if not addressed, they can lead to security risks such as sexual assault, physical assault, retaliation, and numerous other issues.

Sexual Harassment

The US Equal Employment Opportunity Commission [7] defines sexual harassment as unwelcome sexual advances, requests for sexual favors, and other verbal or physical harassment of a sexual nature (including harassment based on sexual orientation). In a workplace, sexual harassment can occur between one colleague and another (usually male to female) or by a superior who is using his influence or position to obtain a sexual favor or to degrade the subordinate of the opposite sex (mostly women). Sexual harassment can be public or secret and can occur in various forms such as sexting (text messages with sexually explicit content), e-mails with sexual content, and verbal harassment. It can occur with the purpose of simply humiliating or as a sexual advance.

Sexual assault occurs when one person is forced into a sexual act without consent. Sexual assault includes any kind of rape (vaginal, anal, or oral) as well as any touching and kissing without consent.

Mobbing

Mobbing is the emotional abuse of an employee by a co-worker, superior, or subordinate. The purpose of mobbing is to discredit someone through rumors, disrespect, humiliation, intimidation, and social and work isolation, and eventually to force this person out of the workplace. As security professionals who should protect the employees in a company, and because of moral obligations, we are required to notice the signs of workplace bullying and request action from competent functions in a company. Victims of mobbing frequently experience depression, severe stress (even posttraumatic stress disorder), and other psychological and health disorders. If not addressed properly, apart from aggravated health of the victim, mobbing can lead to retaliation by the victim against the bullies, including physical assault. However, mobbing is also known to be a common trigger for substance abuse (such as drug and alcohol abuse), and in extreme cases it may even lead to self-mutilation and suicide.

In many countries there are anti-mobbing laws aimed at protecting victims and punishing abusers, as well as punishing companies in case they were aware of mobbing and failed to stop it.

SUBSTANCE ABUSE AND GAMBLING

According to the Occupational Safety and Health Administration (OSHA) in the US Department of Labor [8], between 10% and 20% of American workers who die at work have a positive result when tested for drugs or alcohol. A study by OSHA states that the most dangerous occupations, such as mining and construction, also have the highest rates of drug use by employees. According to the American Council for Drug Education [9], 2 million Americans use heroin, 6 million use cocaine, 18 million have alcohol abuse problems, and an estimated 23 million people use marijuana at least four times in a week.

According to OSHA [8], 74.8% of all drug users are employed and active in the workplace. This means that only in the US, close to 13 million individuals actively use drugs in the workplace. If we would add together all of the illegal drugs that are being used, including the growing problem of abuse of prescription drugs and painkillers, especially at work, the statistics would be even graver.

One role of corporate security is to prevent and detect alcohol and drug abuse in the workplace, including preventing drugs and alcohol from being brought in, preventing the use of drugs and alcohol at work, and preventing employees from working or even entering the workplace while under the influence. Depending on the company and type of industry, detective and preventive measures could include information received from internal intelligence sources, random physical checks of employees entering the facility, an unannounced random breathalyzer, and urine and blood tests.

Aside from obvious health and safety risks, alcohol and drug abuse are, together with gambling, the most common motives for embezzlement, employee theft, and fraud. Employee crime prevention includes looking for early warning signs that could indicate substance abuse and/or a gambling problem.

Unlike with drug or alcohol addiction, with gambling addiction there are no obvious physical signs, symptoms, or incriminating items. Gamblers are typically good at denying or minimizing the problem and will do anything to hide the gambling problem. Still, there are signs that could indicate a gambling problem:

- Frequently borrowing money from colleagues
- High turnover of value items: for example, coming to work with new watches, jewelry, and cell phones, and frequently replacing them
- Large visible oscillations in financial situation
- Offering personal and household items for sale to colleagues
- Occasionally not showing up at work without providing credible reasons
- Frequent mood oscillations

These are warning signs of gambling addiction, but they are also points an investigator will analyze when investigating the possible involvement of an employee in embezzlement, theft, or fraud. However, apart from gambling, these signs can indicate compulsive spending, which is also a personal disorder that could cause employee dishonesty.

INADEQUATE SECURITY RESILIENCE

By security resilience, we mean internal security and security-related setup and performance in terms of their ability to withstand threats and recover from incidents. Although the term "resilience" is usually used to explain the preparedness of an organization concerning business continuity management and disaster recovery, we should understand it in a broader sense. Resilience includes all security and security-related procedures and processes and their relevance in terms of coverage, content, and ability to adapt to constantly changing conditions. Certainly, resilience implies the compliance of employees with internal procedures and proper compliance and performance controls.

Based on the report "Top Security Threats and Management Issues Facing Corporate America—2012 Survey of Fortune 1000 Companies," issued by *Securitas* [10], according to security directors of Fortune 1000 companies that were surveyed, business continuity planning/organizational resilience was ranked the third most significant security concern (out of 24 offered threats and/or concerns). Employee selection/screening was ranked fourth whereas inadequate security was ranked ninth. The survey drew 297 responses from corporate security directors and other executives with primary responsibility for their companies' security programs, and yielded a 25.5% response rate.

Basically, according to the broader understanding of inadequate resilience in terms of an overall security risk for an organization, and not only as an inadequate business continuity management system, it includes all internal weaknesses that can facilitate external risks and worsen their impact on an organization, such as:

- Nonexistent or outdated security procedures and/or business continuity plans
- Inadequate employee screening process
- Noncompliance with information and information communication technology security procedures
- Insufficient internal fraud prevention
- Inadequate security including poor performance of security staff and/or weak planning, physical and technical security measures, setup, and management
- Badly implemented system of security controls, coordination, and management
- Weak cyber and communication security

REFERENCES

[1] 2012 Report to the Nations, Association of Certified Fraud Examiners. www.ACFE.com.
[2] US Department of Justice. www.justice.gov.
[3] Employee Theft Solutions, a Division of the Shulman Center for Compulsive Theft and Spending. www.employeetheftsolutions.com.
[4] US Chamber of Commerce. www.uschamber.com.
[5] Forensic Accounting Firm Kessler. www.investigations.com.
[6] Data Management Institute. www.datainstitute.org.
[7] The EEOC (US Equal Employment Opportunity Commission). www.eeoc.gov.
[8] Occupational Safety and Health Administration (OSHA) in the US Department of Labor. www.osha.gov.
[9] American Council for Drug Education. www.phoenixhouse.org.
[10] Securitas, Top Security Threats and Management Issues Facing Corporate America, 2012. https://www.securitas.com/Global/United%20States/2012%20Top%20Security%20Threats.pdf.

CHAPTER 7

External Risks

OVERVIEW OF EXTERNAL RISKS

Businesses are threatened by numerous external risks. The larger and more complex they are, the more vulnerable they are to a variety of risks. Until recently, threats associated with companies were mostly traditional types of crime such as fraud, theft, and robberies. However, apart from the intensification of such threats, the development of new technologies and a complete change in the way we do business has led to the creation of new methods of committing crime. Not only has crime been able to closely follow legitimate technological invention; it is often the leader when it comes to inventing new technologies and using them to commit crimes.

Moreover, cybercrimes have become the ultimate number one threat in terms of impact. The McAfee "Economic Impact of Cybercrime and Cyber Espionage" report from 2013 [1], which presents data collected from various (unnamed) sources, states that the annual cost of global malicious cyber activity is between 300 billion and 1 trillion USD. However, this research does not show the enormous negative operational impact and annual cost of temporary disruptions of information technology (IT) services (for various reasons) on businesses globally.

The focus on cost savings, such as the reduction of human resources to an operational minimum, the orientation toward technological solutions for processes, the trend of outsourcing all support functions, and the tendency to get the maximum from resources (human as well as physical) and reduction of stock to a minimal operational amount, managed to cut operational costs but increased the vulnerability of organizations and the impact of incidents. It also decreased the ability of companies to ensure business continuity and recovery after a disaster.

The national identity of corporations and frequent orientation toward emerging markets brought types of terrorism (such as nationalistic, religious, and political) that had been reserved for national security to deal with to the front door of corporations. Terrorism suddenly became a serious threat for corporations on all levels, including diverse types of terrorism such as, for example, social terrorism (often referred to as "single issue" terrorism), which includes groups fighting for animal rights and environmental issues, and revolutionary terrorism such as anti-globalization groups.

Terrorism was also affected by the global economy crisis, and some terrorist groups that had been financed by certain Middle Eastern and African states had to look for other ways to survive, such as drug trafficking and kidnapping for ransom, which has become a serious problem for companies operating, for example, in North Africa. In this way, terrorist groups have joined the path of kidnapping for ransom, which criminal groups from Central and South America have been doing for years.

Terrorism became not only a direct threat to business but also a threat used to facilitate terrorism: for example, through the supply chain, money laundering, or financial transactions aimed at financing terrorism.

GLOBAL ISSUES VERSUS CORPORATE SECURITY

Talk about the new, harder wave of economy crisis, especially after the devastating effects of the first wave, has attracted a lot of attention and public discussion. There has been much talk about the probable effects of the new crisis on businesses and unemployment. What about its effects on security? Nobody connected with security issues can pretend that an economy crisis is just a financial or economic issue. In fact, there is a saying that crime is the evil twin of recession. Even without thoroughly analyzing the effects of economy crisis on criminality, we know that crime, which is the most profitable industry globally, especially flourishes in times of crisis.

The first things that come to mind with the mention of recession are unemployment, insecure bank loans, political extremism, uncertainty, and a generally easily flammable situation. On the one hand, for crime it is a situation with endless opportunities. On a state level, recession is a chance for political extremists to gain popularity and power and use the fact that the government is likely to face strikes and demonstrations from public sector employees as they defer wage increases. However, foreign direct investment (FDI) of businesses is related to security in several ways. Investors need to feel that their financial interests will be protected in the country where they are investing, by political stability and existing legislation, and by the institutions responsible for implementing the laws. If there is no assurance that national laws will deal fairly and equitably with foreign investors, but rather will extend preferential treatment indiscriminately to advance this or that political and/or private agenda, the flow of FDI will automatically be reduced. In terms of physical security, the protection of physical assets should also be relatively ensured: That is, the individual company will not be obliged to rely solely on its own internal mechanisms for security but will also enjoy the protection of the police and justice systems.

Recession is an opportunity for organized crime to expand activities. Organized crime quickly enters the business vacuum caused by the recession and gains power. On the other hand, well-established criminal organizations use the effects of the economy crisis, such as the global lack of cash, to invest in legitimate business. On a more personal level, turning toward crime often remains the only possibility of a living for people who were made jobless. On top of that, a state that concentrates on political and economy issues often does not have the will and resources to fight crime efficiently or even turns a blind eye to preserve social peace. In the first wave of the economy crisis, the rise in unemployment and poverty created an increase in petty theft and street crime in all of Europe. Xenophobia and an increase in the number of incidents against immigrants and inter-ethnic incidents are other factors associated with recessions. Acts of violence committed by far-left revolutionary terror groups and single issue terrorist groups, such as animal and environmental protection extremists, experienced the biggest growth in Europe, especially with actions targeting businesses that were identified by the extremist groups as violating the rights of animals, such as performing animal tests or endangering the environment. For example, according to the Overseas Security Advisory Council (OSAC.gov) [2], in Germany in 2009, far-left incidents increased about 50% compared with the previous year.

Other known effects of the economy crisis are the transfer from terrorism to organized crime and the increasingly transnational nature of organized criminal groups. Globally, terrorist organizations seem not to have been well-prepared for the economic crisis and its impact. Main sponsors of terror had to tighten their belts, which left terrorist organizations without sufficient funding and forced them to turn to crime or support criminal organizations to collect funds. In the short term, joint ventures between terrorist organizations and organized criminal groups are a good business strategy; they help criminal groups gain more cash and assist terrorist organizations in becoming transnational.

In the European Union (EU), criminal organizations, mostly those originating from Eastern Europe, are enjoying the fact that their members have become EU citizens and can now move from one EU member state to the next without undergoing border crossing checks and inspections. This is especially visible in the constant rise in the number of vehicle thefts and supply chain crime in most EU states. Supply chain security incidents are particularly interesting: There were sudden trans-European epidemics or Romanian-style thefts of cargo in 2009, which until then mostly occurred in Romania and a few surrounding countries.

Businesses should be prepared for all sorts of problems associated with recession on top of pure economy effects. Illicit trade, brand integrity issues, hardships associated with redundancies, crime on all levels, partner integrity concerns, and corruption are some of the problems known to affect businesses and security in times of crisis.

Corporations are not immune to global politics. As an example of its direct impact, global environmental initiatives such as the Kyoto Treaty affect the cost of energy, whereas the *Organization of the Petroleum Exporting Countries* agreement regulates oil production, costs, and taxation for oil-producing nations.

To lower the costs of their operations, corporations are often pushed into relocating their operations to cheaper emerging markets, which are often characterized by lower costs and higher security risks. On a more indirect level, corporations are the true ambassadors of their founding countries, for good or bad. Any security threat that a country is facing is immediately spread to its trademark companies worldwide. Although a country has planned and anticipated the risks and has a homeland security mechanism in place to mitigate these risks, companies are left alone on a foreign ground to fight against the threats, with incomparably lower resources and capabilities.

CRIME

We can define crime as any act that is unlawful and punishable by a state. Although every crime is unlawful, not every unlawful act is a crime. There are several ways to group crimes. The most common way to group crimes is according to their impact, such as:

- Crimes against property—theft, vandalism, burglary, robbery, arson, extortion, embezzlement, blackmail, etc.
- Crimes against persons—assault, harassment, manslaughter, kidnapping, rape, robbery, battery, extortion, sexual assault, etc.
- Victimless crimes—This group consists of crimes that do not directly violate or threaten the rights of any other individual: for instance, substance abuse and gambling. These crimes are sometimes referred to as "public order crimes."
- Crimes against the state—tax evasion, espionage, etc.
- Crimes against justice—bribery, corruption, obstruction of justice, etc.

It can often be unsatisfactory to group crimes and sometimes is pointless because some crimes appear in more than one group. For example, robbery and extortion are crimes against both property and against a person. There are also numerous other ways to group crimes, depending on the goal of the specific classification. If we were to further analyze crime grouping methodologies, we would notice numerous flaws and inconsistencies. Nevertheless, here are some alternative ways to divide crimes:

- According to perpetrators (organized crime, disorganized crime, employee crimes, white-collar crimes, war crimes, etc.)
- According to motive (poverty, greed, ideology, harm, sex, etc.)
- According to model (virtual, nonviolent, violent, etc.)

We will continue by analyzing gain- and damage-motivated crimes against property and workplace-related crimes against people that are executed by external perpetrators and commonly affect businesses.

Organized Perpetrators versus Individual Perpetrators

When we talk about organized perpetrators, we are not referring only to criminal organizations, but any organized group of career criminals who exercise planned and systematic criminal acts, have an organizational approach and internal division of responsibilities and tasks, and have sufficient logistics that enable them to target higher volumes and values. We will compare organized perpetrators with individual perpetrators who are not career criminals but impulse criminals motivated by immediate needs such as poverty, substance abuse, or gambling debts.

Anticipating the Type of Threat

When we analyzed the concept of values, we mentioned that by analyzing the protected value in terms of a motive to commit crime, we can anticipate the type of threat we are facing. Basically, unlike organized perpetrators, individual perpetrators target immediate value that does not require time, resources, and logistics to bring a profit. Moreover, by anticipating the types of perpetrators, we can anticipate the types of risks and impact.

Impact

An organized criminal group is motivated by greed. It will plan the action so as to get maximum gain with minimum damage. Basically, an organized group of criminals is aware of the consequences of its action in terms of possible punishment and will, in many cases, try to minimize damage. Experience teaches us that an organized group is less likely to assault and harm during an armed robbery than single perpetrators.

On the other hand, single perpetrators often do not thoroughly plan the action but act based on the impulse to satisfy a relatively immediate need. The focus is mostly on smaller amounts of primary value that can provide immediate profit (such as money, jewelry, electronic gadgets, etc.) and they usually have tunnel vision, which means that they focus on the goal and not the consequences. There is a higher chance of violence and injury during a robbery executed by a single perpetrator.

Theft

Theft, especially in the form of shoplifting, is the most common type of property crime that affects businesses. There is no mystery in the fact that retail is the most affected part of business. A shop displays the items that people want to own in an appealing manner while making them visible, easily accessible, and customer friendly. Shoplifting is mostly performed by single perpetrators and the majority of shoplifting is poverty motivated; as such, not surprisingly, food is the number one type of retail stolen merchandise worldwide. However, the focus of perpetrators greatly depends on their age, whether they are single or organized, and their motive for committing a crime. For instance, alcohol is especially popular with shoplifters because it attracts underage perpetrators who cannot purchase it legally, or alcoholics, or gain-motivated criminals planning to resell it. Pregnancy test theft is generally reserved for underage perpetrators who prefer to steal it instead of buying it, mostly because of shame. Addiction is also a top motive for the theft of prescription drugs such as tranquilizers and painkillers, as well as easily resalable items such as expensive alcohol, jewelry, mobile phones and other small electronic devices, perfumes, and clothing.

Apart from a limited number of cases such as, for instance, theft of jewelry, the nature of theft is such that it cannot provide larger gain for the perpetrators during a single action. As such, it is not attractive for large groups of organized criminals. However, small groups consisting of two to three criminals, often involving an insider (a seller or even a shop security guard), target items such as electronics, IT and communication equipment, and expensive branded clothing, perfumes, and cosmetics.

Thieves are not likely to become violent if confronted, so workplace violence during theft is rare.

Car Theft

Another type of theft that frequently affects businesses is car theft. In fact, car thefts are popular criminal acts even when not connected to businesses; however, there are several reasons why corporate cars are especially popular with thieves. First, general company car fleets often consist of common models and brands of vehicles, which makes it easy for thieves to move unnoticed with the stolen car and resell it afterward. Most company cars are not owned by companies but are actually rented or leased and are completely insured. As such, neither the leasing company nor the company that is using the vehicles will invest in security systems. Moreover, companies and company car users will usually not be as quick to report the car stolen as private vehicle owners would be. The main reasons why companies decide to lease cars instead of buying them are to outsource the risk and save costs. Car users are also likely to pay less attention to company cars compared with their own privately owned cars. Furthermore, it is easy to anticipate the movements of a company car and it is convenient to plan and execute the theft, especially if the cars are marked with the company logo, which they usually are. In addition, when one company car is stolen, it is likely that more will follow. All cars used by one company usually have the same security systems, so, basically, after stealing one car, the thieves will know exactly which security systems are being used on all other vehicles.

However, the risks that companies face in connection with car theft consist of more than the inconvenience of their car being stolen. Company car users tend to be reckless not only with the cars they are using, but also with company assets such as, for example, laptops, documents, and other IT and office equipment and items. For thieves, that would be a special free gift, while it would create numerous inconveniences for the company, such as a loss of information, jeopardy to reputation, and additional costs.

Burglary

As much as theft is mostly reserved for single perpetrators, burglaries are often performed by small organized groups of two to three criminals, sometimes involving an insider. We mentioned earlier that the nature of theft is such that it cannot provide larger gain for perpetrators during a single action. On the other hand, an organized burglary with good logistics, whether it is executed against retail or against a warehouse, can generate big profits for the criminals and bigger losses for the company. A criminal is unlikely to plan and execute a burglary to steal one item from a place filled with desirable items. He will likely have accomplices and logistics. Furthermore, because theft mostly targets higher-value merchandise, burglary can target not only high-value items but also large volumes of lower-value items such as scrap metal, wood, and basically anything that has a potential or buyer. It is extremely difficult to prevent theft owing to the customer-friendly nature of retail, but preventing burglaries is not contradictory to good service. Depending on the type of item and type of facility, burglary prevention can include lighting, alarms and alarm monitoring, physical and mechanical barriers, closed-circuit television, guards, dogs, and random patrols.

Unlike with theft, burglars are more likely to engage in violence if they are detected and interrupted.

Robbery

By definition, robbery is taking the property (of value) of another by force or threat of force. Common types of robbery are armed robbery, which involves use of any weapon, and aggravated robbery, which is performed with the use of a deadly weapon. To differentiate, extortion is taking the property of another by using words instead of an action or weapon. Robberies are performed by both single and organized perpetrators. As mentioned earlier, an organized group is less likely to assault and harm during an armed robbery than single perpetrators. To be classified as a robbery, a criminal act must occur during an interaction between a perpetrator and a victim. Moreover, robbery is basically an aggravated act of theft because it not only includes the theft of property but poses a severe risk to the victim. As much as we are protecting value, we must know that our ultimate goal is to protect life, and that is what our protection strategy against robbery should be based on as its primary objective.

Even more so, it is not rare that security measures intended to protect value from robbery actually put human life in greater danger. When designing protection strategies, our goal should be to harden the target to prevent the robbery from occurring; however, once the robbery has started, we should concentrate on protecting life even if that means doing everything not to aggravate the situation, including assisting the robber to escape with the stolen property. We can call this philosophy "hard in—easy out."

We can take bank robberies as an example. Many banks opt to implement the interlocking door system. The interlocking system is used to control entry into a secure area with a system of two or more doors that are electrically interlocked in such a way that they cannot be opened simultaneously. Basically, interlocking systems are made from vandal-proof or bulletproof material and consist of a go-through security booth with two doors. When entering the booth, after the first door closes, a visitor is trapped in the booth where he may be observed before being granted (or denied) entrance through the second door. Moreover, the system works in the same way during entrance to the secure area as well as during exit. Such systems are known to have lowered the number or robberies in bank branches. Unfortunately, no known research has been done to determine whether violence during robberies has increased in facilities equipped with interlocking door systems. However, common sense tells us that it may have. Basically, apart from slowing down the entrance of a robber to a branch, we are slowing down his departure once he has taken the money. By not letting the robber leave, we are certainly making him feel more impatient and threatened, and so are making the situation more danger-ous. Also, unlike in high-security facilities (such as, for example, in embassies and state agencies that are attended by armed and trained security personnel), we have no actual ability to confront the perpetrator. It is probable that the robber will compensate for the lack of control by using a weapon. Also, a robber is usually aware that interlocking doors must be equipped with a panic button system that will open both doors simultaneously, for instance, for the purpose of evacuation, and that it is operated by bank employees or a security guard. In that case, the employee who has control over the doors is endan-gered, as are other employees and customers.

Workplace Violence

Workplace violence is any violence that occurs in a workplace. It can range from threats and verbal abuse to physical assaults and homicide. Workplace violence is a leading cause of job-related deaths globally. It is not reserved for robberies but can occur anywhere. Workplace violence is not only gain motivated but can be motivated by disagreement with the service the employee is providing (for example, cutting off electricity because of unpaid bills) or dissatisfaction with the company and its services. Some occupations are particu-larly at risk, especially those handling cash and goods or providing services to the public: community workers such as inspectors; gas, electricity, and water utility employees; and taxi drivers, especially if they work alone, in small groups, at night, or in high-crime areas.

The key to defending employees from workplace violence is first to acknowledge that it happens. The strategy should include risk assessments and should provide workplace violence prevention programs including trainings for employees such as awareness, reaction to threats, keeping a low profile, breaking routine whenever possible, and so forth. However, in certain cases, global positioning system panic buttons and other electronic safety devices can be considered as well as, for instance, procedures that obligate endangered employees to work in pairs, and special measures for working at night or in high-crime areas.

Vandalism

Vandalism occurs when perpetrators knowingly damage company property. It is a con-stant concern of many businesses.

Location is a key risk factor when it comes to vandalism. This is an issue that can be prevented and/or anticipated with a proper security assessment when considering a location for a business. Apart from high-crime areas, high-risk locations include proxim-ity to sports facilities, areas near bars, sports hooligans' routes, places that are frequently used for demonstrations and protests, and such. Another factor associated with location is standing out. Businesses that stand out in the neighborhood—for example, luxury businesses in poor neighborhoods—are more likely to face vandalism. Operating time also has an important role. Vandals prefer to operate when the premises are not attended. Also, target-hardening measures such as well-lighted facilities and the visible presence of security systems such as alarms and cameras will sometimes discourage vandals.

Motives for vandalism can be numerous. Apart from targeting businesses because they have a convenient location, vandals could specifically target certain businesses as revenge. Reasons may include targeting American businesses to demonstrate dissatisfaction with US foreign politics, and trivial rationales, such as angry minors who were annoyed because they were not allowed to hang around the premises.

Cargo Theft

Based on the 2013 Global Cargo Theft Threat Assessment issued by the Freight Watch International Supply Chain Intelligence Center [3], globally, cargo thefts are experiencing growth in terms of the number of incidents and their financial impact. Organized, often transnational criminal groups are targeting easily resalable goods that have left the safety of a production facility or warehouse and have not yet reached a safe destination. As with other thefts, the criminals are targeting traditionally hot products that are easily disposed of yet retain a high black market value, such as alcohol, cigarettes, branded clothing, computers, mobile phones and other electronic devices, entertainment equipment such as televisions, and prescription drugs (based on data extracted from the 2013 Global Cargo Theft Threat Assessment) [3]. For instance, a truckload of expensive cigarettes may be worth up to 2 million Euros. Still, the focus of the thefts depends on the demand and the goods are often ordered or even presold before the theft.

Also on the rise are the number of assaults on drivers and the increasingly violent nature of supply chain incidents. As presented in the EUROPOL report from 2009 [4], criminals are showing increasing willingness to employ firearms, explosives, and gas and to use violence with little regard for human life. Incidents involving the use of a weapon have significantly increased in several countries.

The impact of supply chain incidents can be devastating for a business whether they affect production through the delay of cargo with necessary raw materials or cause the loss of product during distribution to consumers.

CYBERCRIME AND HIGH-TECH CRIMES

Cybercrime

Cybercrime (or computer crime) is basically any crime that involves a computer and a network. However, there are various forms of cybercrimes, not all of which threaten companies. Like traditional crimes, cybercrimes can be divided into several categories:

- Fraud and financial crimes—theft of funds and vital information, extortion (also in the form of sextortion), embezzlement, blackmail, etc.
- Cyber-vandalism—defacement of a Web site, denial of service attacks, altering or deleting stored data, etc.
- Crimes against persons—cyber-stalking, identity theft, harassment, threats, hate crimes, bullying, online predators, etc.

- Victimless crimes—for example, online gambling
- Crimes against the state—espionage, etc.
- Obscenity—for instance, distributing, downloading, and viewing illegal pornography

The ideas behind cybercrimes that affect businesses are to steal financial and other sensitive information from the business and its customers and partners, steal funds, cause business discontinuity, or cause denial of service to the company's Web site or modify its content so that it damages the company's reputation.

Cybercrimes are not driven only by greed. In fact, because the Internet offers a powerful tool for sending a mass message, cyber-activism (hacktivism or cyber-terrorism) has become a constantly growing threat. Like traditional terrorism, but in a much wider manner, cyber-terrorism is a threat to both national security and businesses. More so, activists use attacks against companies to protest against states. For example, hackers are known to have executed countless attacks against the Web sites of Israeli and US companies after their founding countries' military actions and political moves. This type of terrorism (or activism) is inexpensive and does not require physical gathering but can have many people spread over the world working together from the comfort of their homes. Although cyber-activism may not be greed motivated, its intention is to cause financial loss to the target.

Companies are financially affected by cybercrimes in several ways:
- Direct financial loss caused by cyber-theft
- Loss of sales caused by Web site denial of service
- Business (service, production, etc.) discontinuity resulting from unavailability of systems and applications caused by cyber-attack
- Damage to reputation such as loss of trust of clients if, for example, their personal information were stolen, or because of mass messages about the company's alleged business practices. Customers are not likely to do business with a company vulnerable to attacks.
- Penalties paid to customers for inconvenience, loss, or contractual compensation such as delays, failure to deliver the service or product, etc.
- Fraudulent orders and payments (chargeback)
- Cost of protection against cybercrimes—including expensive software and hardware, hired experts, as well as regular testing and monitoring costs
- Cost of insurance
- Cost of recovery from cyber-attacks

The most significant losses are caused by viruses, unauthorized access, theft of information, denial of service, insider Internet abuse, and laptop theft.

Cyber-attacks are performed by several types of malicious software:
- Malware—a computer code that has a malicious purpose, usually to destroy something on a computer or steal information from it.

- Virus—hidden software that infects a computer. It attaches itself to a file or a program and has the ability to multiply. Viruses can be hard to detect and difficult to remove from a computer.
- Spyware—a type of malware that spies on the victim. There are numerous types of spyware but all are intended to steal information. For example, spyware can record what a user types on a keyboard and in that way steal passwords.
- Worms—The characteristic of worms is that they multiply and can spread across an entire network. Unlike viruses, they can work by themselves and do not need to be attached to other programs and files.
- Brute-force attack—a method of cracking passwords with programs that assist a hacker in trying out all possible letters, numbers, and symbols.
- Dictionary attack—performed by a hacker who is using a program that employs a dictionary to guess a password.
- Botnet—incorporates a group of computers to overpower a targeted network. Sometimes the owners of the computers do not know that their computers are being used for a denial of service (DoS) attack. Apart from flooding a server with an overwhelming amount of data, DoS can also be performed by making a targeted computer reply to fake requests (smurf), or simply by cutting a cable.

High-Tech Crimes

There are many definitions of high-tech crimes. In most cases, high-tech crimes are defined as being equivalent to computer crimes or cybercrimes. Many sources define high-tech crimes as crimes against new technologies. Both definitions are far from precise. I prefer to define high-tech crimes simply as crimes committed with the support of new technologies. According to this definition, cybercrimes are a subgroup of high-tech crimes and not just a synonym for them. To elaborate further, if we take the example of automatic teller machine (ATM) skimming, it is certainly a high-tech crime but it is not computer crime. Also, if we were to define high-tech crimes as any crimes executed against new technologies, we would also classify the use of explosives on ATMs to steal money, or stealing the entire ATM, as a high-tech crime. Moreover, according to that definition, we would have to classify the theft of a computer as a high-tech crime. However, high-tech crimes include ATM skimming and forgeries using new technology.

EXTERNAL FRAUDS

Fraud is basically any illegal and intentional deception enacted for personal gain. Fraud that targets corporations ranges from general fraud that can target any company to industry-specific fraud. However, although fraud is always committed for gain, victims of fraud do not necessarily experience losses.

According to the Price Waterhouse Coopers "2014 Global Economic Crime Survey" [5] conducted on over 5,000 global respondents, fraud continues to be a major concern for organizations of all sizes, across all regions, and in virtually every sector. One in three organizations reports being hit by fraud. According to the same report [5], industries especially at risk from fraud are financial services, retail, and communications.

Types of fraud that commonly affect corporations are:

- Application fraud
- Financial identity takeover
- Check fraud
- Insurance fraud
- Counterfeiting, forgery, and copyright fraud
- Short and long firm fraud
- Procurement fraud
- Corruption and bribery

Application Fraud

Application fraud is a broader name for a group of frauds that include all fraudulent acts committed during an application process. The first thing that comes to mind when we mention application fraud is credit application fraud committed during the credit/mortgage application process, such as presenting fake and forged documents, information, and financial status. Application fraud can be committed with forged personal data, most commonly by presenting false information concerning financial status, particularly by exaggerating income; or by using a stolen or fake identity. Such frauds do not necessarily have to cause loss but they certainly carry a higher risk of loss and in most cases cause loss. For example, a credit applicant can commit application fraud, such as presenting forged documents to obtain a mortgage, but still regularly pay off the mortgage.

Another type of application fraud is job application fraud, such as when an applicant falsely lists a college degree, exaggerates accomplishments, and seriously misrepresents his background. Job application fraud also does not necessarily have to cause losses, but it often does. A bad hire can be extremely expensive for an organization, including wasted training costs; severance pay; loss of productivity; theft of goods, information, and other assets; impact on the reputation of the company; cost of rehiring, etc. On the other hand, a person employed based on a fraudulent application can end up being successful.

Financial Identity Takeover

Financial identity takeover includes all fraudulent acts in which a fraudster uses stolen financial information for personal gain. Financial identity takeover includes not only fraudulent credit applications but also the use of stolen credit cards, credit card skimming, and theft of financial information (such as personal identification numbers) received through social engineering and employed to purchase goods from card-not-present merchants, for example.

Check Fraud

Check fraud refers to the fraudulent use of checks to illegally acquire funds that do not exist within the account balance of the fraudster. The most common methods of check fraud involve taking advantage of the float. In financial language, float is the time between when the check is written and presented and when the funds to cover that check are deducted from the payer's account. For example, fraudsters can use float to take advantage of the delay of notice about nonexistent funds.

Other common frauds include writing bad checks, such as purchasing goods and/or services with a check that will not clear. Sometimes fraudsters will forge checks by adding digits, or even using disappearing ink. In some cases, fraudsters will use chemicals to erase certain information written on the check and adjust it to commit fraud. Another somewhat rare method involves using a completely homemade fake check.

Insurance Fraud

Insurance fraud is naturally commonly committed against insurance companies. The most common and costly type of insurance fraud accounts for false insurance claims. Insurance fraud can be soft fraud, such as exaggerating otherwise legitimate claims, misreporting the condition of the object of insurance to obtain a lower premium on an insurance policy, or over-insurance, when the insured amount is larger than the actual value of the insured property. On the other hand, hard insurance fraud is committed when a claimant invents a loss that did not occur or purposely creates a loss such as by fire or theft, by causing a real traffic accident, or even by committing a murder. Apart from murder, life insurance fraud can be committed by faking a death to claim life insurance. Health care fraud can be committed by a patient or the health care provider, or jointly. Health care fraud ranges from prescription medication fraud to exaggerating injuries and billing for services that were not delivered, by a patient, a physician, or both. A common type of physician fraud is the performance of unnecessary treatment, such as surgery.

The most common types of vehicle insurance fraud are staged accidents and falsely reporting a vehicle as stolen when it has actually been sold by the owner, typically to a foreign buyer. Staged accidents are often carried out so as to involve an innocent party (often targeting new and expensive vehicles), and apart from damage to the vehicle, claim injuries that would be later confirmed by a collaborating physician.

Counterfeiting, Forgery, and Copyright Fraud
Counterfeiting

Counterfeiting is basically creating illegal imitations of genuine products with the intention of fraudulently passing them off as genuine. Products that are especially vulnerable are established brands with a relatively high retail value, such as alcohol, cigarettes, electronics, popular food brands, watches, and clothes. Moreover, illegal imitations include

Web sites that imitate genuine commercial Web sites for the purpose of fraudulent activity, such as social engineering.

Forgery

Forgery is the process of creating, adapting, or imitating objects or documents. The most common forgeries include money, works of art, documents, diplomas, and identification. Forgeries often accompany other fraud such as application, insurance, or check fraud, financial identity takeover, and so forth. In a less traditional sense, forgeries do not have to be physical but may also be electronic, such as fake personal pages on social media Web sites or adaption of e-mail correspondence. Concerning documents and identification, there are several types of forgery:

- Blank documents are real documents, such as genuine passports without personal data or stamped and signed memorandum letters without content. The data are inserted by the forger to support fraudulent activity. As for passports and identification, they are usually obtained with the assistance of officials (police, ministry of interior, embassy, etc.) or stolen. This group of forged documents is difficult to detect.
- Adjusted documents are documents that belonged to someone else but the data or picture in the documents has been changed to fit the carrier. These documents are often stolen from their real owners or bought (the owner is selling documents and then declaring them as missing). Documents that were deliberately damaged, such as those that were washed in a washing machine, belong to this group. Adjusting documents is the most common type of forgery.
- Made documents are completely homemade to resemble real documents. Made documents can be privately made and are often of bad quality and easily detectable. However, documents can be made professionally by criminal organizations that invest huge amounts of money in sophisticated equipment. Also, certain states are known to make fake foreign documents for agents abroad. These documents are almost impossible to detect because they are of superb quality.
- Borrowed documents are often used by illegal immigrants from Asian and African countries who are taking advantage of the fact that most Westerners cannot distinguish different Asian and African features. The forgers use unchanged documents belonging to someone else.
- False documents—Several companies sell documents from countries that have ceased to exist although their names continue to sound familiar, such as Yugoslavia, Czechoslovakia, British Honduras, and Burma. With the passport, a client also receives identification cards, a country club membership card, a driving license, and so forth.

Copyright Infringement

Copyright infringement is the unauthorized use of copyright products and patents. For example, a company that is contracted (and equipped by the copyright owner) to manufacture copyrighted products could use the equipment, technology, components, and design to produce an illegal product under a different brand name and sell it separately or even produce a lower-quality item with the original brand name. Another type of copyright infringement, which is not always illegal, is the production of similar products with a similar brand name. A common example is the manufacturing of, for example, sneakers that resemble the models and logo (but are not identical to the original) of the renowned sports brand Adidas, but add a letter "d" to the name of the brand so that it becomes Adiddas.

Short and Long Firm Fraud

Short and long firm fraud involves setting up an apparently legitimate business and/or falsely building up the reputation of the company and its reliability. Long company frauds are performed so that companies (or individuals) win the trust of suppliers by placing small orders and paying for them. When they establish a good reputation with the supplier, they place a large order and disappear without paying for it. Short company fraud is executed when fraudsters set up an apparently legitimate business with the intention of defrauding its suppliers and customers. Fraudsters can register a company using a stolen identity, set up a legitimate-looking retail space, and use it to establish legitimacy to fraudulently acquire goods, for example.

Procurement Fraud

Procurement fraud is mostly executed by employees, and as such it is one of the most frequent frauds that affect businesses. However, procurement fraud can also be executed by vendors. Common methods of procurement fraud include presenting fake information, delivering lower-quality goods or services than agreed, invoicing services that were not delivered, or exaggerating the delivered service.

Corruption and Bribery

Bribery is a criminal practice of giving something (favor, money, services, product, etc.) to gain an illegal advantage. Corruption is basically receiving something to facilitate an illegal advantage. Corruption involves the abuse of position and trust.

Engaging in corruption and bribery creates an unfair advantage and an unfavorable business environment. Apart from supporting and strengthening organized crime, corruption is one of the primary obstacles to the economic development of a country and is a main risk that could deter potential investors.

CORPORATE EXPOSURE TO TERRORISM

Terrorism is usually defined as employing violence against civilians to draw attention to a cause, endorse political change, or gain power. When we talk about terrorism, we immediately think of Islamic extremists. However, there are many types of terrorism and countless terrorist groups. Terrorism was once an issue associated solely with national security, but the development of different types of terrorism, the development of corporations, and the expansion of ways in which corporations conduct business led to corporations becoming exposed and extremely vulnerable to various types of terrorism.

We have experienced the development of terrorism and its reinvention in different forms, supporting different agendas and using new technologies, but in many cases, terrorism has expanded to organized crime either by supporting it or actually by performing it. In some parts of Africa and the Middle East, joint ventures between terrorist organizations and organized criminal groups proved to be a good business strategy and have helped criminal groups gain more cash and assist terrorist organizations in going transnational. One reason for this business deal was the sudden lack of funding for terrorist organizations by certain governments that were known to support terror but had to tighten their belts owing to the economy crisis. However, this lack of funding also transformed some terrorist organizations into purely criminal organizations. One of the best examples of religious terrorist groups changing to crime is Al-Qaeda in the Islamic Maghreb in North Africa, whose main source of income comes from ransom paid in return for the release of hostages, mostly foreign nationals who are visiting or working in North Africa.

The most common types of terrorism are:

- Religious
- Right-wing
- Left-wing
- Issue-oriented
- Separatist

Some sources also list state terrorism, pathological terrorism, and narco-terrorism as types of terrorism. However, this is disputable because state terrorism is equivalent to dictatorship and does not fit the definition of terrorism. Moreover, pathological terrorism has no agenda apart from terrorizing others. Narco-terrorism is the closest of the three to the definition of terrorism because it often uses terror against civilians to intimidate and eventually facilitate drug trafficking by causing political instability. The best examples of narco-terrorist groups are drug cartels in Mexico and Colombia.

Corporations are affected by all forms of terrorism ranging from cyber-terrorism and actual physical attacks to being used to facilitate terrorism through illegal financial transaction and illegal use of the supply chain. Corporations are targeted by religious and separatist terrorist groups because they are symbols of the financial strength of their founding states, have huge media potential, and still do not have adequate protection capabilities. Left-wing terrorism seeks to establish communist regimes, sees corporations as symbols of capitalism, and perceives corporations as their worst enemy. Issue-oriented terrorism targets corporations because of their effects on the environment or, for example, the use of animals for testing. Right-wing terrorists can target corporations for various reasons such as ownership by members of an ethnic or sexual minority.

Terrorism versus Freedom Fighters

There is a thin and blurred line between terrorism and freedom fighters. Mostly to blame for this unclear division are politics and use of the two terms to justify the support of a state for one foreign militant group and its struggle against another. However, a division between the two exists, at least in definition. We said that terrorism is employing violence against civilians to draw attention to a cause, endorse political change, or gain power. On the other hand, freedom fighting groups are resistance movements fighting against an oppressive political system or a foreign invasion. Freedom fighters target military, police, and security targets and do not employ violence against civilians.

Religious Terrorism

Because of its fanatic ideology, religious terrorism is believed to be the most dangerous type of terrorism, mostly because of the readiness of its members to do practically anything to achieve their goals. They have proved many times that they have absolutely no respect for human life and that they are ready to kill countless civilians regardless of age, gender, and status. Moreover, religious terrorists are more likely to use drastic tactics such as suicide bombing than any other terrorist group. We immediately think of Islamic terrorism and terrorist organizations such as Al-Qaeda and Hezbollah; however, religious terrorism includes numerous other Islamic and also Christian terrorist groups as well as various terrorist organizations associated with almost all existing religions.

Right-Wing Terrorism

Right-wing terrorism often fights against national, racial, ethnic, and sexual minorities. Right-wing terrorist groups include Neo-Nazi groups, the Ku Klux Klan, and numerous fascist and extreme nationalist groups, especially across Europe, in Russia, and in the US. Members of a right-wing terrorist group often share the same religious beliefs.

Left-Wing Terrorism

The goal of left-wing terrorism is to overthrow capitalist economies and establish communist regimes. Although left-wing terrorist groups still exist to a certain level, they are not nearly as active as they used to be during the Cold War era. Known groups included the West German Red Army Faction or the RAF (also known as Baader-Meinhof Group), the Italian Red Brigades, the French Action Directe, the Belgian Communist Combatant Cells, and the Japanese Red Army. However, left-wing terrorism is transforming, and according to some sources, violent parts of the anti-globalization movements could be the new form of left-wing violence. The best-known left-wing terrorist groups that are still operational are the Revolutionary People's Liberation Party Front in Turkey, the Greek November 17th, and the Colombian FARC.

Issue-Oriented Terrorism

Issue-oriented terrorism refers to violence committed in support of certain issues, usually concerning environmental and ecological causes. The most famous issue-oriented terrorist organizations are the Animal Liberation Front and the Environmental Liberation Front. Radical environmental and animal rights groups have claimed responsibility for hundreds of crimes and acts of terrorism, including arson, bombings, vandalism, sinking of ships, and harassment. Probably the best-known animal rights campaign was the Stop Huntingdon Animal Cruelty (SHAC) campaign which began in 1999 with the aim of shutting down Huntingdon Life Science (HLS), the largest European animal testing laboratory. The activists allegedly firebombed houses owned by executives associated with HLS's clients and investors. In 2009 and 2010, 13 members of SHAC were sentenced to jail terms ranging from 15 months to 11 years on charges of conspiracy to blackmail or harm HLS and its suppliers. The best examples of eco-terrorism are attacks on ski resorts, logging operations, and companies involved in genetic engineering, genetically modified crops, and sports utility vehicle sales, executed by the Environmental Liberation Front.

Separatist Terrorism

Separatist terrorists seek to liberate a part of a country inhabited by an ethnic and/or religious minority and establish a new state. The best-known separatist groups are the ETA in Spain, Chechen terrorists, the Tamil Tigers in Sri Lanka, the Kosovo Liberation Army in Serbia, the Kurdish PKK in Turkey, and the Quebec Liberation Front in Canada. Some separatist movements cooperate closely with religious terrorist groups but also with certain states from which they receive support and funding.

NATURAL FACTORS

Natural disasters are not criminal acts and do not happen because of a motive. However, Mother Nature has the means to create disasters, and it certainly does. It is impossible to count the effects of natural disasters on businesses because, apart from their direct influence and damage to a business, natural factors set in motion a chain of influencing events that can have enormous effects on the local or national economy and in that way indirectly affect businesses. Both security and economy are influenced by even seemingly trivial events, such as, for example, refreshing spring showers, and by disastrous events such as tsunamis and hurricanes. Moreover, economy and security continuously influence each other. Still, although we cannot protect businesses from the indirect influences of natural factors, and sometimes not even from direct ones, we can still foresee many events and prepare for and minimize their effect. When we talk about natural factors, we do not mean only the meteorological, geological, and similar natural processes, but also epidemics and other health hazards.

Businesses make two common mistakes when designing and managing business continuity and disaster recovery.

The first mistake is that, in most cases, we perceive business continuity and disaster recovery as a topic almost exclusively related to IT services that support the organization's critical business activities. We anticipate the effects of unavailability of IT services and design a system that should prevent their stoppage, minimize the damage of IT-related incidents and events, and help recover from disasters. Unfortunately, we do not dedicate enough attention to and often even completely neglect the effect that natural factors can have on the business. However, harsh weather conditions can cause severe disturbances to all parts of the business. They can, for example, delay the shipment of products to consumers or the arrival of raw materials; floods can destroy goods stored in warehouses or contaminate the water needed for production; storms can cause problems with the power supply. Moreover, natural disaster will in most cases influence IT services. Epidemics can cause unavailability of the critical minimum number of employees required to execute business processes. Extreme weather conditions can prevent employees from coming to work and cause serious problems for a business.

The second mistake is the failure of business to anticipate events that could cause business discontinuity. What is especially surprising is that even IT business continuity has this weakness because business continuity managers often fail to predict events that can influence information and communication technology services: for example, cell phone networks overload during holidays and cyber-attacks increase during certain holidays. For example, in the US, companies traditionally experience a significant rise in cyber-attacks around Thanksgiving and Christmas, whereas government Web sites experience an increase in cyber-attacks during elections or independence days.

A famous proverb that "A danger foreseen is half avoided" should be an essential principle of effective business continuity planning and management. The good side of natural factors is that they can be anticipated to a certain extent. We basically know what natural risks exist and which are associated with what parts of the year. We relatively accurately know when to expect heat waves, floods, epidemics, and so forth, and based on that knowledge, we can create an effective template for business continuity plans and disaster recovery.

We also should not forget that weather conditions not only influence business continuity, but also the behavior of people, with an increase in violence and crime rates. The heat hypothesis in psychology states that extremely high daily temperatures increase aggressive motives and behavior. For example, more assaults occur during summer months and hot days than during other periods of the year.

Moreover, violent crimes are more likely to occur during summer months but so are property crimes, simply because they are convenient. Summer holiday season is perfect for burglaries. Also, a robber prefers to rob a bank during the summer holiday when there is less traffic (unless he plans to do it at a holiday destination) and when there will be no cold weather and harsh weather conditions that could slow him down or cause his car engine to fail. Pickpocketing may also rise during summer months because of the higher number of tourists and the convenience of summer outfits.

SPECIFIC RISKS TO PEOPLE

People are the most important asset of every organization, and the most important value we are protecting is certainly human life. Security risks differ among locations, exposure of position to risks, organizational hierarchy, gender, and many other influencing factors. Risks are various and can range from theft to threats, assault, kidnapping, and murder. Even domestic violence is not confined to the home and will usually follow a victim to work.

Our main mission is to create a safe working environment and protect employees at work and from work-related security risks, but we cannot be responsible for all off-work security risks to employees. However, we should do our best to protect employees even from off-work risks that follow them to work and also encourage them to come forward with serious private security concerns and advise them on how to handle them or where to seek professional assistance.

Still, work-related security risks deserve the largest share of our efforts. It would be an endless mission to try to list all on-work- and off-work-related risks. Basically, we start by knowing that risks exist, and based on thorough risk and vulnerability assessments that we conduct for every position with higher risk, we create prevention programs including tailored security measures, specified trainings for employees, and emergency strategies.

Some groups deserve special attention, such as expatriates in and business travelers to risky areas. The transnational nature of corporations and their focus on emerging markets create new opportunities for reward, but in many cases they are accompanied not only by investment risks but also by specific security risks to both the business and its people. Opening a business in a less traveled location is an exciting opportunity to conquer the market before the arrival of competition. However, locations that are new to business usually lack highly skilled professionals and practically require companies to import more skilled professionals and experienced managers (expatriate positions); they also require tighter management, including frequent visits to the new part of the business (business travelers). Traditional expatriate and business travel assignments recently started expanding to give companies more efficient models of increasing employees' mobility and creating alternative options for sending employees where they are required. Such assignments include short-term assignments and peer-to-peer assignments. Another thing that is changing is the male–female ratio of business travelers: Female business travelers now comprise almost half the corporate travel market.

Although kidnapping for ransom, hostage taking, terrorism, and political violence are not exclusively reserved for emerging markets but can happen anywhere, such risks are higher in some places than others. The risks could be also heightened by corrupt and ineffective local security forces as well as risk factors such as the nationality, position, and behavior of the employee, the effectiveness of security measures, and the image of the company and its founding country.

According to the number of incidents against foreigners, especially kidnappings for ransom, based on numerous sources and news reports [6–13], the following countries are marked as kidnapping hot spots: Mexico, Venezuela, India, Nigeria, Afghanistan, Pakistan, Iraq, Syria, Philippines, Guatemala, Colombia, Libya, Egypt, Algeria, Brazil, Yemen, Kenya, Malaysia, Bangladesh, Burkina Faso, Cameroon, Chad, the Democratic Republic of Congo, Eritrea, Ethiopia, Mali, Mauritania, Morocco, Niger, Peru, Sudan, South Sudan, Senegal, Somalia, and the area of the Indian Ocean off the coast of Somalia.

According to several news reports from 2013 [6–13], France has the highest number of nationals held hostage worldwide; US citizens are second on the list. However, almost no nations are kidnap-free.

Security risks are not the only risks that business travelers and expatriates face. Other significant risks include disease and epidemics, poor sanitary conditions and food and water safety risks, low quality and limited availability of medical facilities, and difficult access to medications.

Further on in this book, we will analyze practical ways of managing the security of the business and the employees in high-risk environments.

DATA LEAKAGE

To prosper in today's business world, companies need to keep crucial business information confidential. For example, all information about unique processes, specific technology, prototypes, or customers has vast value for the business, whereas its disclosure can lead to serious consequences. All crucial information related to business must be kept secret and requires an efficient internal safeguarding system. Unfortunately, we mostly concentrate on protecting electronic information and often forget the numerous other ways in which information is disclosed.

According to the 2011 survey conducted by Dimensional Research and sponsored by Check Point Software Technologies [14], one-third of businesses do not train employees to avoid social engineering attacks, although half of them said they plan to do so. However, people are a critical part of the security process and its weakest link. According to the research [14], 48% of large companies and 32% of companies of all sizes have experienced 25 or more social engineering attacks in the past 2 years. According to the same report [14], these attacks were frequently costly, with almost half of participants (48%) reporting a per-incident cost of more than $25,000. Again, larger organizations reported even higher costs, with 30% reporting a per-incident cost of more than $100,000.

Cyber-attacks and social engineering attacks are far from being the only methods of data leakage. Traditional methods of stealing information still work. Stealing or just seeing hardcopy documents, overhearing classified information during should-be classified conversations, information disclosed in good faith, and dumpster diving (someone's trash is someone else's treasure) are probably still prevailing techniques of collecting sensitive information.

Sometimes companies have strict clean desk policies which require employees to remove from their desks documents with any information that could be compromised. Still, by restricting the policy to a desk, companies recklessly give employees the freedom to unintentionally disclose sensitive information anywhere else, such as, for example, visibly leaving sensitive documents on the backseat of their car.

It is also common for companies to publish too much information on their Web sites and for senior executives to unintentionally disclose sensitive information on their pages in social media sites such as Facebook, LinkedIn, or Twitter.

Another common way sensitive information is stolen is as collateral damage. A thief would steal a vehicle, a computer, or a cell phone and receive sensitive information as a bonus.

EMERGENCY SITUATIONS

Emergency situations basically can have an extensive impact on life, health, and property. They can be divided into two groups:
- Emergency situations that pose an immediate threat to life, health, and property or have caused loss of life and/or extensive damage to health and property
- Emergency situations with a high probability of escalating and causing immediate danger to life, health, and/or property

Both types of emergencies have to be identified as potential threats and require planning, procedures containing exercised actions, immediate coordinated actions, involvement of all, and a clear chain of command. However, even with a good assessment and plan, unplanned emergencies will occur. It is always necessary to have plans for dealing with unplanned situations that will officially arrange the chain of command and identify the decision makers.

Immediate Threat Emergencies

Immediate threat emergencies range from natural disasters and accidents to manmade incidents and disasters. Performing assessments to establish the probability of the occurrence of natural disasters (such as the high probability of earthquakes, hurricanes, forest fires, etc.) and specific manmade incidents (e.g., crime and terror) will narrow the surprise effect. Manmade incidents include emergencies such as shooting incidents, bombing attacks (including explosive mail, car bombs, and suicide bombers), hostage situations, physical assaults, suspicious objects or persons, and threats (anonymous phone calls, letters, e-mails, verbal threats, etc.).

Procedures designed to deal with emergency situations should contain not only the reaction to an emergency but also measures designed to lower the effects of an ongoing emergency. They can be procedural or technical. An example of a procedural measure could be a system to distinguish hoax anonymous phone threats from real ones. For instance, for institutions with a large number of anonymous phone calls, performing an evacuation after each one would cause serious disruption for the business and morale and endanger the institution in other ways (if, for instance, the goal of the anonymous phone call is for a caller to collect information about the evacuation procedures, or simply to empty the building to commit a theft). Apart from technical measures designed to deter or detect a problem, deny access to a problem, delay it, and defend from it, an example of technical measures implemented to lower the effects of an incident could be a special mailroom with reinforced walls that would dismiss the need for total evacuation in case a mail bomb was discovered.

We divide reactions to emergency into two groups:
- Emergency situations that require evacuation (partial or total)
- Emergency situations that require sheltering

Basically, the reaction depends on the proximity of the emergency (space and time), its position (outside or inside), the mobility of the emergency (stable or moving), and the possible level of impact (small radius, disasters, etc.).

Although it should be clear how evacuations and sheltering are announced, because I have witnessed a complete lack of logic in many institutions, I feel that I should briefly explain it. Because sheltering has a clear direction and is a simple one-choice action (such as, for example, sheltering in the safe room, or if there is no safe room, staying in the office and locking the door), it can be announced with a siren. However, the direction and place of evacuation depend on the location of the problem and can be performed efficiently only in an explanatory manner, such as by verbally stating the direction of the evacuation (e.g., evacuation to the front) or with electronic information screens and signs that point the correct direction of the evacuation away from the danger.

Crisis Management

Crisis management is the process of dealing with a major event that threatens to harm or has already harmed the organization. Although somewhat similar to crisis management and closely cooperating with it, risk management and business continuity management are different concepts. Risk management assesses the probability of threats whereas business continuity proactively plans processes aimed at ensuring the continuity of an organization's operations during a crisis. On the other hand, crisis management encompasses all aspects of a crisis to protect human life, material resources, and the image and reputation of the organization. For example, in the case of a natural disaster, business continuity management and disaster recovery will ensure that the business recovers quickly and continues to perform by moving its key operations to another unaffected site. On the other hand, crisis management deals with the ongoing crisis by controlling damage through conducting rescue operations, evacuating the injured, informing and coordinating relevant emergency services, informing the families of casualties, issuing press reports, and so forth. Also, in the case of a product defect, especially concerning safety issues, a crisis management team will manage the product recall from retailers, issue public statements, and maintain a hotline to communicate effectively with consumers and clients. A crisis is managed by a predefined crisis situation decision maker and the crisis management team by maintaining the emergency chain of command and using clear lines of reporting and communication, both internally and externally.

There are numerous possible crisis situations ranging from those that affect the organization (natural disasters, reputational risks such as rumors and news spins, manmade disasters, etc.) to those inflicted by the company, which can have a negative effect on the public by endangering safety, environment, health, and security, such as faulty products and environmental disasters.

A crisis management team is a management-level committee composed of relevant functions. Crisis management team members can be constant or variable. For example, a team could consist of all top managers and a crisis manager. On the other hand, if the incident is sector specific, the team could consist of a core crisis management group supported by relevant functions that can provide a proper response to the incident. For example, in the case of an incident that could jeopardize the production process, such as water pollution, in addition to its core members, the special situations management team would consist of relevant functions such as production, engineering, quality assurance, and environment, health, and safety.

A standard member of the crisis management team is the spokesperson of the organization, who manages statements and press releases. However, activation of the spokesperson (public relations) is the decision of the crisis management team based on the extent and impact of the crisis.

Emergencies with a High Probability of Escalating

Emergencies with a high probability of escalating range from approaching natural disasters to political violence such as civil unrest and wars. Such emergencies may usually be anticipated, depending on our ability to collect relevant information and process it. However, their effects can be devastating and in most cases cannot be influenced. Efficiently dealing with such emergencies requires detailed emergency plans and an infrastructure that is able to withstand them. For example, large-scale political violence (such as the civil wars that hit North Africa and the Middle East in 2011) would require a good plan for evacuation from the country, diplomatic efforts, and probably the assistance of specialized security contractors who are able to provide logistics, medical assistance if necessary, and transportation out of the country. We will go into detail about analyzing evacuation and contingency planning further on in the book.

REFERENCES

[1] McAfee, Economic Impact of Cybercrime and Cyber Espionage, 2013. www.mcafee.com/sg/resources/reports/rp-economic-impact-cybercrime.pdf.
[2] Overseas Security Advisory Council (OSAC.gov). www.osac.gov/pages/ContentReportDetails.aspx?cid=9010.
[3] 2013 Global Cargo Theft Threat Assessment, Freight Watch International Supply Chain Intelligence Center. www.freightwatchintl.com/node/1602.
[4] EUROPOL Report from 2009. www.reportingproject.net/new/REPORTS/Cargo%20Theft%20Report.pdf.
[5] PwC (Price Waterhouse Coopers). 2014 Global Economic Crime Survey. www.pwc.com/gx/en/economic-crime-survey/.
[6] Rukmini Callimachi, Paying Ransoms, Europe Bankrolls Qaeda Terror, New York Times, July 29, 2014. www.nytimes.com/2014/07/30/world/africa/ransoming-citizens-europe-becomes-al-qaedas-patron.html.
[7] Sergio Ramos, Mexico: The Fight to End Kidnapping, Infosurhoy, April 11, 2014. http://dialogo-americas.com/en_GB/articles/saii/features/main/2014/04/11/feature-01.
[8] Adam Nossiter, Millions in Ransoms Fuel Militants' Clout in West Africa, New York Times, December 12, 2012. www.nytimes.com/2012/12/13/world/africa/kidnappings-fuel-extremists-in-western-africa.html?pagewanted=1&_r=1.
[9] Steven Perlberg, The 20 Countries Where People Get Kidnapped the Most, Business Insider, December 12, 2013. www.businessinsider.com/top-20-countries-by-kidnapping-2013-12.
[10] Risk Map, Control Risks, 2014. www.controlrisks.com/riskmap.
[11] Associated Press, APNewsBreak: 4 Charged in "Virtual Kidnappings," Fox News, November 8, 2013. www.foxnews.com/us/2013/11/08/apnewsbreak-4-charged-in-virtual-kidnappings-targeting-random-immigrant.
[12] France Tops World Hostage List with Latest Kidnapping, France 24, February 20, 2013. http://www.france24.com/en/20130220-france-hostages-world-cameroon-nigeria-hollande-terrorists/.
[13] Somali Piracy: More Sophisticated than You Thought, The Economist, November 2, 2013. www.economist.com/news/middle-east-and-africa/21588942-new-study-reveals-how-somali-piracy-financed-more-sophisticated-you.
[14] The Risk of Social Engineering on Information Security: A Survey of IT Professionals, Dimensional Research, September 2011. www.checkpoint.com/press/downloads/social-engineering-survey.pdf.

Where: Allocate

CHAPTER 8

Physical Security

FACILITY SECURITY

Physical security is a combination of people, physical and technical measures, procedures, and controls aimed at detecting, preventing, and mitigating threats. It is impossible to develop one overall facility security formula that would be applicable to every facility and under all circumstances. The measures depend on the type and nature of the institution, level and type of threat, accepted level of risk, availability of resources, budget, natural and structural terrain in and around the facility, and balance between security and customer orientation.

Apart from classifying institutions and facilities based on their security clearance level and level of security measures, we can classify them in numerous ways according to their nature. For example, facilities can be large, medium, or small; they can be introverted and extraverted according to their accessibility to outsiders. According to their structure, they can be stand-alone, shared, or wall-to-wall, and have an accompanying perimeter or not.

The level of control can range from simple observing via actual physical checks to restriction of access to trusted employees only; logically, the type of security measures is designed based on the type of threat and can be completely different if the probable threat is, for example, theft, robbery, or terrorist attack. Moreover, we can classify institutions based on their entrance and exit setups, such as hard in–hard out (facilities with both entrance and exit controls), hard in–easy out, easy in–hard out, and easy in–easy out (facilities with no entrance and exit controls).

Layered Defense

The main principle of layered defense is to detect and stop an attack at the earliest possible stage and far from the facility. The concept of layered defense is often perceived differently by different security professionals, mostly depending on their backgrounds. It may be defined as a purely physical system of barriers, a technical security system setup, or manned guarding systems positioned in circles. However, the truth is that security layers are multidimensional, multidisciplinary, multitasked, interactive, and overlapping security measures designed to deter, detect, and stop an action in its earliest phase, as far away as possible, to reduce its impact and enable fast recovery. Security layers include all human, physical (natural and structural), technical, mechanical, and procedural boundaries.

What everybody seems to agree on is that the closer a circle is to the protected asset, the more security measures should be positioned tightly, whereas the farther away a circle is from the protected assets, the less dense it is and the wider an area it covers.

We can divide a facility into areas that are observed, physically controlled, and restricted, according to the proximity (or accessibility) of the area to the protected asset.

The common principle of facility security and one of the dimensions of layered defense is 5D1R, which requires that a security system have six functions to be effective. The functions are:

- Deter
- Detect
- Deny
- Delay
- Defend
- Recover

Deter

Deterrence is basically target hardening and its function is to discourage a potential perpetrator. Target hardening can include all elements that would deter potential perpetrators in the phase of collecting information about the target and would make them give up on the target and start searching for an easier one. Apart from visible security measures and deterring environmental design, for a collector of information, the knowledge that he has been detected would most likely discourage him and thus prevent an attack at the earliest possible stage.

Detect

Detection is as good as the earliest stage of an attack that is noticed by security, including the ability of a security system to correctly process the information and appropriately and promptly react to the threat. The objective is to detect a problem at the earliest possible stage and as far away as possible, ideally in the stage of collecting information about the target.

Deny

Denying is the ability of the security system to keep anything and anyone unwanted from getting inside. Denying is influenced by the ability of security to narrow the amount of unwanted entry by deterring and by noticing unwanted entry through detection.

Delay

The goal of delaying is to slow down the progress of any action (attack) before it reaches the protected asset, causing the perpetrator to give up and giving security enough time to react efficiently. By delay, we usually mean physical and technical barriers, environmental design, and procedural barriers.

Defend

Defending is the ability of the security setup to protect valuable assets efficiently. By defending, we do not necessarily mean the combat ability of the security staff. However, in corporate security, it is unlikely that we will have the resources to engage in a combat-like response. Defending is also special technical and physical measures that are implemented to protect specific assets. In addition, defending is the efficiency of our communication to police and their capability of responding.

Recover

The capability of a system to minimize the damage from an incident and recover from it successfully is crucial. The impact of an incident on people, property, morale, and business can be devastating and felt for a long time after an incident.

Perimeter

One of the basic elements of facility security is the perimeter. The perimeter is basically the buffer zone that will prevent an attack from reaching the facility; as such, it should be layered. The perimeter is the physical space that is controlled by the security of the facility and is divided into inner and outer perimeters.

Inner Perimeter

The inner perimeter is the area belonging to the facility and is physically controlled by the security of the facility. Security controls entry into the inner perimeter and can grant or deny access. To establish the inner perimeter, we must first determine what the sufficient length and width of space would be and the distance from its borders to the facility that would, together with our capabilities to control the space and efficiently react in it, prevent an attack from affecting the facility itself. Of course, the bigger the area is, the more expensive and more difficult it is to secure it.

Certainly, we must ask ourselves what could be the probable course of action (PCA), including the choice of weapon, and determine the inner perimeter and the structure of its border accordingly. If a bombing attack is probable, what is the most likely scenario for a bombing attack? Is a car bomb attack possible or probable, or a hand grenade attack, or maybe both? In the case of a car bomb attack threat, the distance of the explosion from the facility and the structure of the barrier are of utmost importance. In general, each 10 m that an explosion is farther from the facility will lessen its impact by 40%. Another factor is the structure of the barrier. If the perimeter border barrier (a wall) that is positioned between the explosion and the facility is likely to fragment easily owing to an explosion, it will probably cause more damage. Moreover, to protect the facility successfully from a car bomb, the distance of the closest place a car could reach from the facility should be as large as possible and not less than 30 m. In case of a hand grenade, the height of the barrier (fence or wall) and terrain will determine how far inside the facility the grenade could fall if thrown from the outside and how far the blast of a hand grenade could reach.

Still, no perimeter makes sense if you do not have the ability to control it, and not only access to the perimeter but events within the perimeter itself. Basically, you will never be certain that you will notice a suspicious object at the moment it is thrown inside the perimeter or be sure that no intruder has managed to bypass the security measures and enter the perimeter without being noticed. To control the perimeter efficiently, we do not rely only on security patrols and electronic surveillance, but have to match these with other security aspects such as, for example, having adequate lighting and keeping the space clean from objects and vegetation that could block our view and disable us from detecting a suspicious object or that could provide an intruder with the opportunity to advance toward the facility without being detected.

The entrance to the inner perimeter must be controlled from the outside the perimeter. Basically, the inspection booth should be positioned so that the exit from the inspection booth is the entry to the inner perimeter.

Outer Perimeter

The outer perimeter is the area that does not necessarily belong to the facility but is observed and patrolled by security to notice the collection of information, preparation for an attack, or the early stages of an attack. In some cases, we will be able to reach an agreement with the relevant authorities to introduce some security measures in the outer perimeter. That will, of course, depend on the level of threat we are facing and the willingness of the relevant authorities to cooperate. However, the measures that we would implement in the outer perimeter do not necessarily have to be described as security measures but may be presented as efforts to improve the area. Using environmental design crime prevention techniques such as, for example, introducing a roundabout traffic arrangement that would slow down approaching vehicles or limiting the access of vehicles by installing planters and fountains could be effective.

We have mentioned routine as one of the most important elements of security. Thus, while we break routine, we must be able to notice any changes in the routine of the area, such as unfamiliar vehicles, vehicles or people who appear out of place, suspicious characters in the neighborhood, and so on.

Security must be aware of points in the outer perimeter that are suitable for collecting information and observe them frequently to try to notice a potential collector of information in the early stage. Also, every attack has a starting point. Starting/preparation points are areas in the vicinity of the installation where an attacker will finalize the preparation for an attack. These points must be close to the facility (so as not to be noticed and stopped by security or police before the actual attack), protected visually so the attacker can become ready without being noticed, and positioned in a way so as to have eye contact with the target. To prevent an actual physical attack in the early stage, security has to know the potential points and have visual control over them.

Neighboring premises can be used to perform an attack against a facility. In case the facility is well-protected and the neighboring premises are easy to access, an attacker can choose to take control over the neighboring facility to perform an attack against the target. The attacks can be performed in many different ways, including planting an explosive device in the neighboring premises in case of wall-to-wall premises.

Depending on the local laws, we might not be permitted legally to check people outside the perimeter whom we suspect are collecting information. Still, it is important to let the collector of information know that he has been detected.

Inspection Booth

The weakest points of the perimeter are its entrance and exit. Ideally, the booth should be positioned on the outside of the inner perimeter. It should be structured so that the first and second doors are not exactly parallel to each other or so that barriers exist between the doors so as not to allow an unwanted visitor to just run through the booth or a vehicle to drive through. It will also prevent the effects of an explosion that occurs in front of the booth from reaching beyond the booth. The doors should be made from a material that is difficult to break and also function as a visual barrier (especially the front entrance). Doors should function so that the second door can be opened only after the first door is closed (interlocking doors). The possibility of both doors being opened at the same time should exist in case of evacuation. In addition to closed-circuit television (CCTV), which would enable the control center to follow the visitor's check process, the booth should be equipped with a listening device (interphone) that would allow the control center also to hear what is going on in the booth during the check, especially during the body search, which would not be monitored by CCTV.

Dividing the Perimeter by Response Areas

Depending on the size of the installation and the position of objects within the perimeter, one way to divide the perimeter is by response areas. If you are responsible for a large area and have positioned all security staff in one place, it would take a lot of valuable time for your staff to be able to react if an incident occurs at a distant part of the perimeter. Response areas are geographical areas divided so as to have better control and a smaller area of responsibility. Ideally, a number of security officers (or at least one) should be assigned to each response area, perform the patrols in the area, and be able to react in case of an incident in the area assigned to him, or to help out with resolving an incident in another response area depending on the type and severity of the incident.

It is absolutely necessary to have a plan of reaction in case of emergency. This plan should contain a description of different threat levels such as, for example, blue, green, yellow, red, and black, and a plan of reaction. In that case, blue is the routine whereas black requires the immediate evacuation or sheltering of the entire facility. For example, the security of a facility is divided into four zones. In each zone there is a security officer on duty who is responsible for that zone. His or her duties are to control the situation constantly in the zone of responsibility and to respond in case of emergency depending on the level of threat. In case of a threat that requires the involvement of more officers, an officer from another zone should assist while the officer from the third zone should take over patrolling the zone that is not attended. For example, in case of a green level threat in zone 1, the officer from zone 3 will leave that zone and assist in dealing with the emergency while the officer from zone 4 will, in addition to his zone, take over the responsibility of zone 3. At the same time, the officer from zone 2 will be on standby to be the next to assist with the emergency. Also, a threat that is green could become more severe. If the emergency in zone 1 is a suspicious object classified as green, once that object is classified as an actual explosive device, the level of threat will become higher.

The system of response areas requires that iron posts be determined. Iron posts are positions that must never be abandoned: such as, for example, gates and the control center.

Daily Protection Routine

A daily protection routine is all of the security elements that perform regular tasks. Daily routine depends on the threats and the security setup.

Routine Patrols

Routine patrols are an important factor in every security system. The purpose of routine patrols is to notice suspicious people and objects, immediate or approaching threats, and any irregularities such as, for example, open doors and windows, breach of security policies, or stay-behinds. Because routine patrols are supposed to be a way to prevent an attack or warn about an attack in the early stages, they must physically thoroughly check the inner and outer perimeters. This is why the routes of patrols must be well determined. However, it is necessary to break routine by not always starting a patrol at the same time or from the same starting point, but still perform the entire patrol.

Staff Rotations

Keeping the concentration, vigilance, and performance of security staff high requires a frequent change of positions and regular rests. Basically, a usual system for staff rotation requires the officer to move from one position after a certain period (usually 1 h) to another position where he or she will perform different processes. For example, a security officer will patrol an area for 1 h, then move to performing entrance control for 1 h before taking a break. After the break, he will be assigned to another area for 1 h before moving to the control center.

Entrance and Exit Control

To set up entrance and exit controls, we first have to determine what we want to prevent from entering and what we want to prevent from exiting. If our facility or some area of the facility is not open for everyone to enter, we should create categories of visitors, implement the system of visitor announcements, and determine check levels for each category. For example, visitor categories could be:

- Announced visitors
- VIPs
- Unannounced visitors
- Service providers
- The press

For instance, special procedures should be determined for the press during entrance and movements inside the installation. We should remember that the press can influence our image and that, generally, representatives of the press deserve special treatment. In case of announced and unannounced visits by the press, security officers should perform questioning and a physical check in the nicest and most polite possible way while paying attention not to under-perform security procedures. Security officers should always be instructed in advance regarding what they can say or never should say and how to behave in the presence of the press.

All visitors who are banned from entering the facility should be blacklisted. The opposite of blacklists are white lists. These should include all visitors who are allowed to enter the secured area freely without being checked every time. However, we should break routine and once in awhile physically check visitors from the white list.

The purpose of visitor entrance procedures is that when your facility is open, no visitor, delivery service person, or unknown individual is able to enter the facility without being both observed (directly or indirectly) and approved. Checking of a person starts by visually observing suspicious appearance and behavior before he or she has entered the checking area. Security is supposed to try to do everything to notice a potential problem as far from the secured area as possible and to deny access to a problem. A thorough physical check consists of several stages:

- Visual check
- Verbal and behavioral check
- Check of the person and personal items
- Luggage check
- Check of documents and credentials

Reports

When starting a shift or changing position, the security officer must receive all information from the officer who previously attended the post, process this information, and use it in routine. If there were unusual situations in the previous shift, a security officer must look for similarities in his shift. The security officer who is finishing the shift must make a written shift report. However, in case of an emergency situation, a report should be made immediately after the emergency situation has finished. All reports should have defined templates covering the 5W1H questions: who, what, how, when, where, and why. These reports are used not only to inform the new officer on duty but also to provide periodic updates and information processing to notice periodic similarities in unusual situations.

Briefings
All security staff should be present at morning briefings and shift change briefings. This is the time to exchange important information from the day before and from the media. Security managers can set working rules for the day based on collected information. Morning briefings are also a good time to refresh security theory and update the knowledge about procedures and threats.

Radio Communication
Simple as it may seem, establishing and maintaining a proper radio communication system requires attention and has certain rules and principles. Codes are essential. Every person involved in radio communication should be assigned a code. Codes are divided into two groups:
- Personal codes
- Position codes

People who do not change position during the shift should have personal codes. This means that, for example, the chief of security and shift leaders will have their own codes that will not change with their movements.

Security guards do not have their personal codes. Instead, they will use the code of the position to which they are assigned. For example, if the parking area has the code "13," every security guard assigned to the parking area will use "13" as his code.

Codes can be names, letters, or numbers. It is essential that codes not have a clear and logical order, to confuse a potential listener–intruder. The chief of security should not have the code "1" or "Chief." Also, the numbers should not be organized in an order that would reveal the number of security posts in the secured area. It is important not to use letters and numbers that make a similar sound and can be confused when pronounced (for example, "D" and "B"; "M" and "N"; or "A" and "K") or letters that are not radiophonic ("S" and "R"). Codes should be used in a routine and in an emergency. Pass on short reports to allow someone else to burst in, in case of emergency. If your report is long, report it in several parts. In emergencies, do not use the order of call and codes but simply report the emergency.

Procedures
Classical facility security procedures are divided into three groups:
- Security unit procedures
- Security clauses in regular procedures
- Security procedures for employees

Security Procedures for Employees

The goals of security procedures for employees are to ensure their safety and raise their awareness (reactions to suspicious persons and objects, etc.), ensure proper reactions in case of an emergency (evacuation and sheltering procedures or reaction to anonymous phone threats), ensure compliance with security measures (e.g., clean desk policy, handling classified documents, proper use of access control system), and so forth. Apart from being officially implemented, filed, and easily accessible, procedures must be communicated through trainings and be periodically refreshed and exercised.

Security Clause

A security clause is the part of regular non-security procedures that regulates the security aspect of regular processes to control associated risks and minimize the possibility of theft, embezzlement, and fraud. The objective is to have a security clause as part of every procedure, tailored to the process it regulates.

Security Unit Procedures

Regular security unit procedures regulate the protection routine and emergency response of the security unit. They basically regulate all processes performed by the security unit. The second group of security unit procedures regulates the actions that security performs to control the compliance of employees with employees' security procedures and regular procedure security clauses.

Facility and Area Files

Facility and area files are an essential part of every facility security system. Area files consist of all information concerning security, including technical information about the secured perimeter and surrounding area. The idea behind these files is to have all necessary information we could need during emergencies and special situations. A good way to make a solid foundation for the file is to include all information that could be useful in case of different emergencies and information about the installation that the police special weapons and tactics team would require (tunnels, wall structure, phone lines, water, etc.) in case it would have to deal with hostage takers or storm into a certain area to perform hostage rescue. The area file must be easily accessible in and outside the installation (in case the one in the installation is not accessible for different reasons). Because some subjects are constant and some are variable and should be refreshed and updated, every section should have a clearly marked revision period (2 years, 1 year, 6 months, etc.) and the date when it should be revised and updated.

Among other information, area files should include:

- Detailed area maps
- Detailed blueprints of the perimeter
- Geopolitical information and risk analyses

- Area information (hospitals, police stations, fastest routes, etc.)
- Detailed information about surrounding objects, neighbors, etc.
- Routine information (traffic, working hours, number of employees, general information about employees, information about frequent visitors, information about repairmen, postmen, other hired services, etc.)
- Detailed information about the building structure (walls, windows, alternative exits/entrances, etc.)
- Detailed information about electricity, water, phone lines, lighting, etc.
- Main/alternative routes from the perimeter to frequently visited places and safe spots
- Position of CCTV cameras, alarms, fire equipment, etc.
- Emergency exits
- Emergency escape routes
- Phone numbers and contact information of all employees
- Phone numbers and contact information of all external emergency services.
- Contact information and availability of all security and non-security staff required in case of need and a list of their special skills that could assist in emergencies (bank of talents)

Use of Firearms and Types of Security Staff

In general, in corporate security when we think of securing a facility, we concentrate on prevention and disaster recovery. Under regular circumstances, for numerous reasons (corporate image and legal restraints are some of them) usually we will not list firearms as part of our protection routine. In most cases, we will be able to use alternative weapons such as teargas, batons, and shockers. Of course, depending on the location and the type and agenda of an institution, firearms might be required to "close the circle."

The use of firearms requires constant training, safety, and control, and even then it is hard to know how an armed individual will react in times of panic. Unfortunately, according to statistics, there are more cases of on-duty and off-duty accidental deaths and injuries caused by the incorrect and unsafe handling of firearms than actual protection successes using a firearm.

In facilities located in hostile environments that face higher threats, we use two types of security officers: observers and reactors.

Observers/Selectors

Observers usually make up some 80% of the force. They are usually visibly uniformed and do not carry firearms. The task of observers is to patrol and search for suspicious objects and persons (suspicious signs in appearance and behavior) outside and inside the perimeter. They are mostly focused on the early detection of threats. They will also inform about the arrival of a VIP or massive arrival so that other security positions can regroup. Observers will inform and approach a potential problem and ask assistance from reactors in case they are unable to solve it by themselves. Observers are mostly positioned in the perimeter with patrols inside the facility but also patrol outside the perimeter. They are also responsible for performing entrance and exit control. They investigate any disturbances or incidents, respond to emergencies, raise the alarm, and take necessary immediate actions including leading an evacuation.

In some cases, security systems require supporting staff such as people dealing with maintenance or logistics to be dressed in the same uniforms as security guards to create the visual illusion that the facility is attended by more security staff and to make it more difficult for a collector of information to count the number of security officers precisely.

Reactors

This group is low-profile (some 20% of the security force or based on threats) and is always supposed to be in visual and radio communication with other teams and members and react (assist other security staff) in case of emergency. Reactors are dressed in civilian clothes and are trained to use firearms and engage in combat. If observers assess that a certain situation carries a higher risk, they will request the assistance of reactors or their closer presence. The emergency reaction of this group requires thorough planning and coordination, including setting the levels of emergency to avoid having all simultaneously react to a certain emergency and leave all other positions unattended. Reactors are mostly positioned inside the facility and in places with higher risk, such as entrances to the perimeter and the facility itself. During an attack, observers lead the evacuation while reactors will deal with the attacker and the security of VIPs.

Female Security Officers

Female security officers are of outmost importance in every modern security system. There are several important reasons for encouraging the employment of female security officers. One is the ability of a female officer to perform a physical check on a female. Another is that, as some researchers suggest, women have a better ability than male officers to notice details, spot suspicious behavior, and remember important information. Also, female officers are believed to be better in applying the worst-scenario principle. Female security officers are valuable in questioning, screening, early warning, and as control center operators. On the other hand, because of physical strength and speed, male officers are often (but not always) better confronters.

Shelters and Assembly Points

According to the reaction of employees, emergencies are divided into those that require sheltering and those that require evacuation. Depending on the proximity of danger, timing, and probable impact, employees can shelter immediately in their offices or in special shelters. Also depending on the emergency, evacuation can be total or partial, and evacuees could evacuate to assembly points in the perimeter, or to a previously agreed-upon spot or spots outside the perimeter, or abandon the facility without gathering. Shelters and assembly points are important elements in facility security setups.

Shelters/Safe Rooms

Shelters are specially designed and constructed rooms able to resist a range of natural and manmade disasters. This means that they should have reinforced walls, safe doors, and blast-proof windows with bars. The room should be sealable so as to protect the employees not only from explosion and hostile takeover but also from chemical or biological threats (aerosols, toxins, etc.). Shelters can be stand-alone or internal. Internal shelters are usually more accessible and convenient for employees and are surrounded by layers of defense, which make them less accessible to perpetrators. On the other hand, external (stand-alone) shelters are separate from the building and therefore are not vulnerable to structure collapses. Basically, the position, nature, and security levels of shelters should be decided according to the risk assessment and probable threats.

Together, the shelters in a facility should have the capacity of sheltering at least 20% more people than the number of employees possibly present in the facility at one time. Also, each shelter should be able to shelter 20% more people than the number of people who would naturally use that specific shelter. The reason is that in case of an emergency, most likely the employees will not be evenly spread around the facility, and not all will be in their offices. They will have to use the shelters close to their current position, causing the over-occupancy of some shelters.

Shelters must be equipped with:

- Alternative power source
- Communication devices and chargers
- Emergency lights and flashlights
- List with important contacts
- 24-h food and water supply
- Access control readers—Having access control readers in the safe room will help rescuers know who is in which safe room and whether someone did not manage to enter the safe room and might be trapped elsewhere.

Assembly Points

Internal assembly points are designated areas in the inner perimeter and away from the facility, intended for gathering employees after an evacuation. They should have enough space for a large crowd. The number of assembly points should be two or more, depending on the size of the estate. They should be easily accessible to employees, close to or in the direction of the exits (or shelters), but still in a place that would, based on the risk assessment and probable course of action, provide temporary security for the gathered crowd. Assembly points should ideally be equipped with access control readers programmed so that rescuers will be able to quickly generate a list of employees who successfully evacuated and the names and most recent positions of employees who might still be trapped in the building.

External assembly points are agreed-upon safe spots outside and in the relative proximity of the estate, to which the employees should evacuate and wait for further instructions. External assembly points could be hotels, police stations, and so forth.

Some Additional Points for Facilities Facing Higher Risk
Morning Sweeping and Lockdown Procedures

Daily routine in facilities that are, for example, facing a higher risk of terrorism but are without a constant security presence would, apart from entrance and exit control and patrols, include morning sweeping against suspicious objects and intruders before employees are allowed to enter and closing of the facility at the end of the work day. Morning sweeping and end-of-day lockdown require a system of positive and negative codes. Positive codes are undercover codes that send a message that everything is clear; negative codes are undercover messages that something is wrong. Positive codes are used by the sweeping team to show to security officers on the outside that the building is clear and safe for them to enter. The code must be agreed on and known to all, but not obvious to outsiders (certain lights on, flag, closed/open windows, etc.). Negative codes are used to inform about a certain problem without an outsider noticing it. They are mostly used in case a person is taken hostage and cannot clearly inform about danger.

During the morning sweeping, you should be able to notice marks of entry or a presence in the building. For example, you can leave certain objects in the way that their position seems accidental to an outsider but so that any change can alert you. Some lights can be left on during the night (different lights each time and not according to a logical order). You can leave some doors closed, some wide open, and some semi open, but in the way that you will notice if the doors are moved even a bit, such as directing them toward a certain object in the room or according to a pattern on the floor. You can mark objects so as to notice whether they were replaced. The mark must be known to you but not visible to outsiders. For example, even drawing a tiny black dot on a sticker of a fire extinguisher will be sufficient for you to notice whether the fire extinguisher was replaced. End-of-day locking procedures should include a visual examination of all areas to prevent stay-behind visitors.

Massive Arrival of Employees

Depending on the type of institution and level of threat, the entrance and exit of employees may deserve special attention. For example, employees could be targeted, especially during their routine massive arrival to work or departure, which would require security to apply special measures during these times. Breaking the routine of arrivals and allowing flexible work hours could be a good idea but is usually impossible because it would probably disrupt the business and its processes. Securing the massive arrival of employees requires patrolling the area around the facility in search of collectors of information or persons preparing for an attack. You also must have lines of communication to inform employees about the problem and prevent them from arriving. Once the area is checked, security officers should be positioned on strategic points in such a way that they are able to control the area, notice any changes, and efficiently react in case of need. Security officers should be positioned in such a way as to have visual contact with each other and arriving employees but still not be in a group. Grouping security officers in one place can do more harm than good because a group of security officers can become a target.

SECURITY OF EVENTS

Because of their nature, venues are vulnerable to catastrophic consequences to:
• People
• Property
• Reputation
• All at the same time and with a domino effect

Probable Course of Action

Correctly assessing an event is the most important part in preparing the security for it. There is no precise mathematic formula that will tell us how long before the actual event we should start assessing and preparing, but it is certainly never too early to start. To be on the safe side, it is always the best to start with the assessment the moment a decision has been made about an event.

When making a security assessment and determining the existence of risk, level of risk, and potential target, we must cover factors that can influence an event. These factors are not only directly related to the event itself but must include a much wider picture.

For a criminal act to occur, three elements must be present:
• Motive
• Opportunity
• Means
   Related to these, our task is to:
• Recognize and understand the motive
• Reduce the opportunity
• Obstruct the means

When we talk about the motive, basically it is unlikely that someone will plan an incident at an event because of the event itself (apart from the problematic agenda of the event), but rather because of the profile of the people attending it, the number of people attending (terrorism), the image and reputation of the organizer (including recent business decisions), and so on.

To determine the potential motive and thus the target (people, property, or reputation) of an attack, we must assess several interactive factors:

Default: Global and local trends and risks such as high crime figures, increased threat of terrorism, increased activity of anti-globalization organizations, animal protection groups, etc. (depending on the industry)

Internal: Anything that classifies the organization such as the industry, a recent massive redundancy, recent business moves (for example, investment in a certain industry or support of a certain agenda such as investment in the military, support for animal testing in the cosmetics industry, etc.)

Event agenda: The cause and agenda of the event are also important parts of the assessment. For example, holding an event to celebrate the victorious return of troops from Iraq certainly raises the risk of a terrorist attack

Attendance: The number of people present at the event and the profile of guests are extremely important for an assessment. For example, a large number of people (massive event) could be targeted because of its massive nature. Also, the profile of our staff, guests, and speakers must be assessed.

Circumstances: These include the significance of the place and date of the event. We must be sure that the event was not scheduled for a significant date that can result in revolt (a day of mourning, religious holiday, anniversary, etc.) or might also be at the same time as and in the vicinity of a high-risk sports event and on the route of hooligans. We must also make sure that the place of the event is such that there is no risk that the place itself could be a target, or that a high-profile neighbor could be targeted. Basically, we have assessed the motive, level, or risk and the potential targets and we just have to match it with the amount of publicity (information) that the event has to obtain a full picture.

The second element, *opportunity*, is related more to the event itself. It is directly influenced by the location and nature of the event as well as by our security setup and control.

Events can be divided into several groups based on their nature and location:

- Division by Nature
  - *Open (public) venues*—anyone can attend without restrictions
  - *Observed public venues*—anyone can attend but the entrance is observed and can be denied according to certain criteria
  - *Controlled venues*—attendance only with a ticket whose distribution is not controlled or is mildly controlled
  - *Closed venues*—attendance only by special invitation with a highly controlled list of guests (VIP, the press, partners, etc.)
- Division by Type
  - *A reception/dinner/event* has a scheduled arrival and departure of guests. *An exhibition* is open the whole day and guests can arrive and leave at any time.
  - Also, an event can be a standing, seated, mingling, or multiple stage event. Also, the level of light, noise, and other factors can provide an opportunity for attack. Certainly, a good security setup and control of the event will reduce the opportunity potential.

- As for the *means*, with good planning of the event as well with the security setup and control, we will obstruct the means. Means are not only objects that can be brought to the event but actually anything that we use at the event (dark, noise, alcohol, glasses, bottles, ashtrays, etc.).
- To have a complete PCA analysis and start making a plan, we must have answers to the following questions:
    - Why: what could be the motive and who could be the target?
    - Who: who could be the perpetrator?
    - What: what could happen?
    - When: at which event stage (arrival, event, leaving)?
    - Where: at what part of the perimeter?
    - How: how could it happen?

Planning

Planning means incorporating the human element, physical and technical security, and procedures to minimize and control hazards and risks.

Human Element

Open/closed events are different considering security positioning. In case of an open event, you might decide to position security staff inside the place of the event. In case of a closed event, you might decide that there is no need for inside security. Also, depending on the type of event, positioning of staff should be considered. In case of an event with a strict timetable when arrival/departure times are more or less set and you are expecting massive movement, you might consider concentrating security on arrival/departure routes at these times. In general, one steward can control 50 people. However determining security staff requirement based on the risk assessment while taking into account all relevant circumstances will be much more efficient than simply relying on the general formula. Incorporating the human element also means coordination and cooperation among all parties involved in planning, organizing, and executing the event.

We must plan the following:

- Number of staff
- Type (VIP, anti-terror, bouncers, simple guards, etc.)
- Positioning—based on the facility and event stages (arrival, event, leaving), breaking the routine and changes of positions
- Male/female ratio—it should be close to the male/female ratio of the event
- Training—proper training for all people involved
- Briefing—good briefing before the event for all people involved
- Command—clear chain of command
- Control—clear models of control
- Backup and satellites—model of resting and model of emergency assistance

Procedures

This includes screening procedures, decisions concerning minors or disabled or disturbed individuals, illegal substances and items, alcohol, and so forth. It must predefine the proper behavior of security and other staff and include special procedures for the press, procedures in case of an emergency, unplanned situations, latecomers, uninvited guests, and procedures to limit occupancy and prevent it from exceeding the operational and legal maximum. We must also have procedures concerning default security risks:

- Anonymous phone call
- Suspicious object
- Suspicious person

Technical

A technical tools plan includes screening equipment, communication devices, crowd communication and control equipment, and such. It is based on the assessment of existing technical tools (CCTV, metal detectors, etc.) and upgrading needs. We must include a plan for immediate access to and control of infrastructures such as power, lights, sound, and fire safety.

Physical Elements

Planning physical elements consists of planning how to use existing physical elements, improve the physical deficiencies, and add features.

Physical elements include:
- Natural terrain
- Physical barriers such as fences, walls, doors, and windows
- Visual barriers, which can be natural (trees), existing physical (walls), and added (screens)

Good security is based on layers that should have the ability to deter, detect, deny, delay, and defend.

Boundaries can be divided into six main groups:
- *Physical*: doors, windows, bars, and fences
- *Visual*: curtains, blinds, and lights
- *Electronic*: CCTV, alarm systems, and electronic access control
- *Human*: security personnel and trained non-security personnel
- *Procedural*: security procedures imposed according to the PCA
- *Intelligence*: disinformation, protection of information, collected intelligence, common knowledge, etc.

When we plan, we must have a strategy for anything that could happen for which we did not plan. It usually involves a clear chain of command, a competent decision maker, and excellent lines of communication. On the other hand, we must plan and control all internal factors that could unintentionally jeopardize the security, safety, and reputation of the event. This comes down to responsibility. Basically, because we (our organization) are the name behind the event, we should be the ones to control the event. We will certainly outsource most of the staff and services but we should not think that a contract with a no-name provider will protect our reputation in case of a failure.

Perimeter Setup

Observation Area

The observation area is located outside the perimeter that we have set. It is the area from where our secured area can be observed, where we basically concentrate on all attack preparation points and points for collecting information. We are trying to single out any suspicious behavior and stop an incident at the earliest stage.

Perimeter

The perimeter is the area that is physically controllable. It is the area that we control, and we can deny access to it. The edge of the perimeter must be distant enough from the installation to efficiently stop any concerns. It is the place where we are looking for suspicious objects and persons and checking credentials. We will not allow any problem which we have identified earlier to enter the perimeter.

Physical Control Point

The physical control point is the last line of defense before entering the venue. It is where we perform the physical check. Still, as much as we try to make the entrance to the event slow and controllable, during the same stage of planning, we must plan quick exits in case of an emergency and efficient evacuation.

Security Positioning and Competences

Security staff should:
- Communicate efficiently during routine events and emergencies
- Ensure the perimeter remains intact
- Query anyone who seems suspicious or out of place
- Look for unattended bags and packages
- Watch, report, and react to suspicious behavior
- React in case of an attack (ideally try to stop it at an early stage)
- Understand, observe, and manage the crowd
- Understand their role in an emergency, including when to leave their post and when not
- Understand that they are guarding an event, not participating in it or watching it. However, they should follow the event to understand its phases and be able to secure it properly and react in a timely manner
- Lead the evacuation

As for entrance control, it is basically a way to stop anything you do not want to have during the event from being brought in. Depending on the nature of the event, you could introduce classic entrance procedures for visitors, such as a metal detector gate, X-ray, body search, or a check of luggage. Depending on the law and the company's policy, you can use alcohol tests as the possibility for forbidding entrance to the event. Still, paying attention to suspicious signs in appearance and behavior is always the most efficient model of control. Moreover, it is never restricted by any policy, and it is always free. In most cases, not permitting entrance to someone who should enter will cause less harm then permitting entrance to someone who should not enter. However, from the reputation aspect, denying entrance to someone based on, for example, ethnicity or disability can have disastrous effects on reputation.

For massive events, we use three types of security staff:

- Observers (20%)
- Physical check and crowd management (70%)
- Reactors (10%)

Observers

The task of *observers* is to patrol and search for suspicious objects and persons (suspicious signs in appearance and behavior) outside and inside the perimeter and to inform immediately. They are mostly focused on the early detection of threats. They will also inform about the arrival of a VIP or massive arrival so that other security positions can regroup. *Observers* will inform and approach a potential problem and ask assistance from *reactors* in case they are not able to solve it by themselves.

Observers are mostly positioned in the outer perimeter with patrols inside the installation but also outside the perimeter.

Physical Check and Crowd Management

This group is the central security function for an event. It performs access control and controls or directs the audience that enters or leaves the event. It recognizes crowd conditions and movement and assists in the safe operation of the event by keeping gangways and exits clear at all times. It investigates any disturbances or incidents, responds to emergencies, raises the alarm, and takes necessary immediate action including leading an evacuation.

These staff are positioned just outside and inside the installation and are controlling the entrances and exits, infrastructure, and crowd (tactically positioned outside and inside the crowd and outside according to the situation [mass arrival, leaving, award ceremony, etc.]).

Reactors

This group is low-profile and is always supposed to be in visual communication with other teams and members and react (assist other security staff) in case of an emergency.

Reactors are the ones that will evacuate the VIP. The emergency reaction of this group requires thorough planning and coordination, including setting the levels of the emergency to avoid overreacting or reacting all at the same time to a certain emergency and leaving all other positions unattended. Reactors are evenly positioned throughout the perimeter and the installation.

Crowd Management

Crowds move in waves that are strongest when they are closer to the focus of the event (e.g., stage) and weaker as they move away. We call this phenomenon the crowd routine. In a crowd, we also concentrate on looking at individuals and noticing anything that does not fit the routine of the place, as well as at the natural movements of the crowd, and look for irregular movements that could be the result of an ongoing incident. It is much easier to notice anything out of the routine in a crowd when we are farther away and above than close and at the same level as the crowd.

Correct treatment of an incident in a crowd comes down to noticing non-routine crowd movement and extreme individuals and their behavior and directing more attention to them or reacting to an incident at an early stage. In reality, crowds are not aggressive. Even when violence occurs in a crowd, it is carried out by a small minority of people, and our task is to notice them and stop the incident at an early stage.

Chill Out

Participating in a massive event can be tough. Dimness, strobe lighting, loud music, crowds, fast dancing, heat, lack of fresh air, and sometimes substance and alcohol abuse can be a real challenge to our bodies. It is absolutely essential that a chill-out area be provided (ideally, several) that will allow participants to cool down.

Routine Crowd Management

Routine crowd management starts with knowing the venue timetable, the target group attending the venue, and the combination of physical barriers and security staff. For large events, it is almost impossible to conduct emergency communication with the crowd (direct the crowd) solely with written signs. Communication must be done verbally. One essential security position during massive events, especially those that involve performers, is close to the microphone. Basically, during an emergency, a steward will take over the microphone from the performers and use it to communicate with the crowd.

Barriers

Barriers have several tasks: to direct the crowd, obstruct an incident against the performers, and allow security staff movement and faster reaction. When setting a barrier in front of the stage, we must be sure that this is a space we can efficiently control. Sometimes it is better to make a double barrier close to the stage than to set the barrier far from the stage. It is necessary to have security staff present at all narrow passages, angles, and curves in the paths. Crowd management requires good positioning, coordination, visibility, and authority.

Emergency

Good reaction in emergencies depends on several interactive factors:

- Emergency planning
- Procedures and setup in case of an emergency
- Area file (a file containing all information about routes to the hospital or police, fire fighter response times, etc.)
- Exercised scenarios
- Clearly set roles and responsibilities
- Internal communication, crowd communication ability, and clear chain of command
- Access to and control of infrastructure
- Adaptive setup (changing the physical setup during different phases of the event)
- Visibility and ability to be seen and recognized as an authority and effectively direct the crowd

We must remember that in case of an emergency we must be able to communicate with the crowd to pass on a message and direct the crowd, but without creating panic, which can make the impact event worse than the initial incident (stampede). This is why we avoid communicating and directing the crowd with alarms, but use only voice and human guidance.

Additional Points

In case we are talking about a high-risk institution endangered by terrorism that is organizing an event, such as a political or diplomatic organization, there are numerous other points to be considered. Because we are researching corporate security and not homeland security, we will mention only some of them.

One thing to which high-risk institutions pay attention in the planning phases is the availability of information about the place of the venue and its accessibility before the event. Basically, the organizer of the event will take into account whether the possible place for the venue has been used in the past by someone who might misuse his proficiency with the place. For example, countries that are endangered by terrorism will want to know whether an embassy of a country that is known to support terrorism has in the past used the same place for their event. This would mean that they are familiar with the place of the venue, probably have blueprints of the building, and certainly know all vulnerabilities, gaps, entrances, exits, and so on. Even if the venue location has not been used in the past, it is important to know how easy is it to collect intelligence and obtain plans and blueprints and whether the venue is suitable for preparing an attack a long or short time before our event.

We are trying to avoid organizing the event every year on the same date and in the same place, which is easily accessible to anyone who might pose a threat. Another point to consider is food safety and the possibility of food sabotage (poison attack). Countermeasures include close supervision of the whole process from food and beverage purchasing to consumption, including handpicking, checking, and monitoring catering staff.

Event Safety

Owing to the possible catastrophic consequences of safety flaws, corporate security cooperates closely with a company's safety management (environment, health and safety; health and safety; and occupational health) that is in charge of the safety of an event. One more reason is the overlap of responsibilities between security and safety, especially concerning matters such as crowd management, occupancy and evacuation. Safety incidents and not security incidents have proven to be the biggest hazards and have caused the largest disasters during events. The best known hazards are fire, over-occupancy, and incidents resulting in equipment not being mounted properly.

CHAPTER 9

Product

SUPPLY CHAIN

The supply chain includes all incoming and outgoing cargo that is being moved by road, rail, sea, or air. Threats associated with the supply chain go far beyond the theft of cargo. The current wave of globalization has resulted in the greater immediate need for resources and products, pushing businesses to transport their products quickly to distant locations and reach new markets. The need for the rapid movement of goods has resulted in an improved transport infrastructure and open borders from which not only businesses and consumers benefit. Criminals and terrorists use the supply chain infrastructure to smuggle goods and people, perform attacks, or hijack vessels for ransom.

As for theft, logically, the supply chain is often the weakest security link in the product lifecycle. We do everything to protect the product in the factory and in retail but usually send a truckload of valuable products from the factory to retail with no security measures. However, loss of cargo can have devastating consequences for the business.

Starting from production, the delay of the arrival of material needed for production can cause serious disruptions to business. The tendency of businesses is not to build stock, so every delay of cargo with raw materials is a threat to the continuity of production.

When we talk about the loss of product during distribution to consumers, apart from the cost of the product itself we risk the delay of product to consumers or even running out of stock at the point of sale. In these cases, not only will criminals profit; so, too, will the competition. Especially in the case of fast-moving consumer goods, consumers will buy the brand that is available at the point of sale at least as a temporary replacement, and will sometimes even turn to another brand permanently. We should not forget that criminals are also competition. Furthermore, the illegal sale of stolen cargo undercuts prices in legitimate businesses. Even retailers will in some cases buy stolen goods from another supplier and order less from us. We must know that as much as we are investigating market potential and working on attracting new consumers, criminals are, too. The fact that our products were stolen means that there is a market for our stolen products. Of course, this market expects regular supplies, and the demand grows with each supply. To make it worse, because we were the victim of a successful theft, we have proven to be a soft target and are proving it more with each theft. It is estimated that, on average, one successful incident leads to 10 more incidents against the same target.

Road Transport of Cargo (Primary Distribution)

The theft of hot products is common. Like any other business, goods are stolen to feed consumer demand; often the goods are ordered and even pre-sold before the theft. Based on the 2014 Global Cargo Theft Threat Assessment issued by FreightWatch International Supply Chain Intelligence [1], apart from metal, whose popularity is increasing, other, more traditional hot products are those that are easily disposed of and yet retain a high black market value, such as:

- Alcohol
- Computers
- Entertainment equipment
- Mobile phones and other small electronic devices
- Name brand clothing
- Cigarettes
- Prescription drugs

Cargo theft is a growing threat occurring across the world. Easily resalable goods represent the largest share of stolen property, but criminals are willing to steal almost anything. Also on the rise are the number of assaults on drivers and the increasingly violent nature of supply chain incidents. Whereas various forms of theft (e.g., "curtain slash/jump-up") are still the cause of most loss, the number of violent incidents is increasing. For example, armed hijacking has shown a significant increase in many countries. A report published by the International Road Union and International Transport Forum [2] in February 2008 highlighted that over the period 2000–2005:

- 17% of all drivers experienced an attack during the 5-year period investigated
- 30% of attacked drivers had been attacked more than once
- 21% of drivers were physically assaulted
- 60% of the attacks targeted the vehicle and its load
- 42% of the attacks took place in truck parking areas
- 30% of the attacked drivers did not report the incident to the police

The most frequent road transportation security threats are:

- Driver involvement
- Curtain slashing
- Moving vehicle attack
- Load diversion
- Impersonation of police officers
- Forced stop

Driver Involvement

Drivers are possibly the weakest link in cargo security. According to many estimates, the number of cargo thefts committed with the involvement of driver is high, whether drivers initiated and organized the theft, voluntarily agreed to participate in the theft, or were blackmailed.

Curtain Slashing

Curtain slashing is the most popular method of cargo theft that occurs at lay-bys, parking areas, and on the road in motion. One method employed by road pirates is to use a converted truck with a secret door on the side. The thieves pull up alongside the targeted soft-sided truck, open their secret door, slash a hole in the canvas, and remove the goods.

Moving Vehicle Attack

The Romanian style theft is executed on the road and in motion. The thieves approach a moving truck from behind, jump from their own vehicle onto the loaded truck, and remove the goods. They often simply throw the boxes off the trailer, which are picked up by another truck. The victim truck is often identified earlier, usually at parking areas, and marked so that it can be easily identified in the dark and followed from a distance. The thieves place a reflective sticker on the back of the truck or break the rear light fixture.

Load Diversion

Load diversion (or the round the corner game) is a popular cargo theft scam. A thief pretending to be a customer calls the driver and redirects the cargo. The truck is then intercepted by the criminals, or in some cases, the thieves pretend to be customers and use fake documents to receive the goods.

Impersonation of Police Officers

Criminals dressed as police officers signal to the driver to pull over. They then take the vehicle by force. The criminals often use genuine uniforms. At night, they might simply use the blue rotating light and a siren to signal to the driver of the truck to stop.

Forced Stop

Criminals block the road or set up a fake checkpoint so that the driver will have to stop and can be taken by force. Alternatively, criminals stage an accident so as to stop the truck and then take it by force. The criminals may also signal the driver to stop for some sham reason, such as a flat tire.

Road Transport of Cargo (Secondary Distribution)

Probably the weakest link in the supply chain is distribution to clients (secondary distribution). The main differences between primary and secondary distribution security threats come from the amount of transported goods and routing. Also, unlike in primary distribution, theft, embezzlement, and robberies are the main risks whereas the use of transport to smuggle people and goods or to perform terrorist attacks, including the risk of vehicles being the targets of attacks, are minimal.

In primary distribution huge amounts of goods are transported by trailers; accurate planning, organization, and logistics are required to steal that much merchandise and avoid being caught. Stealing the content of a trailer requires at least a transportation storage space of the same size, which has to be hidden, not to mention the ability to move goods to and from storage. Another difference is in routing. Primary distribution is preferably performed via highways and involves distribution centers mostly located on the outskirts of large cities, avoiding urban or remote areas as much as possible.

Secondary distribution is performed everywhere there are points of sale for the particular product. Thus, whereas the reward for criminals in primary distribution is much more tempting, it takes a lot of effort. On the other hand, secondary distribution is a much softer target and is equally attractive for organized crime and individuals. In secondary distribution, the worth of the contents of a van can be as much as €100,000 or more, depending on the goods, which is still a good motive.

There are several differences in the modus operandi and levels of threat and loss between crimes performed by organized groups and those performed by individuals. Whereas organized groups target large amounts of goods and high profits and usually go after the product, individuals (often motivated by poverty or substance abuse) are willing to steal almost anything from the product to any item that can be stolen and sold. Organized groups are aware of the consequences of their actions and plan the escape while they plan the whole action. On the other hand, desperate individuals focus on getting what they came for and do not think about the consequences. Therefore, even though the financial loss is usually smaller, other consequences from opportunity crime may be graver.

It is not only criminals who are to blame for the distribution being a soft target. What are the distributors doing wrong? The main security problem not only in transportation and distribution but in everything that is a security concern is routine. Distributors often perform deliveries at the same times and according to the same route plans without recognizing a need to change them or to break routine once in awhile. Performing deliveries according to a pattern is a clear invitation to criminals. After collecting information for a short period of time, they know exactly when and where to wait for the van. Lack of awareness, of training, and of security policies are other big problems. It is common to see delivery staff leaving the doors of the van wide open while they carry boxes to the point of sale. To add to that, unlike trailers, vans are usually uniformed and visibly marked with marketing slogans and pictures of products, making it much easier for criminals to track and follow the vans.

One more threat when it comes to individually performed crimes is the lack of clean workplace policies for vans. Even when drivers are aware of the threat of the cargo being a target, they sometimes leave equipment such as mobile phones, wallets, and laptops in the cabin on the seat, which is an invitation, even for those who were not aware of the value of the cargo, to break the glass and take what they can. The nonexistence of clean workplace policies can be also seen in the example of distribution lists displayed openly in the van, so that criminals can clearly see the value of the cargo and the timing and points of sale of the van's route.

Although more and more distributors are installing security equipment such as global positioning system (GPS) tracking systems, alarms, and cameras, if the human element is not involved they usually prove useless. A popular model of thefts is performed with a frequency jammer that blocks the signal of the remote key and prevents the vehicle from being locked wirelessly. Thefts are usually performed at gas stations and parking lots and in front of shopping malls. When the driver comes back to the van, he notices that the van is open, goods are missing, and there are no signs of burglary.

Armed robberies of delivery vans are also common. However, to plan and execute a robbery successfully, the robber must have precise information about the locations and times of deliveries. Basically, unless the robbery was staged and planned by the driver of the van (which is unfortunately common), breaking the routine of deliveries will do the most to discourage a potential robber, as will properly training drivers in security awareness, how to notice suspicious signs, and how to react during emergencies.

Case Study: Armed Robberies of Cigarettes in Secondary Distribution

In 2007, in Belgrade, Serbia, a premium brand cigarette manufacturer experienced regular armed robberies during deliveries to points of sale. All of the robberies were executed at points of sale in downtown Belgrade during morning hours. The robbers would wait for the van close to the point of sale, take the car keys at gunpoint, and drive away with the van.

Belgrade is the capital of Serbia and its largest city, with a population of up to 3 million inhabitants. Severe traffic jams are regular in Belgrade during rush hour, especially in the morning from 7 to 9 am and in the afternoon from 4 to 6 pm.

An assessment of the situation revealed that all robberies were committed in the center of the city and in the morning during rush hour.

One reason for the downtown locations was probably because the percentage of expensive brands delivered to the center of the city is higher than in other areas of the city. Also, as a large city, Belgrade is more convenient for robbers because, unlike in smaller communities around the country, they can avoid being detected as a result of not fitting the routine of the place. The reason why the robberies were executed during the morning and during the first few deliveries is that the vans were still beginning their delivery routes and were still filled with goods. The detailed assessment also revealed that the robberies were executed next to points of sale located on big junctions close to main roads and with multiple escape choices. Moreover, the robbers always chose locations where their escape would not be affected by traffic jams, in areas not close to police stations or attended by traffic police, and where there was no video surveillance such as city security cameras, traffic cameras, or automatic teller machines nor other external security cameras belonging to businesses.

The vulnerability assessment showed that deliveries were always performed in the same order, using the same route plans, and in the same way and that the points of sale were always visited at the same time. Moreover, the drivers would usually park in the same spot every time. Also, the staff had received no awareness trainings and did not know how to spot suspicious behavior or how to behave if they noticed it or were confronted. In addition, because of numerous successful robberies, the delivery vans were perceived by criminals as soft targets.

The security of the company concentrated on limiting the opportunity for robbers by introducing the system of breaking the routine of deliveries, singling out risky spots and introducing higher-security measures in such places, raising the awareness of drivers and their ability to spot and react to danger, and changing the perception about company deliveries as being a soft target.

The security team changed the route plans by introducing several route options with different routes, a change in the order of visited points of sale, and differing times of delivery. The drivers received the new route plan every morning, just before starting deliveries.

With the clear and predictable modus operandi of the robbers, it was easy for the security team of the company to single out probable locations of future robberies. In such places, the security team introduced random visible escorts by security vehicles during the morning hours.

All drivers received a set of security trainings on how to notice suspicious appearance and behavior, how to prevent being confronted, breaking the routine, the clean workplace policy as a way to protect information, and how to react in case of threat and emergency.

Apart from limiting the opportunity for the robbers, which were also measures of deterrence and target hardening, the security team placed disinformation in the media about new top of the shelf security technology that was installed in all delivery vehicles. In reality, only months later the company installed technical solutions in delivery vans, such as GPS, hidden surveillance cameras and alarms, remote immobilization, divided locking mechanisms (one for the passenger part and a second for the cargo part of vehicle), and personalized radiofrequency identification (RFID) cards, which are required to start the engine.

The security strategy proved to be extremely successful and resulted in the immediate end to robberies of the company's delivery vans, which had lasted for more than 5 years. The result was that the business was the only incident-free and zero-loss company performing deliveries in the entire country. Moreover, incidents against other tobacco manufacturers immediately increased significantly and continued to rise rapidly.

Road Transport Assessment and Security Measures
Risk Assessment
Aside from assessing the value of transported goods and how attractive they may be to different types of criminals, the main element of the assessment should be a risk assessment of delivery routes, including mapping the areas and roads without global system for mobile communications/GPS signal, dark and remote points of sales, high crime areas, places where the drivers do not feel safe, multiple escape choice routes, and places with a history of related incidents.

Probably the easiest way to create an effective route assessment is to involve drivers by performing a risk survey in which every driver is asked to answer questions about every point of sale on the route. Apart from risks, route assessment should also help identify safe havens.

Security Measures

The first and most important security measure is to break routine and avoid visible patterns during deliveries or times and places for resting. Moreover, any security measure, regardless of how advanced it may be, will fail if it becomes routine.

Preferred roads should be the those where it would be more difficult for the perpetrator to force-stop the vehicle, hijack it, and escape with it (such as highways, toll roads, roads with security cameras, roads without escape choices, and/or roads with a heavy presence of police).

Protecting information is also crucial. This includes concealing transported goods and any objects and documents that could be useful to a criminal who is collecting information. Moreover, in case of high threat it is always good to weigh the benefits of having branded vehicles against the benefits of being incognito. On the other hand, in some cases, using especially visible markings on a vehicle that would make it stand out may prevent a criminal from hijacking the vehicle.

Provide security training to drivers with an emphasis on suspicious appearance and behavior, secure driving, breaking routine, and clear instructions regarding how to react in case of an emergency. It is crucial to implement a good program in case the transport vehicle is attacked or the driver is confronted. The driver's life and health are more valuable than the goods or materials; considering this, the driver has to comply with the attacker's request.

Technical solutions in delivery vans include GPS devices that can be set to detect and report numerous events, hidden surveillance cameras and alarms, remote immobilization systems (to the extent allowed by local law), divided locking mechanisms (one for the passenger part and another for the cargo part of the vehicle), and RFID keys. If you have a large number of vehicles and drivers and drivers can be assigned to different vehicles, consider connecting the RFID system with your GPS monitoring center so that you will know which driver is in which vehicle. A GPS system should provide you with information such as a clearly visible location, the direction of the vehicle and its status (engine on/off), speed, the type and amount of goods, the type of alarm, the name of the driver with contact info, etc. All parameters should be recorded and kept in the system for as long as possible. To prevent perpetrators from disconnecting a GPS antenna, consider installing a GPS system with a concealed antenna. In some cases, particularly in countries where thefts and robberies in the supply chain are especially popular, delivery companies mark the vehicles with a number on the roof, in addition to tracking devices, so that the van can be spotted from the air. Vehicles should be provided with two independent means of communication to avoid jamming of telecommunications.

In areas with a high security risk for the distribution of goods, consider security escorts. An escorting system should be random for small- to medium-value transport and always accompany high-value transport. Random means that an escort will be provided to a different vehicle or route each day, with no template or pattern. Escorting vehicles need to be clearly marked, equipped with rotary lights, and visible during escorting to be obvious and harden the target. Escort vehicles need to have constant communication with the monitoring center and with the vehicles they are escorting.

You need to set standards for the vehicle itself. For example, consider using only hard-body trucks, vans, and trailers. Implement a security seal system. Seals or locks should be installed by supply chain or security personnel, not the driver. The seal or lock number should be stated on the documents. However, the security seal is not intended as a high-security measure that would enable someone to physically open the truck. A security seal is a system intended for control, especially in primary distribution, indicating that the locks or seals were tampered with or replaced by unauthorized personnel.

In addition to a panic button in the vehicle, consider using a special phone number, ideally not longer than four digits, that can be easily remembered by drivers and that they can call if they are threatened. The emergency mobile phone should contain all telephone numbers of all drivers and/or delivery representatives. Consider making it a daily routine for the control center to call all drivers several times a day. Use a system of code words in case the driver is threatened.

Maritime Supply Chain

Maritime supply chain security is a science of its own and usually is not managed by general corporate security professionals; it requires the involvement of security professionals specializing in maritime security. However, I will mention the most common risks associated with the transport of goods by sea. According to the article "Modern Piracy: The Impact on Maritime Security," written by Lieutenant Commander Charles T. Mansfield, United States (US) Navy (2008) [3], the hotspots for maritime security incidents are the waters of East Africa and the Gulf of Aden as well as the Horn of Africa and the west coast, especially the Gulf of Guinea, the South China Sea, Southeast Asia and South Asia, the Persian Gulf, and the Caribbean and Latin America.

Risks can be divided into five areas:
- Seizure of cargo
- Use of vessels and/or cargo for smuggling
- Use of vessels to launch an attack/sink vessels
- Sinking vessels to disrupt the supply chain infrastructure
- Hijacking vessels for ransom

Seizure of Cargo

Regardless of contemporary threats that are constantly emerging against global import-ers, traditional models of cargo seizure, such as theft and maritime robbery (piracy), remain a severe challenge, especially for vessels carrying high-value goods and valuable liquids such as oil.

Use of Vessels and/or Cargo for Smuggling

The ability of the maritime supply chain infrastructure to move large quantities of goods provides an excellent opportunity for criminals to facilitate illegal drug trafficking, gun-running, and people smuggling.

Use of Vessels to Launch an Attack/Sink Vessels (Terrorism at Sea and from the Sea)

After the 9/11 attacks, fears arose that terrorists might use a maritime supply chain to perform an attack, such as transporting a bomb by ship and detonating it in a port. How-ever, the vessels themselves may be targets of terrorist attacks. There are numerous exam-ples of terrorist attacks at sea. In 2002, Palestinian Islamic Jihad terrorists detonated a boat bomb off the coast of Gaza, which damaged an Israeli patrol boat. Also in 2002, Palestinian terrorists used a boat bomb to try to blow up an Israel Navy vessel. Some terrorist groups have carried out attacks using explosive devices mounted on scuba-diving equipment, sea scooters, and tourist submarines.

Hijacking Vessels for Ransom

Apart from the well-known hijackings for ransom in the waters of East Africa and other piracy hotspots, there are hijacking cases that are not financially motivated but actually support a specific political (terrorist) agenda. In 1985, Palestinian terrorists hijacked the Italian cruise liner *Achille Lauro* off the coast of Egypt and demanded the release of a group of Palestinians detained in Israeli prisons. During the hijack, a US citizen was killed onboard.

RETAIL LOSS PREVENTION

According to the 2011 Global Retail Theft Barometer survey [4] generated by the Cen-tre for Retail Researching in Nottingham, England, the total annual cost of retail theft exceeds $119 billion globally, amounting to 1.45% of total retail sales. The amount of money spent in 2010 on retail loss prevention totaled $28.3 billion worldwide. Accord-ing to the same survey [4], employee theft accounted for 44.1% of retail shrinkage in North America, whereas external theft, including shoplifting and organized retail crime, was responsible for 43.2%. Products experiencing the highest percentage of thefts were clothing, fashion accessories, and high-value electronics and accessories, followed by health, beauty, and pharmaceutical products.

The most common challenge that loss prevention faces as a discipline is balancing between preventing theft and shrinkage and providing good customer service.

External Theft

Aside from theft, the most significant retail crimes include burglaries, robberies, cash loss, bad checks, refund fraud, and exchanges of product at the counter (replacing the good item with a forged one). Still, the main reason for the loss of product is the simplest form of theft—shoplifting—which is mostly performed by amateur shoplifters and motivated by poverty.

However, the number of thefts executed by career criminals is growing. Organized retail crime goes beyond traditional shoplifting and includes groups that engage in cargo theft, burglaries, and so forth. Organized retail crime organizations have the ability to move large quantities of product both into black market channels and through legitimate business channels once the product has been properly laundered. Career criminals usually target items that are small but valuable. The most common methods of theft in retail are:

- Simple shoplifting
- Box stuffing
- Bar code switching
- Magnetic field jamming
- Double shopping
- Refund fraud
- Exchange at the counter
- Fake or stolen credit cards

Simple Shoplifting

The simplest form of shoplifting involves concealing items in clothes, purses, or shopping bags and walking out without being noticed. Thieves simply walk or run out of the store or use simple techniques to prevent the electronic article surveillance (EAS) towers from sounding, such as holding the items high above the pillars, concealing the item in a hat, going around the pillar, or sliding the item between the pillar and the wall. However, some retailers use fake EAS towers and actually have the equipment attached to the wall and extending higher than the towers.

Another popular method is bottom of the basket (BOB) theft, which is basically to leave an item in the shopping cart "unintentionally" and walk out without paying for it. This type of shoplifting is often performed in stores that are not equipped with EAS towers and have no security guard presence at the exits. Some retailers install BOB mirrors so that cashiers are able to observe the customer's entire shopping cart. Many times, shoplifting is performed at the end of the day just before closing of the store, when employees are focused on closing and going home instead on performing loss prevention procedures with full attention and diligence.

Box Stuffing

Box stuffing is performed by placing a high-value item inside the box of a lower-value item. Some retailers use dummy cases for expensive items. Basically, a box may either be empty or contain a piece of plastic of similar weight as the original item. The customer receives the original item only after the item is paid for.

Bar Code Switching

A bar code sticker of a less expensive product is placed over the sticker of the high-priced item.

Magnetic Field Jamming

There are numerous ways to interrupt the magnetic field. One of the most common techniques is to use booster bags. Booster bags are other items (coat inner lining, umbrella, etc.) lined with multiple layers of aluminum foil to provide electromagnetic shielding and prevent the security tags from being detected. Some retailers use detectors that sense metallic surfaces to prevent the use of booster bags.

Many types of electromagnetic field jammers are used by criminals. The two most common types of jammers are those that prevent the alarm from going off or that trigger the alarm, causing the EAS to lose credibility and be switched off or ignored by store staff. Another popular method used by criminals is to use a magnet to remove a tag from an item, preventing the alarm from going off, or simply to demagnetize the tag. However, numerous loss prevention devices are available that can detect magnets and jammers.

Double Shopping

After the purchase of an expensive item, a criminal reenters the store, takes the same product, and exits, showing the original receipt as proof of purchase. Store security guards can stamp the receipt after inspecting it to prevent double shopping.

Refund Fraud

Refund fraud involves returning goods to a retailer in exchange for money or other goods. The returned products may be stolen or found in a dumpster. Also, a criminal may purchase a genuine product and then return a forged product for refund. Another common model of refund fraud involves switching labels on items to purchase them at a lower price and then returning them for their original value. The effort of retailers to combat refund fraud includes keeping track of returns and flagging customers with a high number of returns over a certain period of time. The efforts also include listing serial numbers of the product (or another hidden code) on the receipt and limiting the refund to an exchange of product and not a cash refund.

Exchange at the Counter

An exchange at the counter occurs mostly with products placed behind the counter, such as cigarettes and perfume. A criminal asks a salesperson to see a product. He then makes a quick switch by putting the item into a bag and taking out a fake similar product, "returning" it to the salesperson. For example, a criminal asks to see a perfume packed in a box and then returns another box of the same perfume, but with a dummy item inside the box instead of the original perfume. Some stores place stickers on the product (every day a different color sticker) to prevent this type of fraud.

Fake or Stolen Credit Cards

Use of fake or stolen credit cards to purchase goods is a common method of retail fraud. Some stores request a personal identification document be presented together with the credit card in the case of a higher-amount purchase.

External Theft Prevention

No loss prevention technology is successful if it is not combined with the determination to fight theft, the awareness of employees and their ability to detect suspicious behavior, the proper reaction, deterrence, and procedures, and crime prevention through environmental (store) design.

Technology

The first thing that comes to mind when we think about loss prevention technology is the EAS system. Contemporary EAS systems are expanding from traditional pillars to systems that cover the entire door opening and have add-ons aimed at detecting jammers and booster bags. New EAS systems also prevent tag crowding by detecting active electronic tags from other shops that are being brought in so that the employees can remove them. Another new feature is the individual tagging of items that will not only signal that the item is passing through EAS but will also inform the staff which item it is. A similar system shows a picture of the product on the cashier monitor when reading the bar code, to prevent bar code switching. Another use of EAS is to control the number of items brought into the fitting rooms. The system notifies the fitting room attendant about how many articles the customer has taken and gives the customer a badge stating the number of articles to be returned later together with the articles. Sometimes, similar systems are used to inform the cashier how many items the customer has when he or she is approaching the register (the number of paid articles should match the detected number of items). The system can also be connected to the doors and prevent the doors from opening in case of an EAS alarm.

However, EAS is far from being the ultimate technical solution to prevent retail theft in itself. Closed-circuit television (CCTV) and other means of surveillance such as mirrors (including BOB mirrors) assisted with proper lighting should cover the entire space without leaving dead angles. Means of surveillance should assist the staff in monitoring the store successfully, noticing suspicious behavior, deterring criminals, and providing evidence after an attempted or performed theft.

Employee Awareness

Unfortunately, many retailers rely completely on technology and use technical devices as stand-alone loss prevention systems without having employees manage and use the systems. The first condition is certainly the willingness of the company to invest in preventing fraud, which includes proper staffing, adequate training, and procedures that allow the staff to monitor consumers successfully and spot suspicious behavior and give the staff the authority and capability to react efficiently to incidents, detain the perpetrator, and collect usable evidence.

Target Hardening

At first glance, target hardening in stores can be tricky because deterrence contradicts the inviting image of retail. However, security has become a natural feature of retail sales, even up to the point that visible security measures add the perception of value to products. Target hardening measures include visible real and dummy security equipment, alert sales and security staff, visible determination of the staff to protect the product including the willingness of the company to go all the way in charging perpetrators, store design, warning stickers, and procedures. Some stores even display CCTV print screens showing actual or staged theft attempts.

One important feature of retail target hardening is the exit from the store. In addition to the presence of security guards, checking of bags and receipts, and other procedures, the actual door has an important role in loss prevention. Probably the best type of door that would deter a potential thief is the revolving (turning) kind. Revolving doors are standard in retail; as such, they do not intimidate customers. Still, a criminal may be deterred by revolving doors because of the slowed exit and the possibility of being trapped.

Store Design

Store design is a crucial element of loss prevention. Store design starts with keeping the store orderly and tidy (including the fitting rooms), which helps employees to see whether something is missing. Loss prevention design includes adequate lighting, wider rows, locating the register next to exits, separating entrances and exits, and using one-way gates to distinguish between the two. Moreover, it requires properly locating valuable items, such as placing small expensive items in locked cabinets behind the counter and not displaying valuable items openly on shelves close to entrances and exits.

Internal Theft

Crimes such as theft and fraud committed by employees, or with the assistance of employees, are the biggest concern of retailers. Apart from stealing the actual product, internal theft includes the theft of cash and fraud against the store and against customers. There are countless models of employee theft and fraud; I will mention the most common ones.

Removal of cash from the register is the simplest form of employee theft. In general, the employee who steals cash often will not try to conceal the crime because he knows that he will be one of many suspects. Other forms of theft of cash include more sophisticated methods such as intentional failing to record a sale or to void it after the customer has left, and then taking the cash (causing the theft of cash eventually to appear as inventory shortage); under-ringing the amount of merchandise; refunding fraudulent purchases; and abusing employee discounts by selling merchandise to accomplices at a lower price and then attempting to return it for a full refund without a receipt in a different store.

Apart from the theft of cash, theft of merchandise is also likely to occur at points of sale. The most common form of theft involves concealing the product and secretly taking it out of the store during breaks. One of the most popular methods of theft is called "sweethearting," which is basically passing merchandise over the counter to accomplices who pretend to buy it as ordinary customers.

Many times, the stealing employee is working with external accomplices (either recruiting or being recruited), and in some cases the theft goes far beyond stealing and involve sophisticated methods to conceal the theft. For example, hackers may reach the retail computer and destroy lists of inventory to cover theft activities.

Moreover, employee dishonesty affects not only the employer but also customers. Theft that affects customers includes overcharging and incorrect change. However, more sophisticated methods include copying a customer's credit card information and using it for card-not-present transactions over the Internet. Sophisticated methods go to the extent of copying the actual credit card with a skimming device and recording typing of the personal identification number with the CCTV camera.

Internal Theft Prevention

After pre-employment background screening, internal theft prevention includes selective privileges given to employees and implementations of strict procedures; control and investigation of loss; and the ability to notice suspicious behavior and deter employee theft using fear of prosecution by being determined to file charges for every case of theft.

Red Flags

It is crucial to perform employee assessments regularly to single out indicators of suspicious behavior. The assessment should include the frequency of refunds, sales cancelations, and so forth. Certain occurrences and behaviors could indicate fraudulent activity at the point of sale:

* Frequent shortages of cash during the shift of a specific employee
* High number of refunds or voids

- Frequent customer complaints about incorrect change, overcharging, or not receiving receipts
- A rise in inventory loss
- Declining number of sales
- Receipts found in trash
  Some behaviors can also indicate financial problems:
- Frequently borrowing money from colleagues
- Frequently changing watches, jewelry, cell phones, etc.
- Large visible oscillations in financial situation
- Offering personal and household items for sale to colleagues
- Frequent mood oscillations

Prevention and Deterrence Measures

The basis of prevention and deterrence can be summed up in a few principles:
- Limited privileges given to employees;
- Establishment of several levels of authorization for vulnerable processes such as refunds, voids, discounts, etc; for example, only managers should be able to return merchandise to the floor after approving the reason for a return or void;
- Frequent announced and unannounced controls of inventory and the register;
- A store or shift manager should be able to know which employee used the register and when. Ideally, only one person should use one register during one shift;
- Keeping track of employees' accomplishments, behaviors, and basically all performance indicators;
- Video surveillance pointed at the register so that it is able to record usable resolution footage of transactions, registering ring-ups and actual products that pass over the counter;
- Determination to take fraudulent employees to court is one of the most successful deterrence strategies.

REFERENCES

[1] 2013 Global Cargo Theft Threat Assessment, FreightWatch International Supply Chain Intelligence Center. www.freightwatchintl.com/node/1602.
[2] International Road Transport Union, Attacks on Driver of International Heavy Goods Vehicles, 2008. http://www.internationaltransportforum.org/IntOrg/ecmt/crime/pdf/08AttackSurvey.pdf.
[3] Lieutenant Commander C.T. Mansfield, Modern Piracy: The Impact on Maritime Security, U.S. Navy, 2008.
[4] The Centre for Retail Researching, The 2011 Global Retail Theft Barometer Survey, Nottingham, England, 2011. www.retailresearch.org/grtb_currentsurvey.php.

CHAPTER 10

Human Capital

HUMAN RESOURCES

In corporations, security cooperates closely with the human resources department, especially in fields such as pre-employment screening, control of employees' user profiles, and mitigation of security risks related to individual job terminations as well as to massive redundancies.

Pre-Employment Screening

A bad hire can be extremely expensive for a company. Direct losses are significant, such as cost of hire, training, severance pay, and cost of rehire. However, indirect losses that occur through the loss of productivity, thefts of goods and information, and the negative impact on the morale and reputation of the company can be devastating. According to numerous sources [1–5], the percentage of bad hires in managerial positions exceeds 50% worldwide. We actually know a lot about the impact of a bad hire on a company but often do not analyze its causes deeply.

Human resources naturally concentrate on the education and skills of the candidate although, in reality, personality factors are the main cause of most job terminations. It is impossible to acquire the exact percentages or check the credibility and trace the original sources of information. However, numerous sources [1–5] state that:

- Almost half of all job applications have intentional errors.
- As many as one-third of all resumes contain absolute lies about work history, accomplishments, and capabilities of the candidate.
- Almost 10% of applicants exaggerate their level of education.
- Some 15% of workers have an addiction problem.

The difference between the human resources pre-employment process and the one performed by security is that human resources pre-employment processes try to determine whom to hire, whereas security pre-employment processes concentrate on determining whom not to hire.

A pre-employment process starts with the vacancy announcement, which can sometimes be reckless and contain privileged information such as the complete job description of a position that should be confidential. For example, a vacancy announcement for the open position of information technology (IT) security specialist can contain information about the IT security systems used by the organization that can greatly assist a hacker in executing an attack.

Certain organizations facing higher risk prefer to publish unidentifiable vacancy announcements. This means that they do not publish the name of the organization. The reason is to minimize the risk of persons with bad intentions using the opportunity to become employed by the organization or getting the opportunity of an interview to gain access to the facility for other purposes. For the same reason, organizations sometimes prefer not to conduct the first round of interviews on their premises but in a different location, such as the office of a contracted headhunting company. They also may not reveal the identity of the company to all candidates, but only to those who have advanced to the final stages of the employment process.

Pre-employment screening is an integral part of the hiring process and is performed by security during the final stages of the pre-employment process. The level of pre-employment screening depends on the position. It can range from a simple check of criminal record and opinion from the previous employer for lower positions to the level that would include thorough interviews, careful checking of documents, and verifications for senior and sensitive positions. Hereafter, we will analyze pre-employment screening for positions that require more attention.

Apart from looking for inconsistencies in the interview and documents, we will verify all significant information received through the interview and through documents by matching them with each other. For instance, we will request documents to back the statements given by the candidate during the interview, and/or verify them in direct contact with a previous employer, school, and so forth. It is important for a pre-employment screening interview, just as for any other type of security interview we perform (questioning, investigation, etc.), that the candidate present as many documents as possible, including identification, diplomas, certificates, and other material proof. Verification of information in direct contact with employers and schools should not be done with the contact provided by the candidate but using a contact received through independent sources.

The interview is the central part of screening. We will thoroughly analyze interviewing further on in this chapter, but here I will mention some of its basic principles. The main goals of interviewing are to notice suspicious signs in behavior and inconsistencies in statements. We can achieve that only if we lead the conversation and prevent the interviewee from taking it into his comfort zone. To keep the conversation flowing, which is the only way to notice changes in behavior and discover inconsistencies, we must ask open questions. These types of questions require the interviewee to answer descriptively instead of responding with short yes and no answers. Another principle is not to jump from one subject to another, but to actually exhaust one subject before moving on to the next. If we prepare questions in advance and do not allow the answers of the interviewee to take us to further questions, we are likely to miss clues. Basically, we will direct the question toward particulars in answers that require more research or appear to be inconsistent.

Pre-employment screening covers three life periods:

- Background
- Present situation
- Future plans

Background

Background checks should focus on the following factors:

- Education history
- Employment verification
- Social aspects
- Stability factors
- Criminal background

Because of the simplicity of producing false certificates in today's world, the only sure way to verify is by directly contacting the schools. One more thing to pay attention to is the fact that the employment market is filled with false diplomas and certificates. Numerous companies offer "life experience" diplomas. In fact, such companies (registered as companies, usually at some distant offshore location) have names resembling the names of real universities: "Bradford University," "Almeda University," and so forth. Moreover, these companies provide clients with verification of the diploma in case of inquiry. Basically, employees in their 24/7 call centers will confirm that the person who is presenting their diploma was indeed a student at their "university."

A complete detailed investigation of the applicant's employment history, including dates of employment, position, salary, job duties, achievements, and work habits, is a must.

A more careful check of social background can reveal troublesome potential. We are hiring not only professionals but individuals who will sit in the office across the corridor for 9 hours every day for the next couple of years and who need to interact socially with others in the workplace. We usually concentrate on the childhood period and investigate the family situation, neighborhood, and school history. More intensive checks that are usually performed by government agencies can involve interviews with anybody who knows or previously knew the candidate, such as teachers, friends, coworkers, neighbors, and family members. However, for private companies, such thorough checks would be over the line, might be illegal, and might lead to a lawsuit.

A common red flag is the tendency toward instability. Frequent changes of job often indicate problems, especially when the moves are not logical in terms of higher salary and larger responsibility.

Criminal background checks are essential. Even minor crimes should raise concerns.

Present Situation

Present situation investigation can provide us with valuable information concerning liability of the candidate. We certainly have to make sure that the person sitting in front of us is really who he or she claims to be. This includes dismissing the possibility that the candidate changed his or her name. Other points to be checked are current financial situation, family or relationship situation, circle of friends, and type of connection with the in-laws, residence and neighborhood, and such. If it is allowed by law, some companies require a thorough check of credit history, medical (physical and mental) evaluation, and drug tests and may even conduct a polygraph test.

One more particular to pay attention to is the spouse of the candidate, including addiction problems, criminal background, or, for example, employment with the competition.

These data will help establish the current economic and social profile as well as views on points that are crucial in your institution. It will also give an indication of the main character features of the candidate.

Future Plans

Determining possible life scenarios is especially important in institutions with strict privileged information and privacy policies. It is important to determine the future plans of the candidate by investigating the motives for employment. We will also investigate future plans, such as formal study, as well as plans that have the potential to change the financial situation of the candidate drastically, such as buying a house, parenting, and so forth.

User Profiles

User profiles are permissions, benefits, and access settings for each position in the company that control what particular employees can receive, access, and do. User profiles are determined based on seniority and position requirements and include features such as whether the employee will receive a desktop or laptop computer and the type of mobile phone, company car, etc., as well as whether he or she is entitled to bonuses and other benefits.

However, the concern of security related to user profiles is the employee's access rights, both physical and electronic. A proper system of controls and approvals of access rights is one of the fundaments of information security and a tool that has an important role in preventing and detecting internally committed frauds, thefts, and information leakage. The philosophy behind user profiles and access rights is the principle of least privilege, which limits the access of employees to sensitive information, crucial services and applications, and physical spaces only to features that are absolutely crucial for their work tasks.

User profiles are the responsibility of the human resources department in companies, but with the close participation of security. Access rights are usually proposed by the direct supervisor, granted by the human resources department after approval by the security department (information security), and are executed by security (permission of physical access including where and when an employee can enter) and information and communications technology (permission to use IT systems including what can be accessed, the allowed hours of access, and the level of permissions, such as to create, read, edit, and delete records).

User profiles can be standard or customized. Standard user profiles could be identical rights given to, for instance, all employees in a department or all employees at the same hierarchy level, or could be predefined rights set for each position. This basically means that there are predefined user profiles and that an employee would get an existing user profile.

On the other hand, custom profiles are considered to be a higher security model of information and physical access control but they require more effort and are more difficult to control. Custom profiles are rights that are given individually to each employee separately based on a request by the employee's direct supervisor. In general, the supervisor would check the boxes on a checklist that contains all physical and electronic features and models of access for each employee. The checklist would be then challenged and approved by the security department before the rights are granted by the human resources department.

Job Terminations

Job terminations are never pleasant. Aside from the aspect of empathy, whether they are individual job terminations or massive redundancies, job terminations carry numerous security concerns and risks.

Every company should have a policy that states who must be notified when someone's employment is about to end, and what each of the functions must do, and when.

An employee who is in the process of leaving still has access to the company's network, information, and assets that, with the fact that he or she might be upset, could result in serious damage. Given the chance, a leaving employee could seriously damage the company's systems, steal information, and/or sabotage equipment, processes, or products.

Ideally, the employee should not be allowed to access the physical and virtual work area starting from the moment he or she was informed about the job termination. However, to have a safe job termination, the company must have a system in place that would facilitate it. Basically, to avoid misunderstandings, all employees should know from the beginning of their employment how job terminations would be performed if they happened. An employee would be much more likely to accept that he or she cannot access his or her work area or tools (including IT systems) or that he or she may be escorted out of the building by security officers, if that policy of the company applies to all employees.

Another condition is the assured continuity of the processes. It would be difficult to terminate the job of an employee safely if he or she holds a crucial position and there is no one who could temporarily replace him or her, or if is he or she is the single point of contact between the company and its key clients. The former employee should be dispossessed of all company-owned property, including technological resources such as computer and mobile phones and intellectual property such as corporate files containing, for example, customer, sales, and marketing information. Also, the company must have the ability to access all data on which the employee has been working, including records, logs, and complete e-mail correspondence. Such ability is important for business continuity, but it could also be of legal significance if the company and former employee engage in a legal battle.

Denial of access should be not only virtual but also physical. Security should immediately cancel all access control privileges granted to the employee and repossess access control badges and keys.

SECURITY OF CORPORATE TRAVELERS AND EXPATRIATES

In past decades, with the need of businesses to seek new markets and lower production costs in remote places, international travel, including long-term and short-term assignments, rapidly increased in frequency and distance. Business travelers and expatriates are vulnerable to numerous risks ranging from pick pocketing, health risks, and accidents to political violence, kidnapping for ransom, and terrorist attacks. In this chapter, we will analyze the duty of care responsibilities of companies for their employees and dependents who travel and live in foreign countries as part of their work duties.

The first thing companies should do to protect employees who are traveling and living in foreign countries is to understand the scope and severity of risks associated with them. The second precondition is the existence of infrastructure involving corporate functions in charge of making decisions and executing tasks concerning business travel. Proper travel management requires close cooperation and a reliable system of approvals between functions, both in the headquarters and in the country of destination, such as business management, corporate security, human resources, persons facilitating travel arrangements (such as secretaries), functions in charge of medical and insurance issues, and the actual business travelers and their dependents. However, corporate security designs the system strategy, anticipates and assesses risks, coordinates and manages other involved functions, and takes practical steps in securing travelers.

Whereas property crimes represent the largest portion of incidents associated with corporate travel, terrorism, kidnapping, and civil unrest are the most significant security risks in terms of impact. Unrest in Tunisia in 2011 and in Ukraine in 2014 reminds us that disruptions and violence may occur at any time and anywhere. The increasing frequency and impact of terrorist attacks all over the world do not offer much comfort.

Moreover, the risk of kidnapping for ransom is a major threat to business travelers. In some countries, kidnapping for ransom of international staff has even become the largest concern of international companies.

Civil Unrest and Riots

Civil unrest and riots can occur practically anywhere. Just in 2011 and 2012, over 150 significant riots occurred across the world, including Africa, the Middle East, Asia, and South America, but also in countries such as Canada, the United Kingdom, Italy, Greece, Turkey, and Bulgaria, leaving over 3,000 dead and thousands injured. The number of casualties among foreign nationals who were simply in the wrong place at the wrong time is significant. Moreover, in some cases foreign businesses and foreign nationals are being targeted. For example, in May 2014, thousands of protesters in Vietnam attacked as many as 200 foreign-owned factories.

Many riots start out as peaceful demonstrations. The time before a peaceful demonstration can turn into a violent one and become a riot, civil unrest, or even a civil war and revolution can sometimes be short.

Terrorism

Apart from ideology-motivated terrorism and the risk to foreigners and foreign businesses of being victimized by either a terrorist group or individuals supporting its agenda, in recent years terrorism has not only intensified but has widened its program by moving closer to organized crime. For example, Al-Qaeda in the Islamic Maghreb in North Africa, which is considered to be one of the wealthiest terrorist organizations, is mainly financed by ransom kidnappings of foreign nationals who are visiting or working in North Africa. However, classic terrorist attacks such as those with car bombs and suicide bombing attacks are popular, especially in countries such as Somalia, Sudan, Nigeria, Iraq, Afghanistan, Pakistan, and North Africa. It is no coincidence that African and Middle Eastern countries, which have the highest number of terrorist attacks, also have the highest number of recorded kidnappings for ransom.

Kidnapping for Ransom

Most kidnapping cases go unreported. According to several sources [6–13] only 10% to 20% of cases are reported, although it is impossible to draw accurate numbers. However, according to numerous reports [6–13], globally between 10,000 and 16,000 people are kidnapped every year. Although it is estimated that foreign nationals represent around 10% of kidnappings, the ransom paid for kidnapped foreigners represents up to 90% of the estimated $500 million annual global takings for the kidnapping industry. The most vulnerable foreigners are not top executives, but actually simple employees who are less protected and often engage in fieldwork. Companies would certainly be willing to pay less ransom for lower-grade employees, but because top executives are more protected, the assessment of risk and reward favors lower-grade professional positions as targets. Successful kidnapping requires collected intelligence about the target and preparation, on average some 2–3 weeks of surveillance, although the timing is becoming shorter as kidnappers increasingly use social media Web sites to collect information. Employees and their dependents who spend a longer period of time in a risky country are much more at risk of traditional kidnapping for ransom than business travelers who are visiting for a few days. On the other hand, victims of express kidnapping (the victim is held for a short time for a small ransom or forced to withdraw cash from an automated teller machine) are usually chosen randomly.

Another form of kidnapping is illustrated in the case of Edo de Ronde, a Dutch marketing consultant who was kidnapped in South Africa after his company answered a fake advertisement for scrap metal, agreed to buy $5.3 million worth of railroad tracks, and sent Mr de Ronde to meet with the sellers in Johannesburg. Before his trip, Mr de Ronde received sellers' financial statements and reports, which were very professional forgeries. Mr de Ronde was kidnapped when he arrived at the guest house where the meeting was supposed to take place. He was released 2 days later when his company paid a ransom of roughly $30,000.

Virtual kidnapping is especially popular in Mexico. For example, a perpetrator may call a family, falsely stating that their family member has been kidnapped and demanding that they quickly transfer money to a certain account to ensure his safe release.

Kidnapping hotspots around the globe have stayed more or less the same in the past decade, with the riskiest countries remaining Mexico, Afghanistan, Iraq, Pakistan, Somalia, Venezuela, Colombia, Nigeria, Algeria, Yemen, and Haiti.

Many kidnappings are resolved in the first few days afterward; as many as 90% are resolved within 60 days. However, only 10% of Somalia piracy kidnappings are resolved within the first 2 months; most cases last over 200 days, and some even last over a year [6–13].

Most kidnappings happen in close proximity to the home or office of the victim and with the help of people who personally know the victim. It is estimated that some 90% of victims survive the kidnapping. In most cases, victims are released after the ransom has been paid with no police involved, whereas a smaller number of victims are released without payment. According to sources [6–13], only 6% of victims are rescued whereas only 2% of victims manage to escape.

For companies, it is crucial to acknowledge the risk of kidnapping and have a clear strategy for dealing with it.

Risk Factors

A company cannot protect its employees from being kidnapped unless the employees completely understand the risks and take on the largest part of protecting their own safety.

In the age of over-sharing, we use social media Web sites to share everything from travel plans and lunch arrangements to wealth information and precise should-be-private information about family members, including their places of work, schools they attend, and photos.

Businessmen are often distinguished by behaviors that expose them to collection of intelligence against them, identification as profitable targets, and, finally, becoming victims of kidnapping.

While working on expanding their professional networks, especially on professional social media sites such as LinkedIn, business professionals often forget to be selective and cautious, especially when the connection seems to have the business potential and the contact may result in a business deal. They may inform contacts whom they do not know personally about exact dates when they will be visiting their country and agree to a meeting or even initiate it. They sometimes even travel to a foreign country to meet a social media connection solely motivated by a bogus story and a hunch.

A good businessman is always on time and consistent and usually is horrified at the idea of varying his routine and being intentionally late to a meeting or showing up early.

Another risk factor is the need to show off and maintain a high profile, including craving attention by being confidently loud, driving head-turning cars, wearing expensive clothes, and flashing status symbols such as expensive watches and jewelry and top-shelf mobile phones and tablets.

Business Travel

The security process regarding business travel is divided into six phases:
- Forecasting security, safety, and health risks
- Hotel and airline (route) clearance
- Preparation for the trip and arrival
- Routine
- Contingency

Forecasting

Forecasting requires a mechanism to collect precise and relevant intelligence about existing and potential security, safety, and health risks; classify the risks; and implement security measures accordingly, including the stoppage of planned travel and safe return of those who are already at risk. Most corporations contract specialized companies that regularly collect and send information concerning the countries of interest. The regular reports contain security, safety, and health information with levels of risk, as well as forecasts and their impact on businesses and people. Emergency reports contain breaking news on immediate risks and incidents.

However, most corporations also require that international affiliates and local security managers produce regular security reports and regularly update travel information guides that contain all of the information required by travelers, such as food and health safety, local customs, do's and don'ts, security concerns, and important phone numbers. Travelers should be able to access the travel information guides easily.

Based on the reports, corporate security teams determine the risk rating for the country. The most common ways to classify risk, especially concerning the risk of terrorism and political violence, are descriptive (e.g., insignificant, low, medium, high, and extreme) and use color coding (e.g., green, blue, yellow, red, and black). For example, the insignificant (green) level represents the regular level of threat; low (blue) requires generally tighter security controls; medium (yellow) requires alleviated measures designed to protect from a specific risk and implies limitation of corporate travel to the country; high (red) requires maximum protective measures, evacuation of all unnecessary staff and dependents, and a strict travel ban; and extreme (black) implies an immediate complete evacuation. The assessment should include risky dates such as commemorations, holidays, or anniversaries of terrorist attacks when travel should be restricted. However, having a proper assessment requires the constant effort of collecting and processing information.

Hotel and Airline (Route) Clearance

Apart from assessing and forecasting the security situation, a proper setup requires that a security assessment and clearance be proactively performed regarding acceptable airlines and hotel accommodations at the destination. An acceptable airline should have a good security record. Ideally, the connection should be a nonstop flight or with as few takeoffs and landings as possible and only using airports with high security standards and a good passenger screening system.

Hotel pre-assessment includes several steps. First, the hotels should be in good neighborhoods, including being relatively close to the office while making sure that risky areas are not on the route from the hotel to the office. Also, if demonstrations and riots are probable, the hotel should not be in or close to areas where demonstrations usually occur. If, for example, there is a risk of sports hooliganism, the hotels should not be on the route of hooligans or close to sports facilities. The hotel itself should have a good level of security. A local security manager is required to communicate with the chief of security of the hotel, be able to request special attention for its guests, conduct security assessments of the rooms, and choose rooms that comply with security requirements. In general, acceptable rooms should be located between the second and fifth floors, away from the elevator or stairwell. Ideally, if the elevators and stairwell are on the opposite sides of the corridor, the room should be in the middle between them. Finally, a local security manager should have facility files for all approved hotels, which should contain security and emergency information such as the phone numbers of hotel management and security, the proximity to medical facilities, main and alternative routes to and from the office, and so forth.

Preparation for the Trip and Arrival

Apart from bookings, which should be in accordance with defined rules, preparations for the trip include awareness training for the traveler and arrangements such as pickup from the airport, an assigned driver responsible for the movements of the traveler during his visit, and, if necessary, security escort arrangements.

Because the arrival phase is especially vulnerable, it needs to be well thought out, prepared, and executed. Many kidnappings occur during pickup from the airport and travel from the airport to the hotel. In some cases, a kidnapper may pretend to be a taxi driver or someone offering assistance, but he may also pretend to be the driver sent by the company to pick up the traveler. There are also known cases of kidnappers hijacking a car that is on its way to pick up a traveler from the airport, waiting for the visitor, and then kidnapping him once he gets into the car. Kidnappers may target expensive-looking cars that are driving toward the airport. After hijacking the car, they may search for a board with the name of the visitor or the name of the company, or simply find the name of the company on other documents in the car and prepare a welcome board themselves. One ways to avoid such a scenario is to give the traveler a file containing the picture of the driver and a welcoming code word before his departure, and to instruct him what to do in case he is approached by anyone else.

Apart from the pickup file, security awareness training (or a security awareness presentation that could be handed or e-mailed to the traveler) should address the following issues:

- Travel—This part of training should contain subjects such as import and export restrictions, proper packing, and airline and airport security measures; protection of business and personal information during travel; airplane seat selection, such as choosing a window or center seat to be less exposed in case of hijacking; reaction in case of hijacking, etc.
- Arrival—Being alert and aware of friendly strangers and sticking to the instructions written in the pickup file.
- Hotel—Protecting information (business, personal, and movements) and property; never leaving the room key at the reception (a room key at the reception is a clear sign that the guest is not in the room); knowing the uniforms of the hotel staff (criminals often pretend to be employees of the hotel); being aware that the room could be bugged and monitored by a foreign intelligence agency that is searching for classified information or weaknesses and vulnerabilities in behavior that could be used for blackmail.
- Routine—Using only reliable transport; not showing off (whether by appearance or during conversation); varying routine whenever possible; being aware of risky (restricted) areas and risky situations, etc.
- Workplace—Not sharing personal information with local staff; not leaving sensitive documents or valuables around the office; being aware that although the

office is probably the safest place to be, there still could be risks associated with it (most kidnappings occur with the assistance of someone who personally knows the victim); knowing that office phones and computers are probably monitored.

- Emergency—Knowing whom to call and how to behave in case of an emergency, whether when feeling insecure after being assaulted or robbed or if the traveler is arrested. Also, a traveler should know what to do in case of, for example, a riot or terrorist attack.

Routine

The daily tasks of the visitor should be arranged so that they allow an unpredictable routine. Also, local staff, including the assigned driver, should not know the complete schedule of the visitor but should receive only need-to-know information at the latest possible moment. If, for example, a certain part of the schedule has been announced in the media, it should require special attention and a higher level of security, including even a security escort.

Contingency

A visitor should know the arrangements in case of an emergency and whom to call and what to do. Basically, upon arriving, a visitor should be given an emergency contact list, a map of the city with evacuation assembly points marked on it, and an explanation of steps to be taken in case of an emergency.

Evacuation assembly points are facilities, often hotels, that are relatively secure and easily accessible to employees and their dependents. In case of need, the employees and their dependents could be safely transported together from the assembly points out of the country, or wait for the threat to diminish. Hotels that are chosen as potential assembly points should also be the ones booked for visitors.

Expatriates

Employees who spend a longer time in a risky country are especially vulnerable to being targeted by terrorists and kidnappers. Moreover, expatriates are exposed to health and safety risks and could be potentially more seriously affected by poor sanitary conditions and low-quality medical care than are short-term business travelers. Expatriates are also vulnerable to more risks such as carjacking and residence intrusion. Some studies suggest that dependents are more targeted by kidnappers than actual business personnel.

Security

Security risks range from random petty crimes and being affected by political violence to targeted burglaries, carjacking, terrorist attacks, and kidnappings.

Securing expatriates requires:

- Continuously assessing and listing probable risks and mapping risky areas
- Understanding local laws and customs
- Providing trainings both for the expatriates and their dependents on specific local issues such as how to mitigate risks, emergency communication, and reaction during emergencies, etc.
- Creating a safe environment including selecting and securing the residence (including arrangements such as fencing, lighting, safe room setup, electronic security devices and alarm monitoring, manned guarding); helping find a safe school; providing a secure but not attention-catching vehicle with no company logos on it, which is thus less likely to be stolen (based on police reports); and providing lists of approved taxi drivers, leisure facilities and restaurants, and restricted areas, etc.
- Providing a secure working arrangement such as allowing flexible working hours that allow routines to be broken; allowing a more relaxed dress code; avoiding situations that put expatriates at risk by providing additional security measures for necessary assignments carrying higher risk, etc.
- Always being available and prepared to respond to an emergency
- Having updated emergency plans for dealing with security issues and lists of contacts who can assist in case of an emergency

Safety

Apart from security risks, expatriates could also be vulnerable to safety hazards that must be assessed and addressed, such as hazardous traffic conditions, weather conditions, and the probability and impact of natural disasters. For example, safety issues should be taken into account when choosing a suitable residence and vehicle or, for instance, when planning a field trip.

Health

Like all other security and safety issues, the issue of health risks such as disease, poor sanitary conditions, inadequate medical facilities, lack of medication, and food safety issues must be transparently discussed with a candidate for expatriation. Any seemingly insignificant health issues the candidate might have, including regular medication or special dietary requirements, should be taken seriously and paralleled with the actual situation and availability in the destination country.

In addition to having health insurance, it is crucial to assess medical facilities and choose appropriate ones, as well as have a contract with the chosen facility to ensure priority treatment.

It is also important to create a system that would ensure that in case of a medical emergency, employees are taken to the chosen facility. One way is to make cards for expatriates (which they would be obligated to carry) that contain instructions in local languages about where to be transported in case of a medical emergency, whom to call, allergies, medication requirements, blood type, and so forth.

Expatriate Files

Although in most cases corporations pay ransom for kidnapped employees, because risks involve more than just kidnapping for ransom it is important to have expatriate files that could assist the police or private contractors in tracking the perpetrators and/or victims. Basically, expatriate files should contain personal information such as fingerprints, blood type, dental records, and specific characteristics such as moles, scars, and tattoos. The file should also contain information that could help track the movement of the victim (or perpetrator) such as credit card information, mobile phone International Mobile Station Equipment Identity number, expensive pieces of jewelry that could appear on the black market, special medications required by the expatriate, and such.

Planning for Evacuation

Efficient evacuation from a foreign country that has become hostile or hazardous requires thorough and careful planning and coordination and speedy execution. An efficient evacuation planning and execution encompasses all actions carried out by internal and external facilitators who are responsible for the evacuation. The facilitators of the evacuation include all external services and collaborators that will provide accurate and timely reports and alerts in case the situation is deteriorating and organize, perform, and assist the safe movement of evacuees and provide temporary shelter; as well as internal elements such as the crisis management team and the evacuating expatriates and their dependents. We can divide the evacuation into five phases:

- Plan
- Awareness/routine
- Standby
- Movement
- Evacuation

Plan

The evacuation plan is made at the beginning of the employees' presence in the remote location; while the general plan is revised and refreshed annually, specific information about the expatriates is refreshed with any new change, such as a new arrival or change of residence. Basically, the general plan should exist before the first expatriates arrive.

The evacuation plan consists of lists, contact information, communication models of all involved parties, division of duties, and responsibilities through all the phases of the evacuation, and detailed evacuation instructions.

The plan must contain:

- Division of responsibilities and tasks during awareness, standby, movement, and evacuation, including clearly defining the models of collecting and distributing information during routine and when the situation deteriorates.
- Briefing for expatriates and their dependents about their responsibilities during evacuation, what to take with them and what to leave, and how to dress. For example, a list of desirable items would be as follows:
  - Clothing:
    - Durable long-sleeved shirt and trousers are to be worn.
    - Neutral colors are preferred: gray, beige, etc.
    - Shoes are to be sturdy with good grip and are to be suitable for running if required.
    - Warm, windproof jacket and head covering
    - Breathable rain jacket (Gore-Tex is preferred)
  - Items to be carried on person:
    - Passport
    - Wallet, containing credit cards and driver's license
    - Quantity of accepted currency (US dollars, euros, etc.) in small denominations
    - Mobile phone and handheld radio (if available)
    - Map of area, with key locations marked
  - Items to be carried in hand luggage (maximum 7 kg)
    - Photocopy of passport
    - Essential documents including: residency documents, birth certificates, marriage certificates, certificates of naturalization, and consular report of birth abroad (all in a waterproof bag)
    - Other items of an important or personal nature, including: photographs, children's school reports, adoption certificates, immunization records, prescriptions, financial records, etc.
    - 2-L water bottle
    - 3 days of lightweight, high-energy food
    - Lightweight waterproof jacket
    - Flashlight
    - Prescription drugs
    - Critical toiletries and sanitary items
    - Toilet paper
  - Items to be packed in luggage to be checked in (maximum 20 kg):
    - Clothing, toiletries, batteries, pocketknife, etc.
- Defined evacuation assembly points: Evacuation assembly points are safe havens where evacuees should gather before being transported in an orderly manner and escorted to points of departure (POD). Evacuation assembly points should be

facilities with the potential to provide temporary shelter to evacuees (often well-secured internationally owned hotels) that are relatively close to residences of most expatriates and easily accessible. They should also be located in such a way that evacuees can use several predefined routes to the main and alternative POD.

- Defined main and alternative POD: Points of departure should be airports, ports, or land border crossings that are easily accessible and likely to be operational during a crisis. It is advisable to exhaust all options for evacuation by air before considering evacuation by land or sea. When choosing the POD, the proximity should not be the only criterion, but also speed, route safety, and multiple available choices. For example, expatriates evacuating from Algiers, the capital of Algeria, would most likely use the Algiers airport for evacuation. However, during traffic jams, travel from the Hydra, the wealthy part of Algiers where expatriates are likely to reside, to the airport can take several hours. Also, in case of riot, downtown Algiers is likely to be blocked. On the other hand, the city of Oran, which is located 350 km to the west of Algiers, could be a better solution owing to a good highway that connects the two cities, the proximity of Oran to the Moroccan border by land and to Spain by sea, and the low probability of riots and violence. The plan should also contain a description of the POD in case the local transport infrastructure is not available and a private contractor is hired to transport the evacuees. Here is a template of POD information with the example of "Es Senia" Airport in Oran, Algeria:

Oran (ORN) Es Senia Airport
Lat/Long: 35.623,858 N/0.621,183 W
Elevation: 295 Feet (90 m)
Location: Near Oran, Algeria
Time zone: UTC+1
Max Runway: 10,039 × 148 feet (3060 × 45 m)
Surface: ASPHALT

- Maps with main and alternative routes from evacuation assembly points to POD with clearly marked reporting spots and safe houses. Reporting spots are defined places on the evacuation routes. Evacuees make a call to the evacuation coordinator when passing reporting spots to inform him about their progress and arrival to the POD. Safe houses are facilities on the evacuation route that can provide safety to evacuees in case of sudden need.
- The plan should also define countries to which the evacuees will be evacuated before being repatriated to their countries.

Awareness

Awareness (routine) requires the security situation to be monitored and security updates to be received regularly. During routine, all members of the crisis management team and expatriates and their families are annually briefed. Newly arriving expatriates should be briefed immediately upon arrival and the evacuation plan must be updated with their contact information. Otherwise, the plan is revised and updated annually. Upon arrival, expatriates and their dependents should register with their embassies, receive a copy of the evacuation plan, and prepare and maintain an evacuation kit.

Standby

Standby is announced by the crisis management team based on information that the situation might be aggravated. During the standby phase, all travel to the country should be banned and all unnecessary staff and dependents should be asked to leave the country. Standby also requires ensuring that all employees and external contractors know what to do and are able to do it. All preparations in case of evacuation should be made, such as identifying main and alternative means of transport, refreshing the agreement with a contracted security company that would escort evacuees to the POD, and ensuring that aircraft and speedboats provided by an external contractor are available and on standby. Expatriates need to have luggage prepared as instructed, a vehicle at hand with a full tank, and a fully charged cell phone; they must inform the crisis management coordinator about movements and be reachable at all times.

Movement

Movement is the phase when evacuation is almost certain. It requires the assembly of all evacuees in the evacuation assembly point (EAP). All evacuees and contracted support should be able to start evacuating on short notice.

Evacuation

Evacuation is carried out according to the plan and is coordinated and monitored by the evacuation coordinator. The POD team tracks the movement of evacuees to the airport, receives them, and escorts them to the aircraft. The reception team greets evacuees upon arrival at a safe haven and coordinates all accommodations and transfer arrangements.

REFERENCES

[1] Jacquelyn Smith, 10 of the Most Ridiculous Lies People Have Told on Their Resumes, Business Insider, August 7, 2014. www.businessinsider.com/ridiculous-lies-people-told-on-resumes-2014-8.
[2] Human Resources by the Numbers, Hire Right. www.hireright.com/Background-Check-Fast -Facts.aspx.
[3] Anne Fisher, Resume Lies Are on the Rise, Fortune, September 10, 2014. www.fortune.com/2014/09/ 10/resume-lies-are-on-the-rise/.
[4] Employment Screening Statistics, Trak-1. www.new.trak-1.com/emp_statistics.html.
[5] Industry Fast Facts: Hiring by the Numbers, Background Checks Express, Inc. www.backgroundchecks express.com/industry-fast-facts/.
[6] Rukmini Callimachi, Paying Ransoms, Europe Bankrolls Qaeda Terror, New York Times, July 29, 2014. www.nytimes.com/2014/07/30/world/africa/ransoming-citizens-europe-becomes-al-qaedas -patron.html.

[7] Sergio Ramos, Mexico: The Fight to End Kidnapping, Infosurhoy, April 11, 2014. http://dialogo -americas.com/en_GB/articles/saii/features/main/2014/04/11/feature-01.

[8] Adam Nossiter, Millions in Ransoms Fuel Militants' Clout in West Africa, New York Times, December 12, 2012. www.nytimes.com/2012/12/13/world/africa/kidnappings-fuel-extremists-in-western-africa .html?pagewanted=1&;_r=1.

[9] Steven Perlberg, The 20 Countries Where People Get Kidnapped the Most, Business Insider, December 12, 2013. www.businessinsider.com/top-20-countries-by-kidnapping-2013-12.

[10] Risk Map, Control Risks, 2014. www.controlrisks.com/riskmap.

[11] Associated Press, APNewsBreak: 4 Charged in "Virtual Kidnappings," Fox News, November 8, 2013. www.foxnews.com/us/2013/11/08/apnewsbreak-4-charged-in-virtual-kidnappings-targeting-random -immigrant.

[12] France Tops World Hostage List with Latest Kidnapping, France 24, February 20, 2013. http://www .france24.com/en/20130220-france-hostages-world-cameroon-nigeria-hollande-terrorists/.

[13] Somali Piracy: More Sophisticated Than You Though, Economist, November 2, 2013. www .economist.com/news/middle-east-and-africa/21588942-new-study-reveals-how-somali-piracy- financed-more-sophisticated-you.

CHAPTER 11

Confidentiality, Integrity, and Availability

CONFIDENTIALITY: BASIC INFORMATION SECURITY PRINCIPLES

In this chapter we will not discuss the technical aspects of information security but will briefly analyze its philosophy and key principles and the logic behind it.

Information security does not equal information technology (IT) security. Information security encompasses all information whether it is electronic, hardcopy, or spoken; as such, IT security is just one part of the concept of broad information security. The basic aims of information security are often summarized in three principles called the CIA triad (no connection to Central Intelligence Agency), which stands for confidentiality, integrity, and availability:

- *Confidentiality* means making sure that information is accessible only to people who have the right to see it.
- *Integrity* requires ensuring that information remains intact and unaltered.
- *Availability* implies that people who have the right to access information can have access to it when they need it. Basically, availability means that nothing should be able to block legitimate and timely access to information.

The exact origins of the CIA triad expression are unknown but the underlying concepts have been operative in a military context for millennia.

Confidentiality

Confidentiality requires procedures and measures aimed at controlling physical and technical access to information. For example, whereas physical security limits the possibility of unauthorized physical access to information (facility, IT infrastructure, etc.), IT security controls access to information through the IT system. Procedures aimed at preserving the confidentiality of information include:

- Management of user profiles and access rights
- Data classification (both electronic and hardcopy)
- Clean desk policy (clean workplace policy)
- Confidentiality and nondisclosure agreements with employees and contractors
- Password policy
- Rules and regulations for employee IT use
- Delivered trainings to employees and implemented procedures aimed at preventing, detecting, and stopping social engineering attacks

Integrity

The aim of the principle of integrity is to ensure that information remains intact and unaltered. An example of the compromised integrity of information can be any change in client information by a bank clerk to commit fraud. Integrity of information can be compromised through numerous fraud techniques such as forgeries, financial identity takeover, and copyright fraud.

Another example of a breach of integrity can be sabotage, such as the destruction of important hardcopy documents or vital information from the IT system. However, a breach of integrity of information does not have to be malevolent; it may be accidental. Information security is required to limit the possibility of a malevolent or accidental breach of integrity of information.

Availability

Denying access to information is a popular method of attack; the denial of service (DoS) attack is one of the most common models of attack. The primary aim of DoS attacks is to crash a Web site to make it unavailable to its users. This type of attack can be costly for organizations, especially for those relying on the availability of their Web site for orders and payments. Other factors that could lead to the lack of availability of important information include accidents, natural disasters, and manmade disasters.

Availability starts with simple backup procedures but also requires a proper business continuity management (BCM) and disaster recovery system that enables the availability of data, such as offsite disaster recovery with duplicated key services and applications.

INTEGRITY: COMBATING FRAUD

Anti-Fraud Circle

Fraud is basically any illegal and intentional deception made for personal gain. Fraud can be internal, external, or combined. Efficient fraud prevention is a systematic, continuous effort that requires close cooperation among all the functions in a company. Effective fraud risk management is an ongoing process of assessing risk, designing and implementing strategies, and evaluating their efficiency. It is managed through controls performed by control functions that have three primary objectives:

- Prevention
- Detection
- Reaction
  However, a complete anti-fraud circle is composed of:
- Prevention
- Detection of fraud or a reasonable indication that fraud has been committed
- Communication and reporting

- Reaction that includes investigation, disciplinary and legal proceedings, and mitigation of damage
- Design and implementation of improvement actions aimed at closing detected gaps

Prevention

Fraud prevention is the most important mechanism for combating fraud. It is imposed indirectly through the promotion of an honest and transparent working environment and activities aimed directly at preventing fraud, such as:

- Fraud risk assessment
- Pre-employment investigations and third-party due diligence
- Least-privilege system implemented through correct user profiles and access rights
- Communication and training
- Controls of specific processes
- IT system settings aimed at preventing internal and external fraud

Detection

The detection of fraud is the act of noticing fraudulent activity or its consequences, or having reasonable indications that fraud is or was committed. Fraud can be detected through regular work activity as result of announced or unannounced anti-fraud controls or through information received from an informer; it can be reported anonymously, or the information can come from a client or a partner in the form of a complaint or concern. Information about committed or possible fraud can also come from the police or through fraud forums (in case another company informs us that it has detected fraudulent activity that also might have affected other companies in the industry).

Detection requires elements such as:

- Hot lines and whistle-blower mechanisms including confidentiality and anonymity
- Controls, audits, and monitoring
- Internal informants
- IT system notifications aimed at detecting unusual occurrences
- Ability to process complaints in real time
- Membership in anti-fraud forums and workgroups
- Good contacts with law enforcement

Communication and Reporting

Prompt reporting through well-defined lines of communication is vital for efficient reaction to fraud. It is crucial for efficient investigation, timely closure of gaps, successful mitigation of damage, and disciplinary and legal measures against fraudsters. A prompt investigation would reduce the ability of fraudsters to cover up their actions. Moreover, the human resources department and legal department could be required by law to initiate disciplinary and legal measures within a certain time frame from the moment a fraud has been committed.

Reaction (Emergency Measures)

When information relating to actual or potential fraud is uncovered and communicated to relevant subjects in the company, it calls for an immediate unprejudiced investigation, closure of gaps, and preparation for potential disciplinary and legal measures. The investigation is usually the responsibility of the security department and internal audit. In case of internal fraud, it is conducted with the active assistance of the management of the organizational unit in which the fraud has been committed, which must provide all necessary data, documents, and required information; the IT department that performs all electronic forensic activities (logs, correspondence, etc.); and the accounting department, which can assist in forensic accounting activities and so forth. Mitigation of damage depends on the type of fraud and may include informing clients about self-protective measures, blocking the bank account of the alleged fraudster, and other measures.

Emergency measures include all actions aimed at closing gaps before sustainable improvement actions are implemented. It can include temporary reorganization of the organizational unit where fraud has been committed and the introduction of temporary emergency leadership of the unit.

Improvement Actions

Improvement (corrective) actions include changing the model of control of a certain process that appears to be vulnerable, changing procedures, improving the IT system setup, and so on.

Principle of Least Privilege

Least privilege is one of the key elements of fraud prevention. The principle of least privilege (POLP) is the practice of limiting access to the minimal level of people who will allow the normal function of a process. Applied to employees, POLP translates into giving people the lowest level of user rights that they can have and still do their jobs. The principle is also applied to programs and processes, not just people. The aims of the principle are to limit the possibility of fraud (by limiting the opportunity) and to lower potential damage of any security breach. It is also crucial for detecting a fraudster during a fraud investigation because it limits the number of people who have the opportunity to commit a fraud in certain parts of processes. The POLP principle would, for example, require that an entire process be executed by several people, where each person can have the procedural and technical ability to execute only his part of the process.

Control Levels

Control levels are an integral part of a company's anti-fraud system. An effective system of control levels is based on the control structure setup, which involves the segregation of duties and a clear definition of control activities at every level. Basically, control levels are composed of a combination of layers of control, including:

- Vertical hierarchical control (approval by higher hierarchical positions in one department)
- Horizontal controls (division of control responsibilities according to a natural professional division of a process: departments that perform parts of a process)
- Control functions (controls performed by several different functions that are responsible for the professional control of a process or part of process, such as process owners, security, compliance, and internal audit)
- Combination of diverse methods of control (checking logs, generating reports, approvals, observation, routine controls, unannounced audits, system settings, queries, four-eyes principle, etc.)

First Level of Control

According to the control levels model, the departments that own and perform a part of a certain process are the first level of control for that process. In a hierarchical dimension of the control, employees performing a certain activity are required to apply all rules that are part of the fraud prevention system, the team leader controls the employees, a supervisor controls the team leaders, a manager controls the supervisors, and so on. For example, employees control each other using the four-eyes principle of control; a team leader inspects the signatures to verify that the four-eyes principle was indeed used; a supervisor performs routine and unplanned inspections and receives systems reports if certain actions did not match the set parameters, etc. When a department has performed its part of the process, the second part of that process is performed in another department that checks the performance of the first department and is hierarchically controlled like the first one.

To simplify, in the case of a bank credit application process, the first department is the *front office* (employees working in the branch), which is responsible for the first part of the process, which consists of collecting all required documents, checking their authenticity, filling in the request, and sending the application to the *back office*. The *back office* is responsible for the second part of the process, which is to review the credit potential of the client based on the collected documentation. The first check the *back office* will do is to check whether the documentation collected by the *front office* is complete, whereas all additional steps in the approval process require the approval of a higher hierarchical level in the department. If, for example, the requested credit amount exceeds the approval competences of the *back office*, the back office will send the application to *credit risk*, which is then responsible for approving it according to documentation collected by the *front office* and the assessment performed by the *back office*. These departments horizontally share a process and are the first level of control of that process.

Second Level of Control

The second level of control is performed by control departments such as security and compliance. Security and compliance both check segments of the process that are within their scope of responsibility. For example, security will check whether all anti-fraud measures were implemented and whether a fraud occurred during the process, whereas compliance will check whether the first level performed its activities according to the laws, regulations, and internal procedures, as well as whether all activities aimed at preventing and detecting money laundering and terrorism financing were carried out. Both security and compliance will use different methods to execute their controls, such as randomly checking files to determine whether the documents were forged, all approvals were performed, and the whole process is compliant with laws, regulations, and procedures.

Third Level of Control

Internal audit is the third level of control. The internal audit department is in charge of performing scheduled and random audits to determine whether the systems of controls executed by the first level of control and the second level of control are indeed effective and properly set and performed according to procedures. Based on audits, the internal audit department will issue audit reports that contain an overview of deficiencies and the list of measures for improvement to be undertaken by involved departments, aimed at improving the entire process or its parts and closing gaps.

INTERNAL INVESTIGATIONS

Companies frequently face situations that call for investigations. A carefully structured approach is important for a systematic and well-timed investigation. However, the sensitive nature of investigations requires more than just structure, expertise, and creativity. It requires the commitment and support of the management, a balance between efficiency and privacy rights, and the proficiency of the investigator with local laws and company culture. You might solve the case, but failure to comply with these requirements could lead to lawsuits and serious damage to the reputation of the company.

There could be countless reasons for conducting internal investigations. The grounds for starting investigations could be property crimes, fraud, noncompliance with internal regulations and misconduct, sexual harassment and mobbing, alleged substance abuse, plagiarism, or employment application fraud (bogus degree or unfair candidate selection).

Possible Obstacles in Conducting Investigations

Corporate investigators face numerous internal and external obstacles that make investigations challenging. The most obvious external obstacles are legal boundaries that could restrict key elements of an investigation, such as certain forms of interview and certain interview questions, examination of e-mail correspondence, phone records, and any form of digital forensics, restrictions concerning video and audio recording without consent, and so on.

However, internal obstacles are much more influential than external ones. Without the full unlimited support of management, it is impossible to conduct unprejudiced and uninfluenced investigations. In most cases, investigations will not only fulfill their task but also reveal other wrongdoings that were ignored, supported, or even initiated by the management.

It is common for investigations to be guided by management and intentionally directed away from the actual target. Reasons are numerous and range from protecting certain people in the organization to hiding other flaws, misleading the investigation, and forging its results to achieve other objectives. Other objectives may include falsely accusing someone as a way to terminate his or her contract or turning the investigation findings toward situations that are insured. For example, a company may be insured against losses caused by external fraud and in case of internal fraud may try to present it as external to collect insurance. However, even after an uninfluenced investigation and its correct findings, in some cases companies may decide not to prosecute perpetrators so as not to jeopardize the reputation of the company or reveal other wrongdoings or misconduct. For the same reason, companies sometimes may not even employ internal disciplinary measures to punish the perpetrator. However, this would undermine the authority of the investigator and encourage further fraud.

Another serious obstacle is the seniority of the person who is being investigated, who may even be the direct supervisor of the investigator. Moreover, investigating colleagues may make it difficult to preserve good working relations and much needed communication and collaboration with peers. In many cases, security managers may opt to hire external investigators and not risk jeopardizing their working relationship with peers and superiors, and sometimes even their jobs.

Apart from receiving unlimited support and authority from management, which we have mentioned, the investigator must have access to all necessary information related to the case and processes, permission to inspect the physical workspace, the ability to conduct interviews with witnesses, and expert support in areas such as information and communication technology (ICT), accounting, legal, human resources, and issues related to specific business areas with which the investigator is not proficient.

Investigation Principles, Elements, and Structure

Whereas every investigation is different and each case requires a different approach and resources, principles and elements are required to have a successful investigation. Key principles of an investigation are:
- Independence of the investigators
- Authority

- Expertise
- Unprejudiced approach
- Well-organized and structured investigation
- Ability to think out of the box and be creative (the perpetrators certainly have it)
- Finding a balance between legal and ethical boundaries and the need to gather information
- Discretion
- Tact and diplomacy

The structures of investigations, including their key elements, are usually similar. The elements are as follows:

- Reaching a decision as to whether to start an investigation
- Identifying the lead investigator
- Preparing the scope, plan, and timeline of the investigation based on a premise
- Sealing off the virtual and physical crime scene
- Collecting and reviewing evidence
- Conducting interviews with witnesses
- Conducting interviews with suspects
- Documenting the investigation
- Reaching a conclusion
- Producing the final report

Reaching a Decision Whether to Investigate

In general, the decision whether to open an investigation depends on conflicting facts. Basically, if the perpetrator was caught red-handed and admits to committing a crime, there are no conflicting facts. However, we have to ask several questions to determine whether an investigation is required:

- Do we have enough material evidence for legal action against the perpetrator?
- Are we sure that we know the true extent of harm?
- Is there a possibility that other people were involved in the crime?
- Is there a possibility that other crimes could have been executed by the same perpetrator(s)?
- Is there a legal obligation to investigate?

Identifying the Lead Investigator and Team

Primary criteria for identifying the lead investigator are investigative knowledge and experience and specialized expertise. Not every investigator is able to lead all investigations and be equally successful in, for example, investigations that mainly examine accounting matters, digital forensics, or physical crime scenes. Certainly, for minor matters, and if there is no potential conflict of interest, an appropriate investigator could be the manager of the affected business unit. However, graver allegations call for more formal and independent investigations conducted by high-profile investigators.

The investigator should be someone who is impartial and unprejudiced. If the company is opting for an internal investigator, it must consider the internal hierarchy of the organization to avoid compromised objectivity.

In some cases, the investigator would be required by law to have necessary licenses that should be examined whether choosing an internal or external investigator.

The investigator should consider whether specialized expertise is required (such as IT, accounting, or legal), and if so, build the team of experts accordingly.

Scope, Plan, Timeline, and Methodology
Scope
Most investigations are based on a hypothesis, except those in which the scope of the investigation is simply to collect evidence to support an undisputed conclusion. Hypothesis-driven investigations can concern the identification of factual situations, root causes, roles, and perpetrators.

Investigators should avoid the trap of identifying a hypothesis too early in the process without considering the full range of reasonable theories. In that case, pieces of evidence that support a single presumption could be regarded as more significant than they really are, whereas other, more important pieces of evidence that do not support the presumption could be unintentionally disregarded.

Starting principles when determining the scope of an investigation are to consider multiple hypotheses and actively investigate them, as well as seek discomforting evidence. Basically, instead of trying to support a hypothesis with an investigation, we should attempt to prove it wrong.

During the course of the investigation, the investigator may become aware of issues that are not included in the original scope and continue to explore them with the approval of the stakeholder.

Plan and Timeline
In a nutshell, the approach toward internal investigations based on presumptions is not much different from the scientific hypothesis conformation experiment. The investigation plan should be based on three cyclic groups of activities:
- Coming up with hypotheses
- Gathering evidence
- Assessing the evidence

After coming up with the hypothesis, the next steps in making a plan are: understanding how to obtain and protect evidence; identifying required resources and specifics of the investigation; building a team and allocating duties based on expertise; making a time frame that consists of deadlines for specific actions performed by team members and a plan for how each step of the investigation supports the next step; setting the deadline for completing the investigation and producing the final report; and determining models of communication among team members, including the frequency of communication.

Methodology

Probably the most common method of structuring evidence during a hypothesis investigation is called hypothesis mapping (HM).

Hypothesis mapping is basically determining which hypothesis is true by graphically diagramming the investigation thinking process. It is carried out by visually sorting supporting and discomforting arguments, evidence and findings, and additional questions and steps needed to support or dismiss arguments. The process may eventually lead to a weak hypothesis being dismissed and a strong hypothesis being identified and reinforced with arguments and evidence.

Practically, HM consists of boxes and arrows linking the main question to the hypotheses, which are further linked to supporting and dismissing evidence. It starts with the main question that is the motive for the investigation. The question should be open-ended ("Who has committed the fraud?" rather than "Is John the person who committed the fraud?"). Under the main question, and graphically linked to it, we will list all probable answers: "John committed the fraud," "Peter committed the fraud," "Paul committed the fraud," and so forth. Under each answer we will add evidence and open questions, and under each question the list of further actions to be made. We might have to add answers during the process and link evidence dismissing one hypothesis to another which it supports. We will basically proceed until we identify the correct answer and have collected enough evidence to support our agenda.

Sealing Off the Crime Scene and Collecting Evidence

Making sure that evidence remains intact and is not tampered with is a crucial condition for collecting reliable evidence. In case of a discrete investigation, the actual sealing off of the virtual and physical crime scene (records freeze) is the moment that reveals the investigation. For example, seizing the computer and denying access to Microsoft Outlook and the company intranet to one suspect at a time and not all suspects at once may alert other involved employees and give them enough time to destroy evidence. This is why sealing off the crime scene and collecting all items that could provide evidence should be well thought-out, planned, and performed at once. Records freeze should include physical evidence that would require the physical space to be sealed off and seizing documents and other physical evidence, as well as electronic evidence that would require denial of access to IT systems.

Many companies have document destruction policies and schedules that could be required by law or based on internal regulations. Nevertheless, a freeze order, whose aim is to remove relevant documents from the destruction schedule, should be issued.

A freeze order should be an official internally approved document template that regulates the behavior of employees during an investigation and restricts their access to identified evidence.

Evidence may include physical objects, office space, vehicles, closed-circuit television footage, internal documents and files, access logs, expense reports, evidence of communication including e-mails and phone records, notes, computer hard drives, and basically anything that may be useful to the investigation.

Interviewing Witnesses and Suspects

Interviewing is one of the most important elements of an investigation. The basic goals of interviewing are to receive information that we are still missing, confirm the information we already have, obtain new leads, notice suspicious signs in behavior, and discover inconsistencies in statements and discrepancies between statements and evidence. This basically means that we need to have hypotheses, leads, information, and evidence to be able to conduct a successful interview.

Probably the most common mistake regarding interviews is that they are often carried out too early in the investigation process when we still do not have enough information and evidence to conduct a productive interview. Documents and evidence are an important part of the interview. Well-organized files with documents and evidence brought to the interview will not only help the investigator as references and argument tools, but will show the interviewee that the investigator is prepared and informed and has evidence at hand.

Other basic preconditions may make a difference between a fruitful interview and a bad one that could even jeopardize the investigation. The first precondition is the need to categorize interviewees in a logical ascending order of importance, starting with interviewees who have a lower profile and know less about the matter, to build up knowledge about the case and prepare for high-priority interviews. Preparations also should be done for each separate interview, which involves making a plan that arranges key points to be investigated and verified, including points learned or raised during previous interviews.

An important part of preparation, not only for an interview but for an entire case, is an investigation of the background and the key witness (suspect) and discovery of red flags in history or behavior patterns that should be addressed during the interview. Areas to look at are financial information, job performance, character features and relations with colleagues, criminal history, and so on. Depending on the nature of the case, we will want to look for relevant behavior patterns that could point to the suspect, such as signs of financial trouble or gambling addiction.

If you are not able (e.g., restricted by law) to record the interview, it will be difficult to keep track of questions and answers, pay attention to suspicious signs in the behavior of the interviewee and notice inconsistencies, and simultaneously take notes. It is advisable to have an assistant during the interview who will take notes and may act as a witness in case the interviewee later decides to change his statements.

The investigator is the person who leads the interview and should prevent the witness from taking control of the conversation and steering it to his comfort zone. Every interview should start with the investigator presenting the ground rules of the interview, including explaining who has authorized him to conduct the interview.

To have the conversation flowing, which is the only way to notice changes in behavior and discover inconsistencies, we must ask open-ended questions. Open-ended questions require the interviewee to answer descriptively instead of giving short yes and no answers. Another principle is not to jump from one subject to another, but actually to exhaust one subject before moving to the next one.

We certainly have to plan the interview and prepare subjects to explore and key questions. Still, if we prepare all questions in advance and do not allow the answers of the interviewee to take us to further questions, we are likely to miss clues. Basically, we should direct the question toward particulars in answers that require more research or appear to be inconsistent. The interview should be conducted in a professional manner but without hesitating to confront the interviewee on false statements. In later stages of the interview, backed with evidence and conflicting statements, the investigator should not be indecisive about asking difficult, direct, case-solving questions.

One more thing to pay attention to is the tone of voice and speed we use during an interview. Basically, a constant, monotone, low-speed interview is likely to give fewer results than an interview that features changes in conversational speed and voice pitch.

Suspicious Signs in Behavior

The ability of the investigator to notice suspicious signs in the behavior of the interviewee may be a game changer by directing the focus of the interview toward real issues.

The first thing we need to know is that people lie. One of our objectives as investigators is to notice specific signals that the people in front of us emit when lying. However, these signs are different from the expected generally nervous appearance caused by the discomforting situation of being interviewed.

As a result of an adrenaline rush caused by conflict, our bodies experience changes that produce a range of involuntary psychosomatic signs. Before an attack, just like during any other extremely conflicting activity such as lying, the human body goes through some changes owing to an adrenaline rush. Knowing these signs is also important in recognizing suspicious signs in behavior. Blood moves from the periphery blood vessels to the muscles and the brain. This will cause less bleeding in the case of a wound and will make the muscles stronger and the brain think faster. It will also make the skin paler. The pupils become wider and eye movement becomes faster. All of this happens to increase eyesight. Muscles become stronger and movements become faster. The body becomes less sensitive to pain. It also causes a delay in the need to satisfy physiological demands such as thirst, hunger, and urination. The heartbeat becomes more frequent because of the need to pump more blood to the muscles and brain. The skin starts to sweat so as to become slippery and cool down.

However, we are usually instinctively aware that our body can betray us by producing certain reactions. We know that our eyes will seem different, that we are sweating, and that we are probably emitting suspicious signs. We will perform certain actions to minimize the visibility of these signs, which will create another set of suspicious signs we usually call nervous/stress symptoms: avoiding eye contact, rubbing hands and the forehead to wipe off sweat, hiding or holding hands to conceal shivering, trying to make the body look smaller by bending, and so on. Classic suspicious signs in behavior are avoiding eye contact by looking down and to the side and touching the nose. When a person lies, he has a "Pinocchio effect," which is believed to be manifested by an increase in temperature around the nose and in the orbital muscle at the inner corner of the eye.

Certainly, the signs are individual and differ from person to person. An investigator who is experienced in behavior detection will try to single out signs that indicate lying through testing composed of both standard questions and delicate questions and to observe uncontrolled physical responses to both regular questions and the ones causing heightened stress.

Documenting the Interview

The best interview report is one that is prepared immediately after the interview. An interview is as usable as the report that documents it. When documenting the interview, we must keep in mind the purpose of the interview, which is to integrate evidence, fill in the blanks, and completely understand the case. Failing to produce an accurate written report that contains relevant information listed chronologically could result in the investigation being unusable and dismissed owing to a lack of evidence. If our goal is to use the interview as evidence in court proceedings, it should be documented in an appropriate usable format. The investigator should consider using quotation marks when directly quoting the interviewee.

Documenting the Investigation

The investigator must record all of the steps taken during the investigation, including his decision-making process, to produce a reliable record of the evidence and show what he has relied upon in solving the case. Apart from the facts of the case, the investigator should document obstacles that he encountered throughout the investigation as well as all of the methods used to verify the accuracy and authenticity of information and evidence.

Final Report

The template that should be used to summarize the investigation depends on the goal of the investigation. It is different depending on whether the report will be used internally or in a court. However, standard elements of the final report include:

- A detailed explanation of the issue that triggered the investigation
- Key elements of the issue on which the investigation was based
- The thinking process of the investigator
- An explanation and chronology of the investigation

- All people and events that were part of the investigation, with detailed records
- Evidence that backs statements on which the investigator relied
- A statement of the investigator's findings
- Final conclusion

AVAILABILITY: BCM AND DISASTER RECOVERY

Business continuity is a management process that identifies potential impacts that threaten an organization and provides a framework for an effective response to safeguard the interests of its key stakeholders, reputation, brand, and value-creating activities. It identifies the risk of exposure of business processes to internal and external threats, quantifies and mitigates their impact, and ensures fast and efficient recovery in case of a disaster.

No one can predict with certainty when and how a serious disruption to business will occur. Business continuity can be affected in many ways. Natural disasters that destroy the premises and property and stop the business, extreme weather conditions that disrupt the supply chain, pollution of water required for production, product recalls, epidemics, power cuts, and the failure of critical ICT systems and applications are some examples of events that can affect organizations, causing business discontinuity and costing millions, and sometimes even billions.

Key Elements of BCM

A *business impact analysis* is the process of differentiating between critical and noncritical functions (processes, people, and technology). Functions are considered critical if the implications of their unavailability are regarded as unacceptable, whether in terms of loss and damage or if they are required by law. The analysis must identify minimum application and application data requirements as well as the time frame in which the minimum application and application data must be available. Usually, a business continuity coordinator is in charge of guiding and challenging other departments (process owners) in identifying crucial functions. However, typically the top management of the company will approve the business impact analysis.

A *business continuity plan*, which is a crucial part of business continuity management, is a roadmap for continuing operations under adverse conditions.

Disaster recovery is the set of processes, policies, and procedures that prepare the recovery of crucial IT and technical systems after a natural or human-induced disaster.

A *disaster recovery site* is a secondary site located away from the original business site that contains duplicated, independently hosted crucial IT systems that can provide normal business operations in case of a disaster.

A *secondary location* is a location where business processes can continue to be performed in case the primary location is unavailable. In many cases, the secondary location is the same as the disaster recovery site, but it can be a different location. In that sense, there are three types of secondary locations:

- A cold site is a secondary location that provides a basic space where employees can continue to work. However, it often does not have the necessary IT infrastructure but requires additional time after the disaster to have the operation running.
- A hot site is a duplicate of the original business location and has duplicated crucial systems and infrastructure, usually backed up with real-time synchronization between the original site and the secondary location.
- A warm site is a compromise between the features of hot and cold sites. These sites have hardware and connectivity already but on a smaller scale than hot sites, and require some setup and fine-tuning to be usable.

Threat (risk) analysis refers to the process of identifying, prioritizing, and quantifying probable threats.

Business continuity plan documentation is a set of response and recovery procedures and actions that enable effective business continuity efforts.

A *cost–benefit analysis* (the difference between cost and benefit) is performed to justify investments in the business continuity management setup. For example cost–benefit analysis is often used to challenge the findings of the business impact analysis and concentrates on the cost of unavailability of functions that are believed to be critical compared with the cost of investment in resilience.

Testing (exercise) basically implies the periodical, theoretical, and practical challenge of the effectiveness of business continuity management strategies, plans, and measures. Tests are performed annually at a minimum. Exercises must be carefully planned and executed to make sure the exercise would not unintentionally cause business discontinuity.

- A simple exercise can be performed in the form of a workshop involving a small number of participants (up to 20) and concentrate on a specific part of the business continuity plan. It may involve an entire team (e.g., department, unit) or a single representative from several teams. Typically, participants will be given a simple scenario and then be invited to discuss and challenge the plan.
- A medium exercise may take 2 to 3 hours and involve several departments; it may be conducted in real time and be performed in the virtual world. The exercise may test real reactions and reflect a realistic situation. A medium exercise may require a realistic environment and the number of participants that reflect a realistic situation.
- A complex exercise is not only performed in the virtual world but requires actual travel to the secondary location. A complex exercise may be announced or unannounced, provided that it not disrupt business processes.

Training is a crucial part of BCM and should concentrate on increasing the knowledge and awareness of all employees and ensuring that they are familiar with plans and strategies and will react properly in case of the activation of business continuity measures.

Compliance monitoring concentrates on establishing compliance with the BCM and disaster recovery standards and regulations. It also requires checking the compatibility of our BCM with the requirements of clients and partners, and the compatibility of the BCM setup of service providers and suppliers with our BCM needs and demands.

Based on the type of incident, *communication flowcharts* should indicate appropriate individuals in the organization who should be notified and join the core special situations management team in resolving the special situation. Commonly, communication flowcharts are created after a threat analysis and identification of probable threats.

Anticipating

Although no one can predict with certainty when and how a serious disruption to business will occur, that does not mean that we should give up on anticipating when, where, and why threats to business continuity may occur. A famous Cheyenne proverb is: "A danger foreseen is half avoided." This should be one of the essential principles of effective business continuity planning and management. The good side of natural factors is that they can be anticipated to a certain extent. We basically know what natural risks exist and which are associated with what part of the year. We relatively accurately know when to expect heat waves, floods, or epidemics, and based on that knowledge, we can create an effective template for business continuity plans and disaster recovery. We also know that cell phone networks overload during holidays and that increased numbers of cyberattacks occur during certain holidays.

Common Planning Flaws

Unfortunately, we often perceive business continuity and disaster recovery as a topic related almost exclusively to IT services that support the organization's critical business activities. However, even when we count in natural factors, we mostly concentrate on physical and technology elements that can disrupt the business and rarely take into account the effect an event can have on the most critical element of business—people. For example, harsh weather conditions can prevent employees from coming to work and may cause serious problems for a business, whereas epidemics can cause unavailability of the critical minimum number of employees required to execute business processes.

Moreover, not only disasters can disrupt business. A proper business continuity plan must account for events that are not disasters but may cause unavailability of the critical minimum number of employees, such as the vacation season or important religious holidays.

Another mistake we usually make when we create business continuity plans is to concentrate on the immediate threat and not anticipate events that could be chained to main events. For example, although we protect from the direct impact of natural disaster, we sometimes forget that floods, fires, and earthquakes can cause other business disruptions, such as damaged power, unavailability of IT infrastructures, epidemics, and violence.

SECTION 6

When: Measure

CHAPTER 12

Analysis, Assessments, Planning, Control, and Administration

THREAT ANALYSIS

The Four Phases of Threat Analysis

Threat analysis is the mother of all security analyses. It is performed through four main steps:

- Identifying the value we are protecting (motive)
- Identifying the threats based on the identified value
- Anticipating the probable course of action (PCA)
- Anticipating the level of risk

Identifying Value

We have mentioned the concept of value several times throughout this book. Basically, after identifying the assets we are assigned to protect, we must search for points that make each of asset desirable for a perpetrator in terms of the motive to commit a crime, an act of terror, and so forth. Among other assets, we will assess products, equipment, people, information, and the symbolism of the organization and its agenda to determine whether something about these assets could be a motive for action against the particular asset or against the company as a whole. We should take into account all possible internal and external risks.

Moreover, we will classify value (in a security sense) as primary or secondary. Primary value is the immediate value of the asset. If we talk about a product, primary value items can be used immediately by a criminal or easily sold, whereas secondary value applies to items that have no value in their current form but have to be processed or added to another item to have immediate value. Also, large volumes of primary value become secondary value because executing a theft of large volumes requires planning and logistics.

Because the value also depends on the volume, part of the process, and location, we assess threats for each location of the target of protection and each part of the process. For example, cigarettes that are packed onto pallets and transported by trailers carry different risks and require different modus operandi by criminals than do single packs of cigarettes at the point of sale. If we talk about the risks to people, for example, local Swiss employees who work for the Israeli embassy in Switzerland are at risk from a terrorist attack that could be executed against Israeli targets, but only when they are at work. A terrorist may make a statement and receive media coverage even if the attack is against non-Israeli staff if the attack is logically associated with the Israeli embassy. However, the same employees are not at risk from a terrorist attack when they are off work. On the other hand, Israeli diplomats are at higher risk from terrorism and are threatened both at work and off work.

Identifying Threats

Based on the desirability and value of the protected asset, we can determine the type of threat that is targeting the specific asset. For instance, small quantities of primary value assets are attractive to single perpetrators whereas large quantities of primary or secondary value items attract organized criminals who have sufficient logistics to execute the crime, move and store large volumes, and eventually sell the assets.

Anticipating the PCA

After we have identified the threats, we have to determine how the actions can be performed. Determining the PCA comes down to anticipating probable scenarios (modus operandi of perpetrators). For example, theft of goods from a trailer can be executed with the involvement of the driver, curtain slashing, a moving vehicle attack, load diversion, impersonation of police officers, a forced stop, and so on.

Anticipating the Level of Risk

Anticipating the level of risk of each identified threat is the final step in creating a threat analysis. When we have determined probable threats, to design successful protection strategies, we have to establish the level of risk associated with each threat. To determine the level of risk, we have to take into account two interactive elements: likelihood of a particular threat and its worst-scenario consequences. We establish the likelihood based on previous experience, knowledge, and logic, whereas we count the consequences based on the maximum damage that could result from the particular action.

However, just as with any statistical model, we have to be careful not to misinterpret the information upon which we are basing the likelihood. Flipping a coin once will not tell us anything concerning the likelihood of the result of the next flip.

We can use a matrix to count the level of risk (Figure 12.1).

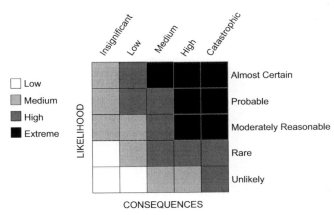

Figure 12.1 Risk measurement matrix.

VULNERABILITY ASSESSMENT

In general, vulnerability assessment is the process of identifying, quantifying, and prioritizing security weaknesses. A threat that is not eliminated or mitigated is vulnerability. After we have identified the threats and their motive, probability, modus operandi, and level of risk, the next step is to assess the preparedness of our organization to address the threats successfully (limit the opportunity). Vulnerability assessment is the basis for a security plan aimed at closing gaps and improving the overall performance of the security setup.

Vulnerability assessment is a multilayered, multidimensional analysis that challenges all elements of the security system (people, physical, technology, information, communication, procedures, and management) against all identified threats in all processes, parts, and elements of the business and during all phases of the incident and protection periods (preparation/prevention, action/response, and aftermath/recovery). It is performed as a specific project and is regularly tested through drills, exercises, and penetration tests.

To conduct and complete an effective vulnerability assessment, we are required to:
- Identify threats
- Catalogue assets
- Identify vulnerabilities of each catalogued asset based on the identified threat
- Quantify the impact of probable incidents on assets
- Perform a cost–benefit analysis to identify risks that can be accepted and ones that should be mitigated or completely eliminated
- Prioritize vulnerabilities as the basis for the security plan that will follow

There are some common mistakes associated with performing assessments. First, we have to make sure not to confuse threats and vulnerabilities. However, they are closely related because vulnerabilities depend on threats but are different. Second, a vulnerability assessment and security plan are not the same. Vulnerability assessment identifies all vulnerabilities whereas a security plan addresses only vulnerabilities that were identified as priorities. The third common mistake is the failure to assess the vulnerability of assets during entire processes and lifecycles. For example, we might identify vulnerabilities associated with the product but fail to assess vulnerabilities related to raw materials required to manufacture the product. Finally, assessments are based on probability and not possibility. Basically, possibility is not measurable whereas probability is based on an empirical approach. To be more specific, the type of probability at which we are looking is called a priori probability and represents a probability that is objective and based on deduction and reasoning about a particular case.

SECURITY PLANNING

Strategic Approach to Security Planning

A security plan is a strategy that arranges and guides security organizations through actions aimed at mitigating threats, closing gaps, and fulfilling the security needs of the companies they are protecting.

As a starting point, a good security plan is based on key issues identified in risk analysis, vulnerability assessment, key performance indicator (KPI) reports, budget overviews, and performance evaluations of employees and contractors. The goal of the security plan is to list and arrange all actions (or parts of actions) aimed at addressing identified issues over the period of 1 year. Because of its strategic nature and influence on the budget, the plan should be approved by the top management of the company. In addition to actions aimed at directly closing security gaps and mitigating security risks, the plan addresses indirect actions such as developing team members, training needs of security and non-security staff, and keeping vigilance high with the performance of exercises and drills. Certainly, the security plan must be linked to the overall strategy of the organization.

The security plan should not be confused with the security master plan. Basically, the security plan is a changeable part of the security master plan. Whereas the security plan is created on a yearly basis, the security master plan is a general document that explains the general direction, values, commitment, and philosophy on which the security organization is based, including its overall strategy. It also contains explanations of all processes performed by the security organization.

SMART

The SMART methodology addresses the basic principles for setting goals and objectives:

- Specific
- Measurable
- Achievable
- Realistic
- Timely

Plans sometimes turn out to be unsuccessful mostly because of the failure to challenge objectives and make sure they are SMART. Whereas the security master plan contains general goals, the security plan is a commitment that contains specific actions aimed at reaching the general goal. Each specific action must have a quantifiable goal and milestones so that its progress can be evaluated; it must be achievable in terms of abilities, timing, resources, and budget; it has to be doable; and it must have appropriate timing and deadlines.

Budget Constraints

The budget and plan are interactive. One reason why our security plan is annual is because the budget is always created on a yearly basis. Thus, we create the plan proposal according to the budget, but we also create the budget based on the security plan. The reality is that the only way to plan and execute long-term strategic projects successfully is to segment them into short-term, quick-win projects. Actions listed in an annual security plan can be part of a project that will last for more than a year, but they should be presented in the form of smaller quick-win projects, all of which have goals, timing, and budget. For instance, a chief executive officer and top management of a company will most likely hold the positions for a short period, maybe a couple of years, before moving on. Having a long-term return on investment will practically mean that, for instance, money was invested in a project during the term of one top management team that could only report expenditure, whereas their successors will claim the results with no spending. Such projects are likely not to be approved.

Classification of Actions

When we create an annual security plan proposal, we must keep in mind that stakeholders are not security experts and that the most common criteria regarding their decision of whether to approve the plan will be based on importance versus cost. One way to classify actions before proposing them is to mark them in a simple matrix that would give a good indication of the ratio between importance and cost and determine cost-efficiency (Figure 12.2).

Another crucial element required to obtain the full picture concerning proposed actions is to quantify them by anticipating the savings resulting from actions and their return on investment. Savings could be achieved by having less loss or by improving processes that would save costs.

Another aspect to take into account is the justified cost of security measures compared with the cost of loss. Basically, investment in security measures must not exceed the cost of incidents over a reasonable period of time. Organizations prefer not to lose money regardless of where the money is going. Security does not generate profit; its mission is to protect the profit and save costs. If your security measures are more expensive than the incidents, your organizations will opt to accept the risk and lose less.

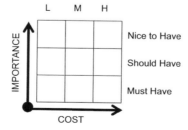

Figure 12.2 Cost-efficiency matrix.

SECURITY METRICS/KPI

In addition to improving security processes, one of the best business inventions and practices and the best tool to assist in bringing security and business closer to each other is key performance measurement or metrics, often referred to as KPI. Key performance indicators are crucial factors for measuring the success of any activity. They are an efficient assessment tool for any type of incident and the progress and efficiency of activities aimed at influencing it. I will mention a few basic rules for a proper KPI:

- Consists of data that can actually be constantly collected
- Can be measured continuously
- Can be influenced
- Must be clear and accurate, simple, meaningful, and understandable
- Must be relevant
- Must have logical timing
  On the other hand, we should avoid traps when setting up the KPI system, such as
- Lack of commitment
- Measuring too much
- Collecting irrelevant data and measuring irrelevant things
- Having imprecise calculations
- Using metrics to evaluate individuals
- Misinterpreting results

To be more specific, we should not use the KPI system to measure weather conditions, for example, because they cannot be influenced and most probably would not interest stakeholders. You can still collect data about the weather if you find them relevant, but do not confuse collecting weather data with KPIs.

When we talk about security, you can choose to measure a particular segment of security incidents, for example. For the measurement to be precise and meaningful, you must decide which segment of incidents you want to measure, what are you going to measure it with, and what part of the business you are looking at. Of course, you must define clear objectives to influence each KPI you are measuring. If your objective is to reduce losses resulting from theft of goods during transport, your KPI should be loss of transported goods, the department of concern is distribution, and you can, for example, base the measurement on the ratio between the value of transported goods and the loss over a measured period. The measurement period should be decided according to the frequency of the incidents you are measuring. To be more specific, if you know that an incident occurs every few weeks, your measurement frequency should be set so that you can clearly understand trends and test the efficiency of the actions you have implemented. For such a frequency of incidents, measuring and comparing them every week would be too soon to understand trends, whereas measuring them once a year would be too late to address issues efficiently and implement timely adjustments. This KPI is relevant for the business because it addresses losses and would definitely be interesting to stakeholders.

Example for Loss of Product KPI

To show the system of security metrics practically, I will take the example of a KPI for the losses of product (finished goods) during distribution.

To have precise metrics, we have to define all particulars related to the measurement. For example:

- We are measuring loss
- The sector that we are measuring is sales and distribution
- The area that we are measuring is metropolitan
- Our objectives are to follow the loss of finished goods owing to security incidents and test the effectiveness of steps taken to improve performance
- Our type of measurement is quantity
- The measurement frequency is quarterly
- The explanation of the method of measurement is a comparison of the number of product units lost versus the previous measurement period. An index is created according to the number of product units distributed versus the number of product units lost. Data are to be collected according to accurate reports from the sales and distribution department.

We will measure the number of products lost compared with the number of products distributed. Thus, the values we are measuring are:

- Total volume distributed
- Loss

X = total volume distributed (million items)

Y = loss (1,000 items)

The loss index would be:

$$\text{Loss Index} = \frac{Y}{X} \times 100$$

If the amount of distributed goods over the measured period is 6 million, our X value will be 6. If the amount of stolen goods is 3,000 our Y value will be 3. Our loss index for the measured period (for example, the first quarter) will be 50:

$$\frac{Y=3}{X=6} \times 100 = 50$$

If, for example, in the second quarter our loss index was 33.3 and in the third it was 16.6, this means that the KPI is showing a positive trend.

Example of Incident Measurement

When we measure incidents, we can be misguided if we measure only one dimension of incidents, such as their direct financial impact on our organization. For example, if we measure only loss, we will not know whether the loss occurred because of the small number of large-scale incidents or many minor incidents. However, this information is crucial if we are planning to design a successful strategy aimed at mitigating losses. Basically, we want to classify incidents that occurred over a certain period, based on two factors: loss and frequency. Moreover, we want to have a standardized approach to measuring that would allow us always to have the same standards when classifying incidents.

Loss

To have a standardized approach, we will simply classify the financial loss that occurred over a certain period of time: for example,

- Low loss—under €1,000
- Moderate loss—between €1,000 and €10,000
- High loss—between €10,000 and €50,000
- Extreme loss—over €50,000

Frequency of Incidents

We can have a standardized approach to measuring the frequency of incidents by, for example, creating a simple index based on the number of days a measured period has and the number of incidents that occurred during that period. If our measurement period has 30 days, we can decide that:

- Low frequency—up to five incidents
- Moderate frequency—between 6 and 15 incidents
- High frequency—between 16 and 30 incidents
- Extreme frequency—over 30 incidents

Matrix

To follow the incidents graphically based on severity and frequency, we will mark the spot on the matrix as in the example shown below (Figure 12.3).

Apart from just marking the incidents on the matrix, we will mark the place that represents the feasible objective we are trying to achieve with our security measures.

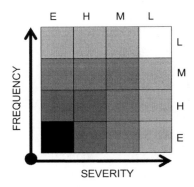

Figure 12.3 Incident measurement matrix.

Severity of Incident

a) Fatal consequences	600
b1) Major injury	500
b2) Moderate/minor injury	200
b3) No injury	0
c1) Armed assault	110
c2) Unarmed assault	100
c3) No assault	0
d1) Loss over 10000 EUR	250
d2) Loss between 1000 and 10000 EUR	100
d3) Loss under 1000 EUR	50
d4) No loss	0

Severity Index = a + b + c + d

LOW	< 50
MODERATE	50 < 250
HIGH	250 < 600
EXTREME	> 600

Figure 12.4 Example of an incident severity table.

Standardized Approach to Classifying Incidents according to Severity

We can use a simple matrix or checklist to help us have a standardized approach when counting the severity of each incident. We can use the kind of matrix that is presented in the example above (Figure 12.4).

TRAININGS AND EXERCISES

During both emergencies and routine, people tend to react in a way with which they are familiar. It is essential to conduct trainings, drills, and exercises to make sure that all people in an organization will do their part to prevent an incident, react to it, and mitigate its impact on themselves and the organization.

Conducting efficient trainings, drills, and exercises requires a methodical approach, regularity, planning (especially concerning safety), close monitoring and control, analysis, and evaluation.

Safety

Safety is the crucial element of training and exercise. There is no point in training and testing the security and safety if the actual exercise and test puts employees and assets in jeopardy. Accidents happen, and unfortunately, they happen often. The safety of exercises and trainings requires thorough planning, monitoring, and complete control including anticipating and proactively eliminating risks and the ability to successfully stop them immediately at any time.

There are key principles for performing safe exercises and trainings. First, we must physically prevent the instinct of participants from overpowering the instructions. In general, people find it difficult to overcome the competitive spirit and to intentionally fail a test. For instance, even if your exercise is planned as a low-speed evacuation, some participants will feel the urge to be the first to get to the assembly point. Controlling the exercise requires placing exercise coordinators alongside the evacuation route to slow down the evacuation. When we conduct virtual exercises using the IT infrastructure, we must make sure that participants are unable to cause unintentional damage to the system. The same risk goes for any vital infrastructure and assets such as the production floor and products. Also, we must never perform a shooting incident drill to check the reaction of an armed security officer, for example, because he is likely to use his weapon instinctively.

When performing drills, we must clearly mark the objects that we use, to avoid confusion. For instance, when performing a drill about an explosive device during patrol, place a clear sign "Drill" on the object. The security officer who discovers the device must know what he should do and must not do in case of a drill (for example, he should not announce a real evacuation). However, you can also write a short reminder of do's and don'ts on the actual object. You should also be in close proximity to the drill to stop it if anything goes wrong.

Another principle is to exclude the possibility that anyone who should not be part of the drill or exercise is participating in it. This includes anyone who could endanger the safety of the exercise by not being properly instructed or controllable or by not being aware that the event is actually an exercise, such as visitors to the facility, bystanders, and police officers nearby.

One more crucial aspect is to have a mechanism to inform about a real threat during an exercise and to react to it. For instance, a real shooting incident can occur during an evacuation exercise.

An exercise must have a beginning and end. All the participants must be clearly informed that the exercise has started, as well as when it has ended.

Training Matrix

A training matrix is the annual plan of trainings and exercises whose purpose is to identify, arrange, and plan the security training needs of an organization. Every member of an institution is responsible for security on some level. Whereas some employees have more direct responsibility than others, everyone requires training. Basically, not all training subjects are for everyone. Also, different functional groups of employees require different levels of knowledge on the same subject. For example, not all employees need training on how to react to an anonymous phone threat; only employees who actually answer external phone calls require such training. On the other hand, all employees must know how to react (search, evacuation, etc.) in case a threat is real. Moreover, not all

	TRAINING X			TRAINING Y			TRAINING Z		
	Level 1	Level 2	Level 3	Level 1	Level 2	Level 3	Level 1	Level 2	Level 3
HR	X				X			X	
PRODUCTION	X				X				
OFFICE STAFF		X			X		X		
SECURITY			X			X			X
IT		X			X				
MANAGEMENT					X				X
CONTRACTORS	X								

Figure 12.5 Training matrix template example.

employees should receive the same level of training. If we again take the example of anonymous phone threat training, call center personnel must know how to react, what to pay attention to, and whom to inform, whereas a security supervisor should be trained to evaluate the threat and decide whether it is real or a hoax. The training matrix should be created so that everyone knows his part in the overall security setup. When creating the training matrix, we should also take into account the required level of simplicity and complexity as well as the use of terminology tailored to the audience and the audience's ability to listen and observe.

Here is a simple example of a training matrix template (Figure 12.5).

Trainings

In reality, trainings are mostly delivered as lectures and presentations. However, information retention will be improved by involving participants: for example, by initiating a short discussion about a case study and by encouraging questions during and after training.

Security Refreshers
Because learning is a continuous effort, training should not always be performed in the form of a lecture or presentation. Weekly refresher meetings, posters, and e-mailed security tips of the week are also methods to achieve ongoing training for security and non-security staff.

Induction Trainings
Induction trainings are delivered to newcomers to the company. Generally, from the moment they start employment in a company, new employees are required to know and obey the basic security principles and rules of the company. Typically, induction trainings include topics such as getting to know the security unit, its people, and responsibilities; entrance and exit procedures; basic information and ICT security; procedures for reporting security violations; evacuation procedures; general do's and don'ts; and so forth. Depending on the frequency of new arrivals to the company and the sensitivity of the new employee's position, induction trainings can be

performed immediately after the employee has signed a contract, or by grouping new employees once a month for joint induction training. A weak and inefficient substitute would be to send new employees an induction security presentation only by e-mail.

Exercises

Theoretical Exercises

A theoretical exercise format is mostly used during regular security staff meetings to keep the vigilance of security staff high. For example, you can choose a place and routine situation, such as a visitors' inspection booth, make a drawing of the booth, and decide a type of emergency, such as a knife attack. Ask security staff to explain what kind of reaction they would have in such a situation. For security supervisors (shift leaders), ask them to draw the positions of security officers in the facility and then explain the response actions during a specific emergency situation. Theoretical exercises, however different, are also used as a way to test the feasibility of business continuity plans.

Information-Chain Exercise/Simulation Exercise

Information-chain exercises are aimed at training staff to pass information correctly and quickly in case of an emergency. The exercise starts with a presentation of the emergency to the first line of participants. Participants receiving the information are supposed to inform the next persons in the chain of command and relevant institutions (extension telephones in the facility can have the role of emergency services). Correctly deciding whom to inform and passing relevant information quickly should be taken into account. This exercise aims to train the reactions of participants during and after an event.

Role-Playing/Scenario Exercises

Role-playing exercises can be used to train the reactions of security staff during all kinds of emergency situations. Certainly, safety is the most important aspect of the exercises. Never use real weapons or anything that can be used as a weapon. Make sure that no persons involved in the exercise are armed. Make a clear division between the exercise area and the area that will be off-limits and keep all weapons off-limits.

It is crucial to plan the exercises well and have clear instructions. Actors in the scenario exercises can be divided into three groups:

- Security officers
- Attackers
- Crowd

The last two groups should have clear missions and know their tasks while the first group is tested.

The crowd should behave according to your clear instructions before the exercise: for example,

- The crowd can obey the instructions of security officers
- You can choose persons from the crowd to act as victims of a sniping attack
- The crowd can mingle and create confusion

Officers acting as attackers must know the exact moment when they will start the attack and the way they will perform it. You should give them a secret sign as to when to start. They should be instructed to be obvious. For example, a person acting as a suicide bomber should wear an item that clearly resembles a suicide belt and exercise obvious behavior.

The team acting as security will be informed only about the situation. For example, "It is now 8:00 am and employees are coming to work," or "It is 1400 h—routine." Always be sure to stand next to the action so as to be able to stop the exercises if anything goes wrong. Always mark the beginning and end of the exercise. After the exercise, always perform a debriefing and discuss the weak and strong points.

Tests

Penetration Testing

Typically, the term "penetration test" refers to an attack on a computer system with the intention of testing it by finding security weaknesses and potentially gaining access to it, its functionality, and data. Physical penetration tests are also a form of testing vulnerabilities within a company's physical controls or resilience to social engineering. Physical penetration tests are not announced and basically come down to the tester trying to gain unauthorized access to the facility, collect information with social engineering techniques, test visitor entrance procedures, steal assets and take them out of the facility, check whether a suspicious-looking envelope would be discovered or distributed to the receiver in the facility, and so forth. Because such exercises are not announced, special precautions must be taken to ensure the safety of the tester in case he is discovered by the security officers, for example. The person controlling the exercise must be able to stop the exercise if there is even a remote possibility that anything could go wrong.

Drills

Drills can be performed during every stage of routine work of security officers. There are many ways to perform a drill, such as staging a suspicious object during search/patrol. The object should be clearly marked and not resemble a weapon, so that the patrol officer will immediately know that it is a drill and not a real emergency situation. Still, the controller of the drill must be in full control of the situation and be able to stop the drill immediately to prevent any kind of hard reaction from the security officer.

Exams

Exams aimed at evaluating the security staff to ensure that they possess the required knowledge and skills can be formative or summative. In general, formative exams (also called diagnostic testing) are all part of the learning process and professional shaping of the employee. Formative exams may be drills, scenario exercises, information–chain exercises, and theoretical exercises. The assessment of employees' performance during formative exams must be noted in their files and used to improve future performance.

Summative exams, on the other hand, are conducted with the purpose of making sure that employees are skilled and competent to perform their tasks. Summative exams should be performed annually in the form of exams and tests that may be written, verbal, or practical and test crucial subjects such as knowledge of specific laws and internal procedures, technical skills, professional knowledge, and physical abilities.

However, constant failure to perform according to expectations during formative exams may be considered a lack of competence.

Web-Based Exam/Quiz

Exams in a Web (quiz) format are considered an efficient way to refresh the knowledge of non-security employees in a company. The main advantages of Web-based trainings are that many employees can take the tests at once at their convenience during a certain predefined time frame, using their computers and without having to leave their desks. They can also take the exam anywhere in the world. Moreover, their participation and success are recorded. There are numerous software solutions for creating and running Web-based exams. Most have a variety of setting options and analytical functions.

INDEX

Note: Page numbers followed by "f" indicate figures respectively.

25788182R00134

Printed in Great Britain
by Amazon